YOU HAD
A JOB
FOR LIFE

T0246280

Jamie Sayen

YOU HAD
A JOB
FOR LIFE

*Story of a
Company Town*

Brandeis University Press
Waltham, Massachusetts

BRANDEIS UNIVERSITY PRESS

First Brandeis University Press edition 2023

Originally published in 2018 by University Press of New England

Manufactured in the United States of America

Designed by Mindy Basinger Hill

Typeset in Adobe Jenson Pro

For permission to reproduce any of the material in this book, contact
Brandeis University Press, 415 South Street, Waltham, MA 02453,
or visit brandeisuniversitypress.com

Library of Congress Cataloging-in-Publication Data

Names: Sayen, Jamie, author.

Title: You had a job for life : story of a company town / Jamie Sayen.

Description: First Brandeis University Press edition. | Waltham, Massachusetts : Brandeis
    University Press, 2023. | "Originally published in 2018 by University Press of New
    England"—Title page verso. Includes bibliographical references and index. Summary:
    "Drawing on conversations with scores of former paper mill workers in Groveton, New
    Hampshire, Sayen reconstructs the mill's human history and the devastating impact
    of global capitalism on a small New England town. This is a heartbreaking story of the
    decimation of industrial America"—Provided by publisher.

Identifiers: LCCN 2023014720 | ISBN 9781684581849 (paperback) | ISBN 9781684581856
    (ebook)

Subjects: LCSH: Paper industry—New Hampshire—Groveton—Case studies. | Paper
    mills—New Hampshire—Groveton—Case studies. | Labor—New Hampshire—
    Groveton—Case studies. | Plant shutdowns—New Hampshire—Groveton—Case
    studies. | Unemployed—New Hampshire—Groveton—Case studies. | Groveton
    (N.H.)—Economic conditions.

Classification: LCC HD9828.G76 S29 2023 | DDC 338.4/7676097422—dc23/eng/20230516

LC record available at https://lccn.loc.gov/2023014720

5   4   3   2   1

For Rachel O'Meara

I think back then everybody had a good job, was making good money. I don't know if everybody was happy, but at least they had a pretty secure place to work. Right now the town is, I think, in turmoil. Nobody has a job; well, they have jobs, but they're not making twenty bucks an hour like they were in the mill. Once you got in the mill back then, unless you chose to leave there, you had a job for life. I think times were a lot better in Groveton back then. There was beer joints all over the place, and everybody was making a living, and everybody was happy. We lived right across the tracks, and I used to bitch about the sound of the mill in the summer when the windows are open, but it was a pretty good sound when you was working here. I didn't have to drive to work. Five minutes, I was in my job. Unbelievable.

LAWRENCE "LOLLY" LAPOINTE | worked at the mill for over thirty years

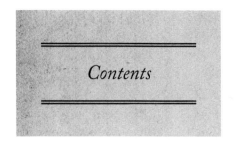

Contents

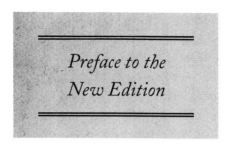

Preface to the New Edition

REREADING *You Had A Job For Life* summoned forth voices of departed mill workers who had graciously invited me into their homes. I recalled the expressions on their faces and their eagerness to tell someone the stories of their life in the mill: their job, the mundane routine, the dangers, fatigue, camaraderie, sense of community, foolishness, and tragedies.

More than twenty of the good souls I interviewed have passed away since publication of *You Had a Job for Life* in December 2017, including Jim Wemyss Jr., whose father, Jim Sr., acquired the Groveton Paper Mill in August 1940, and Greg Cloutier, son of two mill workers. Young Jim dominated the mill from the late 1940s until the James River Corporation acquired the mill's fine papers operation in 1983. Thereafter, he ran Groveton Paperboard until his retirement in 1998.

Jim hired Greg as an engineer in charge of completing the difficult conversion of the boiler from oil to wood chips in 1981. Greg worked at the mill, and later at Paperboard until 1997. Thereafter, he built up a thriving, small-hydroelectric business. Around the time I began to interview former mill workers, Greg and his wife Rita saved the 1930s-era movie theater, the Rialto in Lancaster, the village just south of Groveton. Their modest investments in renovating downtown buildings eventually bequeathed the community a bakery, the Polish Princess, an indoor farmers market, the Root Seller, an art gallery, the William Rugh Gallery, and a local brewpub, the Copper Pig, that have revived Main Street, day and night. The example of Greg and Rita offers a model for other suffering rural downtowns to revitalize their local economies through smart, modest investments. Greg's generous support of the Groveton Mill Oral History Project enabled the publication of *You Had a Job for Life*.

Groveton's economic recovery since the mill shut down in 2007 has been slow. Shortly after *You Had a Job for Life* went to press, NSA Industries LLC, a Vermont metal fabrication company, moved into the old Campbell Building, one of the few remaining mill structures. It employs approximately 100 people.

Otherwise, the Groveton-area economy remains depressed and lacks diversity. About one-third of the storefronts in its downtown support businesses, and the other two-thirds present empty storefronts or vacant lots. New Hampshire's economic revitalization strategy for Coös County has delivered massive ratepayer subsidies to the 75 MW biomass electricity plant that utilizes the boiler of the Berlin pulp mill that was demolished in 2007, and an all-out push to divert ATV riders to Coös County, and away from more settled, affluent communities downstate. These high-carbon-emission endeavors exacerbate the climate crisis, encourage whole-tree harvesting—vacuum cleaning—of our battered former industrial forests, and polarize quiet rural communities overrun by ATVs that generate dust, mud, and erosion, as well as noise that negatively impacts wildlife and low-impact, nonmotorized recreationists.

The epilogue of *You Had a Job for Life* outlined a series of economic lessons the mill's demise teaches. As of this writing, the state and its economic development agencies have shown no interest in linking the fates of our natural and human communities as we seek to build an economy based upon the acknowledgement that human aspirations are circumscribed by the climate crisis and natural limits—an economy that delivers frugal prosperity *and* healthy forests. They continue to cater to global capital intent on exploitation instead of nurturing.

Reviews for *You Had a Job for Life* were gratifying. A favorable review in the *Wall Street Journal* concluded with a Jim Wemyss rant against "speculative" capitalism: "'These people in Wall Street have been disgraceful,' he told Mr. Sayen. 'What they've done in the last fifty years in this country.'"[1]

That review caught the eye of a retired mill manager from Iowa who informed me the forces that led to the demise of Groveton Paperboard and the Wausau operations at Groveton had shuttered his mill at the same time. His letter confirmed my conviction that the story of a small paper mill in northern New Hampshire resonated across the country.

The hollowing of manufacturing in the United States over the past several decades has devastated countless rural and urban communities that had depended upon a textile mill, a coal mine, an industrial forest, or an automobile plant, to name just a few. Many of the forces that doomed Groveton's mill devastated these other mining and manufacturing communities. Some variant of Groveton's story has played out in many communities throughout the United States and abroad.

You Had a Job for Life appeared two years before the outbreak of the COVID pandemic briefly confined us to our homes. Our initial collective response to COVID is instructive. Stories of community musicians serenading their neighbors and tales of kindness directed to the elderly, disabled, and ailing reinforced one's faith in the basic decency of our fellow citizens.

Carbon emissions dropped sharply in the first month of the lockdown, suggesting that we can survive with less carbon and consumerism. In a related development, many people learned that, while they could adjust to a more austere material existence, they could not so easily flourish without access to green spaces—where we humans evolved. It seems an affinity for wild nature is baked into our genes.

If climate and environmental justice campaigns align with wildlands preservation, we may begin to transform our carbon-intensive economy, reverse atmospheric carbon levels, restore justice to victims of environmental injustice, preserve unfragmented habitat for climate-stressed species, and reduce our lethal consumption of energy, raw materials, and manufactured, often toxic, nonessentials.

For decades, our democratic institutions have failed to respond to global ecological and climate crises. Species extinctions and extreme weather events are now almost certain even if we act with the urgency these crises demand. Continued dithering and denial promises even more frightful consequences.

We must develop a politics that is resistant—hopefully immune—to authoritarian demagoguery and politically motivated divisiveness. We need a politics that recognizes and protects the rights and needs of all species and unborn generations by respecting natural laws and limits.

In the United States, neither the Republicans nor the Democrats articulate viable policies for revitalizing rural natural and human communities. Republican politicians, instead of endorsing realistic, locally appropriate solutions to our entwined ecological, climate, cultural, social, and economic crises, have descended to name-calling, conspiracy theories, and hatred, as the party grows more authoritarian by the day.

Democratic politicians give the impression they have abandoned rural America. I believe that if the Democratic Party embraced a strategy for economic revitalization along the lines of the economic lessons former mill workers taught me, the Republican dominance of rural voters could be neutralized, and perhaps reversed.

The reissue of *You Had a Job for Life* coincides with the publication of my forthcoming *Children of the Northern Forest: Wild New England's History from Glaciers to Global Warming* (Yale University Press, 2023), which tells the story of the land use and conservation history of northern New England's forests. Together, these books offer struggling rural resource colonies and abandoned urban manufacturing centers a more hopeful pathway to a fairer, brighter, and more desirable future that effectively combats the climate and extinction crises and toxic politics.

Note

1. Richard Adams Carey, "Requiem for a Paper Mill," *Wall Street Journal*, February 25, 2018.

YOU HAD
A JOB
FOR LIFE

BUILDERS
AND
DESTROYERS

JAMES CAMPBELL WEMYSS SR. purchased the bankrupt paper mill in Groton, New Hampshire, in 1940. "Old Jim," as he was known around town, revived the mill and the town's fortunes. His son, Jim Jr., was seriously wounded as a nineteen-year-old soldier in 1945. He joined the family business three years later. Father and son diversified the mill's product lines and doubled the size of the mill in the quarter century following World War II.

The senior Wemyss owned the mill outright until the Wemyss family merged with Diamond International in 1968. Jim Jr. continued to rule over the mill and the village of Groveton for another fifteen years as vice president of Diamond and a member of Diamond's board of directors. In 1982, the Anglo-French financier Sir James Goldsmith completed a hostile takeover of Diamond International. Jim Jr. no longer controlled the northern New Hampshire paper mill, and the era of engaged local ownership of the mill ended. The following year, Goldsmith sold the mill to James River of Richmond, Virginia. The new owner eventually starved the mill of investment capital. Late in 1992, Wisconsin-based Wausau Paper Mills Company bought the dying mill for the bargain price of $20 million. Wausau invested lavishly until 2000; thereafter, austerity reigned. In 2007, Wausau closed the Groveton mill without consulting local management. A "covenant" Wausau placed on the mill deed forbade future owners from making paper.

For over thirty years, Jim Wemyss Jr. was involved in every aspect of the mill's operations. When the paper machines were making bad paper, young Jim was renowned for throwing his coat on the floor, stomping on it, and then ranting and raving at the unlucky superintendent of paper machines. Wemyss was also a notorious practical joker who might light a cherry bomb and fling it anonymously into the office of one of his mill managers, or fire off his small cannon to entertain an IRS agent assigned to audit the mill. Many

From the air, the Groveton Papers mill appeared as a large rectangle that was oriented from southwest to northeast. This aerial view, looking southwest, taken in 1993, shows the mill complex. The sections nearest to the Upper Ammonoosuc River were the oldest. They contained (from top of photo to bottom): the wood room, the old pulp mill (removed after 1972) and the Groveton Paper Board pulp mill, the bleach plant, the water filtration plant, and the boilers. The large middle section housed Number 1 and 2 paper machines (Number 6 replaced Number 2 in 1972); the electric and maintenance shops; the stock prep department; the building housing Number 3 and 4 paper machines, and old Number 4 finishing room. The long flat-roofed Verrill Building that was added in 1960–1961 contained the main office, the fine-papers finishing department, and the warehouses and shipping department. The section at the far right was the Groveton Paper Board addition of 1966–1967 that housed Number 5 paper machine. (Courtesy GREAT)

of his employees loved Wemyss; others loathed him. Most respected his encyclopedic knowledge of the mill, his loyalty to his workers, his commitment to promote union men to management positions, and his willingness to pitch in during a crisis.

On one occasion, a hose had fallen into the stock chest and become entangled in the agitator; the crew was about to drain the tank when Wemyss appeared and countermanded the order: "I'd just come from a party, and I had a tuxedo on. I said, 'Anybody with a sharp knife?' All paper people had knives. I took my bow tie, coat, and shirt off and dove into the stock chest, deeper than this room. I'm a scuba diver. I knew where the agitator was, and I went down and grabbed it [the hose] like an octopus, and cut it all off in hunks and came up, handed it to them, and said, 'Let's start this goddamned place up.' I came out to the car; my wife said, 'What's all that black all over you? Go home. Get in the shower. You look terrible' [*laughs*]. We did crazy things; that's all. Don't ask me why."

Greg Cloutier, today a successful hydropower developer, was the son of two mill workers, nephew to a dozen or so more, and a childhood chum of Jim Wemyss III. Greg earned a degree in engineering and eventually returned to his hometown. For fifteen years he worked intimately with Jim Jr. at the mill. Like his boss, Greg has an alpha male temperament. Both men cared passionately about the mill, and this often led to conflict. "Fought him all the time," Cloutier told me with a smile.

Shirley MacDow, Wemyss's top assistant for over half a century, had the unenviable task of restoring the peace — or, better, of heading off the next explosion. MacDow also had to give employees "performance reviews." "I hated to give performance reviews," she said, "but it was part of the system, so we did it." Although she thought Cloutier "was a very capable young man," she recalled he scored poorly on the category "Learn to get along with Mr. Wemyss." "I think he got zero on that all the time," she laughed. "I knew when things were getting a little touchy, when to try to do whatever it took to avoid that, which might be telling Greg 'Go away for a little while. Come back tomorrow.'" Cloutier praised her gift for keeping the peace: "Shirley was a lot better manager than I think she got credit for because she did a good job at soothing Mr. Wemyss. If I kept her informed of what was going on, she kept Mr. Wemyss informed. And that kept the fire down."

Not always. In separate interviews, Cloutier and Wemyss told me about an epic battle over whether to change a felt on the paperboard machine. I have taken the liberty of weaving their stories together as if they had been told in the same conversation.

CLOUTIER: It must have been three o'clock in the morning, and he and I had a hell of a blowup. I think everybody left the machine room, and I stormed out.

WEMYSS: These felts used to cost ten thousand bucks apiece. One of our managers [Cloutier] — and he's a good man — said, "I've got to shut it down and cut the felt off." I looked at him and said, "No, you're not cutting anything off. Go get that car washing machine that has three-thousand-pound pressure outlet. Go down to the basement and wash the damn felt." "I won't do it; I'll quit." I said, "No doors are locked. I'll go down and wash it."

CLOUTIER: "I can't do this. This is not the way I want to leave this." So I came back.

WEMYSS: I started washing the felt, and I looked around, and he was right next to me. I said, "You hold it for a while," and we cleaned the felt up, and it ran for thirty days after that. I said, "You had a plugged shower in the back; you didn't see it." Showers have nozzles, and if one gets plugged, it's pretty hard to see with the steam and heat like that. If the felt gets dirty in that area, it can run a wet streak. I guess I've been around so long you've got to learn something.

CLOUTIER: I had a chance a little while ago to thank him for that because I know I would not be successful today if I had not learned some of his techniques.

SAYEN: Studied with the master?

CLOUTIER: I did. I did. Like I said, I spent a lifetime working for him. He gave me a lot of latitude to build, and it was fun.

Despite their frequent blowups, they never stayed angry with each other. The outbursts were triggered by frustration that the mill was not meeting production goals, rather than personal animosity. "We were both pretty adrenaline junkies," Cloutier laughed. His parents had long ago advised their son: "'You've got to show the man respect, but don't take any shit from him.' I always did respect him."

In the summer of 2016, Greg and I visited Jim Jr. As we were saying goodbye on the driveway, Greg asked me to take a photo of the two men. Instinctively, the ninety-year-old Wemyss and his sixty-five-year-old protégé squared up like prizefighters. As I snapped the picture, Wemyss's middle finger emerged from his fist.

ONE LOVELY SUMMER AFTERNOON six years earlier, Jim Wemyss Jr. and I were sitting on the shore of Maidstone Lake, Vermont, a twenty-minute drive from Groveton. Wemyss was railing against Wall Street financiers in general and Sir James Goldsmith in particular. He blamed them for the decline of the United States paper industry. "It's terrible. It's terrible," he raged. "It's destroyed the industry as far I was concerned. What the hell are you going to do about it? What's going to start this mill up? They ruined it with that damned, stupid idiot [Goldsmith]. There's nothing in the world that will ever start that mill up again. It's destroyed because of this idiot. I hate them with such a passion."

I was startled by Wemyss's outburst. "I thought you were a capitalist," I spluttered. "I'm a building capitalist," he shot back. "I'm not a person who tears things apart for gain. I never did that. I wouldn't do it. These people in Wall Street have been disgraceful. What they've done in the last fifty years in this country."

THE DEMISE of the Groveton paper mill devastated the region's economy and brought despair to the community. The covenant was the ultimate insult. Even more than the mill closing, the accursed covenant left scores of former mill workers feeling betrayed. In the first interview I conducted for the Groveton Mill Oral History Project, I asked Francis Roby: "If one of the big guys at Wausau walked in here, what would you say?"

"I'd tell him to get out," he answered tersely. "Point blank. I don't want him in my home. That's what I think of Wausau."

Many of the mill workers served in the nation's military in times of war and peace. At the mill, they endured stressful, dangerous working conditions, morning, afternoon, and night. When the mill was struggling to survive, they did everything asked of them to keep the mill running. Global economic forces beyond their control and decisions made in corporate headquarters a thousand miles away killed the mill and took away their livelihood.

After 2000 the nation's paper industry sank into a prolonged slump. Commodity paper prices declined as demand for fine papers fell and low-cost imports flooded the market. Following Hurricane Katrina in 2005, natural gas prices soared, and the mill's energy bill ate up profits.

Under increasing pressure from corporate headquarters, the mill's last superintendent, Groveton native Dave Atkinson, reminded mill employees that because they could not control unfavorable energy and commodity prices, they should focus on "controllables," such as reducing energy consumption, water use, workplace accidents, and generation of unsellable paper, called "broke." "We need to stay focused on what we can control," he emphasized month after month. "We can't control the market. All we can control is how efficiently, how cost-effectively we work. Focus on that, and we'll be OK." The mill workforce performed miracles to improve productivity, reduce costs, and keep hope alive.

The litany of uncontrollables that doomed the Groveton mill is familiar to rural and urban communities throughout the United States that have lost an auto plant, or a steel, textile, or paper mill: absentee owners with scant commitment to the local community; declining investment in modernizing the aging machinery and infrastructure; soaring energy prices coupled with stagnant or declining commodity prices; and competition from mills and factories located in other regions of the United States or in foreign countries where wages are lower and environmental protections are lax to nonexistent. "Everything you see is made in China, right?" Wemyss angrily declared as we gazed upon the shimmering lake.

"That's why I'm not a big fan of free trade," I responded.

"I'm not either," he agreed.

Without the mill, the region's economy collapsed: taxes soared; families reluctantly pulled up roots in search of gainful employment; school enrollment declined; and politicians offered empty promises to solve the crisis. To some, the fabric of the community seemed to be unraveling.

Nearly a decade after the Groveton mills ceased to make paper, the greater Groveton economy remains shell-shocked. From time to time an out-of-state entrepreneur rides into town with plans to build a wood-burning energy plant, a liquid natural gas distribution center, a furniture plant, even a medical marijuana farm. Hope soars . . . and nothing happens. Time after time, the hope bringer did not have the requisite financial backing to pull off the miracle that would revive Groveton. Today, in the heart of Groveton, along the banks of the lovely Upper Ammonoosuc River, in a valley dominated by the Percy Peaks, Sugarloaf Mountain, and Cape Horn, most of the old mill complex has vanished, and the downtown business district has twice as many empty storefronts as flourishing businesses.

It is time to explore alternative approaches to economic revitalization. For Groveton and the communities of the Upper Connecticut River Valley to gain control over their economic and cultural destiny, they need to address these questions:

+ Why was the mill prosperous for so many years?
+ What caused the mill's demise?
+ What lessons can residents of the Groveton region learn from the successes and failures of the mill as they strive to build a vibrant local economy?
+ At a time of rapid, human-caused climate change, how can we design a prosperous, low-carbon economy that makes creative use of our natural landscape while conserving, preserving, and restoring the ecological integrity of our native ecosystems?

Communities throughout the United States that have lost their economic mainstay must grapple with similar challenges. Each community is a reflection of its unique topography, climate, ecology, and land-use history. In times of economic crisis, each must discover its own distinctive path to revitalization. The experiences of other communities' struggles to revive a failed economy can provide former mill and factory towns with valuable insights. I hope the stories in *You Had a Job for Life* offer consolation, inspiration, and a few laughs to those who are struggling to regain control over their own destinies.

A NOTE ON THE GROVETON MILL ORAL HISTORY
PROJECT AND EDITING ORAL HISTORY TRANSCRIPTS

When I began to gather stories for the Groveton Mill Oral History Project late in 2009, the Groveton Paper Board Company had been closed for four years, and the Wausau-Groveton mill had ceased making paper two years earlier. Former shipping department employee Bruce Blodgett gave me a tour of the dank, dark mill colossus a few days after Christmas. The flat, industrial roof had more than a few leaks. The cavernous interior had been stripped of most of the machinery. Fortunately, Wausau's two fine-papers machines were still more or less intact, and I was able to visualize the papermaking process. Those monstrous machines, installed in 1907 and 1972, were considered small, slow, and old. A year or so after my initial tour of the ghost mill, the paper machines were yanked out and scrapped behind the mill. In the autumn of 2012 a wrecking crew began to demolish the mill.

The Groveton Mill Oral History Project began as an assignment in a graduate ethnography course taught by Millie Rahn at Plymouth State University in the winter of 2009–2010. I soon realized I was a willing captive of a far greater project. By the summer of 2013 I had accumulated over one hundred hours of taped interviews with fifty-six individuals who had worked at the mill or grown up in Groveton.

The transcripts of these interviews fill more than two thousand pages. The careful reader of this book and those transcripts will detect that I have edited the transcriptions to assure greater clarity, to eliminate redundancies and digressions, and, whenever possible, to remove my questions and comments. I have endeavored to assure that the editing process maintained the integrity of the spoken word and kept faith with the meaning and intent of my generous informants. This book would have been intolerably long, and at times confusing, if I had not edited the raw transcripts.

Sandy White was one of the first women to work on a paper machine crew. In the passage below, she reflected on the mill closing. To demonstrate how I edited transcripts, I supply the raw transcript, followed by the edited version. The retained passages of the raw transcript are shown in italic.

SANDY WHITE'S RESPONSE TO THE CLOSING
OF THE MILL: RAW TRANSCRIPT

Sandy White (sw): *It gives you a sick, sick feeling when any of these mills go down.* Of course that one especially. Campbell was bad enough. This one, *I think everybody was in total shock when this one went down. And I'll never understand why. I cannot make myself believe that this mill was not making money.*

I know better, and so does everybody. I don't know whether it was transportation, but then rail come in; they built this terminal up here for shipping and everything else, so to me that can't be the cop-out. Who knows? *We've got guys out there that are playing God with a lot of lives. I know the paper industry is really catching hell everywhere.* But when they send — I think *Groveton Paper Board*, I think *their machine went to Vietnam. I mean, what's wrong with this picture? Because they can make it for half what we can*, apparently. *That's the name of the game. Anybody that can make the most money, that's what's going to happen. Never mind the little guy. They don't count anymore. Haven't for years. It's money; the only thing that counts. It makes me bitter*, but facts are facts. *I don't know what their real reason was.* They could make anything you wanted for paper on those machines and make it well. That I do know. The old guys — they could make paper without all these modern instruments. I don't know — and the money they put in that mill. That's another thing that puzzles me. Why put all that money in that mill and then shut it down. It makes no sense. Maybe they can make me understand; I don't know. But nobody's offered to [*laughs*].

Jamie Sayen: I don't get a sense that there were a lot of people from headquarters in Wisconsin who spent a lot of time here trying to help us understand it.

sw: No. *From what I understand, they just came in one day and said, "This is it; you're going down." No options, no reasons. Nothing. They didn't give them an excuse or a reason.* Something's wrong with this picture. *That shouldn't be allowed. Even a good lie would have helped.*

EDITED VERSION: It gives you a sick, sick feeling when any of these mills go down. I think everybody was in total shock when this one went down. I'll never understand why. I cannot make myself believe that this mill was not making money. I know better. We've got guys out there that are playing God with a lot of lives. I know the paper industry is really catching hell everywhere. Groveton Paper Board, their machine went to Vietnam. I mean, what's wrong with this picture? Because they can make it for half what we can. That's the name of the game. Anybody that can make the most money, that's what's going to happen. Never mind the little guy. They don't count anymore. Haven't for years. It's money; the only thing that counts. It makes me bitter. I don't know what their real reason was. From what I understand, they just came in one day and said, "This is it; you're going down." No options. Nothing. They didn't give them an excuse or a reason. That shouldn't be allowed. Even a good lie would have helped.

I HOPE MY EDITS have retained the spirit, intent, and humanity of the storyteller, even though I have had to delete interesting information. I also hope that some readers will be impatient to read the original transcripts or, better yet, to listen to the interviews themselves. They are available in the Northumberland Library, Groteton, New Hampshire.

Chapter One

THE LIFE
OF THE TOWN

FOLLOWING THE CIVIL WAR, as demand for paper products soared, scientists developed methods for the mass production of paper using wood fibers. Investors began to build paper mills in New England towns with access to softwood forests, railroad service, and river power. In 1891, three investors began to construct the Groveton Paper Mill on the bank of the Upper Ammonoosuc River, where two major railroads converged. The mill was part of an emerging national and global economy: it depended on outside investors; it required raw materials from other regions; it needed far-flung markets to sell its paper products; and it competed with other paper mills.

The village of Groveton is located in the township of Northumberland, lying along the Connecticut River, north of Lancaster, south of Stratford, and west of Stark in northern New Hampshire's Coös County. For centuries, Abenaki hunters had pursued game in the region, but there is scant evidence that they established permanent settlements. Northumberland was settled in 1767 by two frontier families. When they arrived, the vast old-growth forests of red spruce, balsam fir, white pine, sugar maple, yellow birch, and American beech teemed with moose, wolves, bears, lynx, otters, foxes, martens, mink, muskrats, woodchucks, and passenger pigeons. The rivers and streams abounded with Atlantic salmon and brook trout. Agents of the European fur trade had extirpated beaver in the previous century. Wolverines had also disappeared. By the end of the nineteenth century, land-clearing for agriculture and commercial logging, along with swamp drainage, dams, sawdust pollution from sawmills, and reckless overhunting and overfishing, provoked the Coös County historian to lament: "Coös, from being the finest sporting ground in the world, is now about the poorest."[1]

Eighteenth-century Northumberland farmers built small sawmills and gristmills as soon as they could. The remoteness of the region protected the old-growth forests of northern New Hampshire and northeastern Vermont from commercial lumbering until the Grand Trunk Railway crossed the Upper Ammonoosuc River four miles north of Northumberland village in 1852. The railroad men recognized that the uncleared woodland on the western bank of the Upper Ammonoosuc, about a mile north of its confluence with the Connecticut River, would make an ideal spot for a new village that could supply the steam engines with wood, water, and other necessities. They named it Groveton, in memory of the grove of trees that had been cleared to build the rail depot and village. John Eames, grandson of a leading early settler, immediately began construction of a store and a hotel, the Melcher House, along the tracks just west of the station. The population of Northumberland nearly doubled during the 1850s.

In 1863, Eames and partner Charles Bellows built a dam and a sawmill on the Upper Ammonoosuc, just south of the railroad bridge. The first house of worship, the Methodist Episcopal Church, was constructed in 1869. That year, Gilbert Soule, a Maine lumberman, acquired controlling interest in Eames and Bellows's sawmill. Soule and his sons transformed it into the village's largest manufacturer. Groveton also boasted smaller clapboard and shingle mills and a tannery.

In 1870, Eames and two partners, the Holyoke brothers, acquired the uninhabited township of Odell, east of the Nash Stream and northeast of Groveton, for roughly a dollar an acre. Lumbermen dammed a boggy area in Odell to create the Nash Stream Bog. From the bog, Nash Stream flows south ten miles to its confluence with the Upper Ammonoosuc about four miles north of Groveton.

A second railroad line, the Boston and Maine, connected Groveton with Concord, New Hampshire, and Boston in 1872. The following year, George Holyoke sold a huge shipment of lumber to New York City, unwisely accepting housing as security. When the 1873 financial panic wrecked the nation's economy, Eames and the Holyokes were forced to sell Nash Stream to Gilbert Soule.

Groveton's steady growth stalled in the early 1880s, owing to a decline in housing prices. By 1889, the economy had revived, and Groveton's greatest decade of growth commenced. Investors from Massachusetts sank $150,000 into the construction of the Weston Lumber Company sawmill and a dam half a mile south of the Soule Mill. Weston's mill burned down in August 1890 and was immediately rebuilt. By 1898 the Weston mill complex included a box factory, a gristmill and grain elevator, a large general store, a wagon and sled construction and repair shop, and a harness department. Weston had acquired two-thirds of Odell Township, and throughout the 1890s the mill sawed approximately twelve million board feet a year. It employed 125 men during the sawing season and 300 men and 100 horses during the winter logging season.

After 1901, the paper mill dominated the tight-knit, remote community. Most everyone in Groveton shares Hadley Platt's belief that "the mill was the life of this town." Kathy Mills Frizzell reflected upon how the Groveton Paper Mill affected her childhood: "There's the kids' perspective of growing up in Groveton with the mill here. How you incorporated the whistles, the smells. We had the nine o'clock curfew whistle. We went home with the noon whistle. It was a presence in our lives in many ways — the woodpile. Just what it looked like, and what it felt like being in Groveton from the kids' perspective."

Herb Miles, born in 1920, lived on a farm in Stark, the township east of Northumberland. He recalled there were farms in downtown Groveton in his youth: "A fellow by the name of Swift had a farm right there [in town], a barn, had eight to ten head of cattle. In the summer he drove them up to Moore's pasture — grazing, and bring them back, milk 'em."

Cars were scarce. Miles and his sister traveled by horse: "I remember the gravel streets, the watering troughs. You drove horses in the winter. My sister and I would come downtown to the company store. We were eight, nine, ten years old. We'd hitch up a driving horse, a sleigh. Mother would write out a list. We'd cross the river right there on Brooklyn Street at the far end over to the company store to get groceries."

On Saturday nights, Miles went to the movies: "I had a cousin who lived out beyond the Red Dam [a mile upriver from town]. I'd come out and stay with him and then we'd walk over to the street on Saturday night. We would go to the movie theater. The first movies I went to were silent. That's how old I am. They didn't have the talking machine, talking movies. Finally they had it; that was something. 'Squawk, squawk.' But it talked. George Russ had a diner right there by the theater, and you could buy a hot dog and a bottle

Main Street, Groveton, looking north, ca. 1930. At the intersection, just before the nearest car on left, one could make a left turn onto State Street. A right turn onto Mechanic Street led to the mill. The Eagle Hotel, at the north end of Main Street on the right, was demolished in 1999. (Courtesy GREAT)

of sody pop and go to the movies for a quarter. George's son would give us a bottle of pop once in a while, and that would give us five cents [extra] to buy a bag of popcorn when we went in the show."

Len Fournier, born in 1925, lived in one of the mill tenements: "My father worked in what they called the 'bull gang' in the mill. They did everything, moving stuff, unloading. He earned twenty-seven dollars a week." Len played around the mill: "I can remember when we were kids down here, we used to get ahold of them horseshoe nails and put them on the track and make the train run over them and make a pair of scissors. It would weld them together. Me and the girl who lived a couple of houses down used to go over in the sawmill yard. Sometimes there would be extra long boards sticking out. Boy, they'd make a good teeter board. After we broke off two or three of them, we got driven out of there."

Fournier remembered an old man who fished near the mill: "An old guy by the name of McGreavy used to fish out of the river all the time. Of course the sewage used to go into the river down there. He'd pull eel and fish out of there. I don't know if he ate them or not." Although Albert "Puss" Gagnon couldn't swim, he remembered family outings to the river, upstream of the mill: "We used to go out Red Dam, and we'd swim in between the pulp logs. After a while, they put a stop to that. For years my father and my mother would take us out there to that dam."

As a boy, John Rich took a hot dinner to his father at the mill: "I could bring my father's dinner pail in. That's all my father wanted me in there. There was a lot of places to get hurt there. He'd go to work in the afternoon or the evening; I'd bring it in five o'clock, something like that. He'd have something hot."

Shirley Brown remembered walking through the mill: "During the winter, when it was cold, we'd walk to the end of the mill and walk all the way through the mill just to keep warm. It was pretty scary."

Coal and chemicals befouled the air around town. Many children suffered from asthma, and when the air was especially bad, they had to remain inside, where there was a good chance someone was a heavy smoker. "But that was part of life back then," Hadley Platt observed with a fatalism common to natives of Groveton.

Platt also remembered that people scavenged coal cinders: "Around the mill, there was a lot of free heat because the mill burnt coal at the time. They had coal cinders, and people used to get it by the truckloads, and sift it, and burn it in their stoves. We burned it at our house. We'd go down there with a truck, and load them, take them home, and take them to different people. Then they'd sift it out and put it in their stoves and burn it."

The company store near the river, where Soule's sawmill had stood, supplied most mill workers' families with necessities during the hard times of the 1930s. "My mother was born in '27, and my grandfather worked at the mill," Bill Russ said. "She never remembers them having any money. Everything that they had was purchased down at the store. It was almost like: you worked there, you were rewarded; you get all your food you needed there. Everybody was so happy to have jobs. They could eat."

Shirley Brown thought the mill paid only in script redeemable at the company store: "My dad, all the years that he worked in the mill, never got a paycheck. He got a yellow slip. We lived in the company houses; we got our groceries at the company store. The oil and wood was through the company store. If it hadn't been for the company store, a lot of people in this town wouldn't have survived. When you went to work in the mill, it was almost a contract that went with it; you deal with the company store. We never got anything that didn't come from the company store."

"The big old company store, we used to buy our groceries there," Hadley Platt said. "Nobody had any money on payday because they owed it all to the store for groceries. Times were hard. Everybody bought their groceries there who worked in the mill. They were lucky if they got a dollar in change, because most of it went for groceries."

A horse named Old Billy Call pulled the company store delivery wagon, Raymond Jackson recalled: "My father used to go round to the houses on Crow Hill. He'd see the woman who'd tell him, 'I want a pound of hamburger, flour, whatever.' The next day he'd deliver it to her. [Old Billy] had been on the job quite a while, and my father would go into one house, and he'd go back out and go to the next house, and the horse would kind of follow up the street behind him." In the mid-1930s, a Model A truck replaced Old Billy, enabling Edwin Jackson to drive to far-flung places, such as Auburn, Maine, for supplies.

Puss Gagnon remembered that during those years, downtown Groveton was "lively. Goddamn lively. You had one, two, three, four, five beer joints. You ain't got any no more. That ain't counting the Moose Club, neither. There was one in the Eagle Hotel. The Tip Top, the next building, that was a beer joint. [Everett's] Diner was a beer joint. Dinty Moore's was a beer joint, and up to the Union Hotel was a beer joint. Liveliest little town you ever see. Deader than a son of a bitch now. Back then, you go down Saturday nights, you never could find a place to park the car anywhere, the town would be so full. Now you go down, there's all kinds of room."

The movie theater had discount nights, Gagnon recalled: "Had movies every night. One night was chum night. I remember when I was too young for anything, go down and stand in front of the picture hall, chum night, somebody would be coming by themselves — they'd haul you in. Two for the price of one. They had one night that was half price. Then they had bank night. They'd draw money, bank night. Quite a nice movie house."

After Rosa Gaudette Roberge's father died in late 1942, her mother was forced to rent an apartment above the recently closed company store down by the mill's converting plant and print shop. "Our apartment was small," she remembered. "We were on the opposite end of where the furnace was, and

State Street, looking north, in the early 1940s. The paper mill is behind the photographer, and the Opera House tower with its clock is at the north end of the street. One interviewee recalled running over the traffic dummy at the intersection of State and Main one Sunday morning while hauling a truckful of bark from the drum barker. (Courtesy Becky Craggy)

boy, we didn't get much heat, I'll tell you." The apartment had no hot running water: "When us kids would play, of course it was dirty down there where all that coal, soot, and crap. There was a pipe coming out outside of the print shop, and it spit hot water. So we'd take a pail over and put it underneath and get hot water to dump in the tub. We'd go off and play, and when it was full, we carry it upstairs. That was memorable."

Fred Shannon's family moved into one of the mill tenements shortly after the war ended. He was ten, and he discovered the ideal playground. "We used to play in the mill, everywhere," he said. "At night we were pretty sneaky. Kids will be kids. We'd go in there and get a piece of cardboard, and slide down the conveyor belts. A couple of them would run ahead and get the wheels all spinning, and then we'd go down through out on the shipping dock. When I stop and look back at it, yeah, it probably was [dangerous]. Like swimming over there to the [Brooklyn Street] Dam. They'd have the gates half open, letting the water out, so we'd climb up there and jump off on them. I often think, how come we didn't get sucked right down through? But we did come through them gates one time during the [maintenance] shutdown. They had the gates wide open; the river was drained so they could work on the dam. We went up by the old railroad bridge with a plank — three or four of us. We'd get on that plank and we'd come right down through the little channel. Right on through those gates going like a bat out of hell. The current would be strong, and away we'd be going. We'd get back to shore just before we'd get to that covered bridge, and we'd get off. Carry it all the way back up and do it again."

After the Second World War ended, the mill and the town, along with most of the United States, entered an extended period of prosperity. In 1946 the mill produced ninety-four tons of paper a day. After two decades of relentless activity, the old, rat-infested mill had been transformed into a modern mill that had nearly doubled in size; by 1967 it turned out 450 tons a day. Just about anyone who wanted a job at the mill could get one.

Shirley MacDow was hired in 1951, right out of high school. She recalled downtown Groveton in those years: "There were several stores, and the towns-people would sit on the street at night and talk to everybody on the street in your car. It was very laid back. But it was a busy little town. There was all kinds of stores, restaurants. Everett's Diner [would] have a dance there every Sat-urday night, so everybody would go downstairs to the dance. You hardly ever went out of town. And then, you'd go up to Dinty Moore's Diner, after you'd had a few drinks, and have something to eat before you went home at night."

Dinty Moore's on State Street served beer on one side and soda pop on the other. Neal Brown described how the clientele for the two operations occasionally mingled: "The woods people were a little bit more apt to be the wild and crazy guys. They lived a pretty rough life. I don't want to be dispar-aging; there were a lot of good people who worked in the woods. But there were some pretty rough-and-tumble guys who lived out in the logging camps, and then they'd come in on the weekends and raise hell all weekend. Dinty Moore's had a bar on one side, and they'd hang out there. One of them would run out of money, and then he'd come outside, and all of us guys would be out there. He'd lay down on the ground and tell everybody they could jump on his stomach from the railing, and if he didn't flinch, we had to give him a quarter. Get some money and go and drink some more."

Thursdays were paydays. "It was a busy little town on Thursday night," Thurman Blodgett remembered. "Sat on the street and watched the people walk by. That was big excitement. That's when everybody was doing their shopping. Watch the drunks fall out of the beer joints. Go to the next one, somebody'd get to fighting. I didn't know they was mill guys, but after I got in the mill, some of these guys are still working there."

"When the mill blowed them stacks off," Blodgett shuddered, "you wanted to get out of town. Stank like a son of a gun. They'd probably blow every three–four hours. That old sulfur; you could see it just laying right into town."

"Oh God, you'd get that old sulfur smell in the morning and sometimes it would be like a cloud right down on the town," Fred Shannon added. "Sulfur from the cooking of the chips. It was pretty nasty in the mill. Some places you had to go, if they had just got done blowing one of the digesters, and then they'd bleed off the pressure, boy, you couldn't see; if you needed to go through there, you had to hold your breath and run like hell through and down the stairs. If you didn't know where you were going, you'd probably die. It was pretty strong, oh, yeah, real strong in the town."

Sylvia Stone said you simply had to endure the smell: "In the Old Red Office we'd get the sulfur smell terrible. Some days you'd have to sit all day with a tissue over your nose, it was so bad. If you wanted a job, you had to do it. There was nothing we could do about it. It would happen off and on. Not all the time. There were days it was really bad."

Neal Brown was almost always outside playing as a youngster in the 1950s: "Groveton did not smell nice. If you got a weather inversion in the summertime, you kept your houses closed, no matter how hot it was — the strong sulfur smell that you had down there, the rotten egg smell that would come out of the mill. You got a little bit used to it, but you still knew it was there."

Tom Bushey's father told him about hunting downwind of the mill in the 1940s and 1950s: "He said you'd walk through the snow, and it would be up over your knee oftentimes, and he'd step into the snow, and you could see the layers of black and yellow and white, black and yellow and white. The stratification." Soot, sulfur, and snow.

Groveton residents drew some consolation from the belief that the smell wasn't as bad as the stench emanating from the much larger Kraft pulp mill in Berlin, twenty-five miles to the east. "That was our claim to fame," Kathy Frizzell remarked with gallows humor. She remembered that the mill would blow two quick whistles to alert asthma sufferers to get inside because a particularly nasty blast had just been emitted from the digesters.

Coal dust was another hazard from the mill. Shirley MacDow remembered having to rewash the laundry many times, thanks to the mill's boilers: "My husband and I lived over on West Street in a small apartment. They were burning coal at the mill then. And to put out a laundry, you knew when you brought it in, it was going to be black. But you know what? We all lived the same way. 'Oh, the mill just blasted us with some more coal dust.' You didn't hear people grumbling about it. I'd grumble, but it was sort of, 'Oh, well, I've got to wash my clothes all over again.' Every time the boiler would burp, out come the coal dust. It was just a way of life. I guess we all thought, 'If you are going to live here and work here, this is what you are going to have to put up with.' You didn't get into all this clean air stuff. Back in the old days, my God, everything went into the river, up the smokestack." Her longtime boss, Jim Wemyss, asked a group of former mill workers: "What color was my house when I lived in town? Black! I painted it black because that way nobody could say my house doesn't look good." The mill switched to oil around 1958, and thereafter the laundry remained white, although it might still smell of sulfur.

"Back then there wasn't the concern about environmental hazards and the connection to your health," Kathy Frizzell explained. "I'm aware of a high cancer incidence in Groveton, and I can't help but think the smells we lived with in Groveton, what was released into the air, could have had an impact on us. It was taken in stride. It was our life. Other kids would say, 'Oh, you're from "Stinky Groveton."' I think that impacted us because I think I used to say, 'I'm from the armpit of the North Country.' Lancaster and Littleton are so lovely and genteel, and Groveton was just stinky, smelly, and dirty." When she lived with her grandfather, the house had a coal furnace: "He smoked a pipe, my mother smoked, the mill spewed [laughs]. You put up with things. I do have a susceptibility to bronchitis, and I do have a calcified spot in my lung, and I can't help but think it's all the stuff I grew up breathing."

Shirley Brown reflected on the health hazards of mill towns: "Groveton, Berlin, and Lincoln have the highest cancer rate in New Hampshire. When you used to walk downtown, or when we were kids, you'd get home, and you'd look yourself in the mirror, and you could see in your eyes and mouth, that everything was black and sooty." Her son, Neal, added: "We went through a period of time where we had six or seven people in town who died of heart attacks in their thirties and forties, and early cancers, people dying of cancer when they were in their early thirties."[2]

Strong community and family bonds in Groveton helped to overcome the unpleasant smells, the filth, and the illnesses. As America became increasingly mobile and rootless in the postwar, automobile culture, isolated Groveton remained a remarkably stable community. "Somebody said you could throw a blanket over this town, and it would be one family," Jim Wemyss joked. "One day I was talking about somebody in this town," he said on another occasion, "and [town manager Bob Mayhew] said, 'Jimmy, you can't talk about him; he's my third cousin.' I said, 'For Christ's sake, Bob, is there anybody in this town you aren't related to?' He said, 'Yeah, you' [*laughs*]." Lolly LaPointe recalled a friend whose father and grandfather were both working at the mill when he was hired. "Three generations worked there," he marveled, "until they retired."

Groveton kids roamed the streets and neighboring woods without adult supervision. "We were let out in the morning. When the noon whistle would blow, we had to come back for lunch — gobble, out for the rest of the afternoon. When we got older, we were also out at night," Kathy Frizzell recalled fondly. "We had a gang, the Roughriders. It was kids of all ages, boys and girls. The big kids took care of the little kids. Gangs in a good sense. We had a fort, a playhouse; we were organized; we played baseball. We were roaming all over the hill. Parents were not involved in this. We had rules; we couldn't go in the river. It was a safe environment. Any parent could discipline you. There were kind of eyes on you, but for the most part they didn't know what you were doing, and we didn't need them to know. We were very industrious in our play, and very self-directed. I'm quite nostalgic about that kind of play being lost in the world."

Bill Astle remembered the trucks that hauled the bark away from the mill's drum barker: "Boy, one of my earlier memories of the mill is living on Odell Park. Ten-wheelers would haul the bark to the bark dump. They had holes in the tailgate that allowed the sap to flow out, and it would be like you had a water truck going down the road. We were all out there playing barefoot — five- or six-year-old kids. You had to time it so you could get across the street before the next truck came through because the sun would dry it out in a matter of a couple of hours. If you walked across it, it would be sticky and you'd end up stuck to the pavement — not to the point that you couldn't get away. They dumped the bark down where the town has its clarifiers now. It was all wooded then. It would make all these little moguls there. It was a great place; all the neighborhood kids would be down there playing army, whatever. You'd jump down behind one mound and pop up kind of like whack-a-mole or something."

As a young man, before taking a job at the mill, Astle was a social worker for several years. He learned that not everyone had enjoyed the idyllic childhood he remembered: "There were things going on in their homes I never would have dreamed of. I'd always assumed that I grew up with *Ozzie and Harriet* and so did everybody else. I came to find it was a much different place than it appeared on the surface. Groveton has always been a tight-knit community. It takes care of their own, rallies if someone comes on hard times."

Kathy Frizzell's father never worked in the mill, and she grew up poor, yet she never felt stigmatized: "I was friends of Holly Schumacher [niece of Jim Wemyss Jr.] early on. I went out to the red house by the railroad trestle, swam in the pool, and went ice skating. Birthday parties and things like that; it was very nice. I was always kind of aware of this sort of fantasy life. A life that would never be mine, but privy to a glimpse of it. It was sort of like, 'Wouldn't it be nice?' I really appreciated the exposure I had when I was invited out to the swimming pool or the birthday party, and the toys that they had." Kathy later reflected on how she viewed the Wemyss and Schumacher families: "It was, I guess, the way a child would think about a rich, kindly, but demanding, grandfather. You were aware that you were at the mercy of his benevolence."

Even as a child, Kathy was a worrier: "We lived with the river, and I re-member in my younger years the pulp in the river, the smells from the river, when the river was high, when the river was low. Was there enough wood on the woodpile? Were they going to be able to make paper for a while longer? Is there enough water in the river to get the pulp down? There was a threat of fire in the woodpile. Accidents. One of my classmates' father was missing an arm from the mill. It was just worrying about the livelihood of the town. What if something happened to the mill? Because even as a kid, we realized it was a one-horse town, and we were at the mercy of how well the mill did."

Kathy and her playmates worried when union contracts were under nego-tiation: "I remember as a kid, and I was seven, eight, ten years old, schoolyard conversations would be, 'What's going to happen if they go out on strike? There won't be any income. What if the mill closed?' I remember this sort of being a threat, like a bogeyman. People would generally get along, but at times of possible strike and negotiation, you really felt that separation of the workers and the management. So it was terrifying as a kid."

Albert "Puss" Gagnon (pronounced "Gon-yer") was nicknamed "Ti-Puss," or "Little Cat," by his mother. He had one of the most extraordinary careers at the Groveton Paper Mill. Hired at age fifteen, fired — and rehired — at twenty-nine, he retired at age forty-five after a near-fatal accident. At age eighty-four, two months before his death in March 2010, Puss cheerfully described his hell-raising career.

Hired at fifteen: Puss was thirteen when his father, a woodsman, died at age fifty-three in 1938 following a two-year illness. The family was poor, and in the summer of 1940 Puss decided to get a job at the mill. *How did you get a job that young?* "I lied to them to start with. There was two of us. One kid, he was pretty near eighteen; so Red [O'Neil] came up to him:'How old are you?' 'Seventeen. I'll be eighteen in a couple of months.' 'Come back in a couple of months.' He came over to me, and I knew by then, lie or I wasn't going to get a job.'How old are you?' I says, 'Eighteen.' 'Get your card.' That's when the [mill] timekeeper sent me up to the high school because he knew goddamn well I wasn't old enough. And when you get them permits like that, you're not supposed to work no overtime; you're not supposed to work nights. I worked both."

I was hot: "I remember going in there [to the boiler room] one night, they had to have a guy lead me down to the mill. I was so goddamned hot. I went down there. It was me and Albert Auger on these hand fires. When I first started in the mill there, there were three wood fires. I tried to pick these long pokers to poke the fire because the steam was going down. Couldn't hit the hole. I threw the poker on the floor and lay down and went to sleep. The head fireman came over, and Albert says to him, 'Puss is awful drunk, ain't he?' 'No, no,' Carl says. 'He's sick.' So he worked for me all night. He was the boss."

Fired: Puss and his two crewmates were fired on July 22, 1954, because they were caught sleeping by engineer Bill Verrill, not once, but twice on the night shift. "When I worked in the fire room, time dragged. Sit there and do nothing. On the big boilers there's nothing to do. It's all automatic. You've just got to watch the board. I got done because they caught us sleeping on the job. 'You ain't heard the end of this.' You know fuckin' well you ain't, especially when the big boss catches you — Bill Verrill."

"You can't let the steam get to four hundred pound pressure. It would blow them to hell if the pop-off belt didn't release," electrician Herb Miles explained. "Bill Verrill, the engineer, walked by and woke them all up. When he came back, they were asleep again. They fired them all, but you know Wemyss hardly ever fired a person. Most guys that got fired, he would bring them back." Gagnon shared with me the memo about his rehiring. It read, in part: "These men will be re-hired with loss of old departmental seniority. . . . Management will endeavor to furnish continuous work during the year period, but will not guarantee that this will be done. Present mill seniority will be restored at the rate of 5 years for each year worked, based on date of re-hiring."[3]

Rehired: "[After the firing] I went over on Littleton dam. What I didn't like about it was traveling. You're using a lot of your wages just for running. I run into Bill Swift [foreman of the wood yard]: 'You want a job? C'mon down; I'll give you a job.' So I went down on the barker."

Run over: In June 1970 Puss Gagnon was working in the rail yard of the pulp mill. "We was moving one car, and I slipped off the ladder in the back and fell on the ground and underneath it. It went down, oh I would say, probably a couple of hundred feet, dragging me down under them pockets. I couldn't fit under them; I was too fat. All my ribs is broke; back was broke; fractured skull. I know Doc Hinkley was telling everybody when they took me with the ambulance, he says, 'When he comes back, it'll be in a pine box.' I was in Hanover for a month. When I got there they said I'd be there six months at least. I didn't break no bones below [his legs], just up in here [chest]."

Puss drew workers' compensation, and he became a junk dealer. "All I done is bought and sold junk. Just something to do. I remember one time, the little guy down here at the mill office — he looked after, I guess, insurance things — he says, 'You know, you ain't supposed to be doing that.' I said, 'I don't give a fuck what I'm supposed to be doing. I'm doing it; I'm going to keep doing it.' They never bothered me, neither. And I used to bring stuff right in back of the mill office building. They'd see me; a lot of fellows said, 'I don't know how you get away with that bullshit.' I says, 'Fuck 'em. They think I'm just gonna lay down and die, I'm not.' You've got to do something."

Chapter Two

FEEDING

THE MILL

PRIOR TO 1972, you could not miss the seventy-five-foot-high piles of pulpwood as you approached the village of Groveton from the south. The woodpiles formed a haunting symmetry with North and South Percy Peaks in the Nash Stream watershed, seven miles northeast of the Groveton Paper Mill. For nearly a century, loggers working in the Nash Stream and surrounding forests cut the wood destined for those piles that fed the mill throughout the winter.

The forests of northern New Hampshire had survived the farmer's and woodsman's ax almost to the end of the century because of the region's remoteness, rugged mountains, and lack of reliable transportation to major urban areas. In the summer of 1891, the lyrical "Locals" correspondent to the weekly *Coös County Democrat* celebrated the end of that era: "Now that the Concord and Montreal [Railroad] have got through the village [of Groveton], the way is open for them to escape for the mountains where a great amount of lumber is waiting to be handled by the cars. Unbroken forests farther than the eye can see — dense, silent, beautiful. Great trees, both soft and hard, seem crowded for room. The stillness in those great forests sometimes is too much for any man to bear. Beautiful, because natural, the various scenes — the shadows, the valleys, the hills, and various shades of foliage all combined will bring the sublimest thoughts to those who view the scenery from the hilltop or the valley."[1]

Intensive logging of New England's old-growth forests, dominated by two-foot-diameter red spruce, supplied the lumber to construct the mid- and late nineteenth-century industrial cities of the northeastern United States. Reflecting populist sentiments of the day, the *Democrat*'s editor in 1894 lamented that absentee corporations, not farmers, owned most of the region's forests: "But very little timber is owned by private individuals. We are perfectly safe in asserting that the farmers throughout the Coös country do not own enough timber to supply the home market, and most of them do not own enough for their own building purposes."[2]

The roof of the wood room and the woodpile, looking south, in the early 1950s. (Courtesy GREAT)

Paper was made out of old rags and was relatively scarce and expensive until scientific advances in papermaking after the Civil War allowed mills to manufacture paper using wood fiber. The sudden abundance of cheap paper toward the end of the nineteenth century enabled the mass production of newspapers, magazines, books, and toilet paper. Around the time the old-growth forests were vanishing, paper mills with new, high-speed paper machines began to manufacture paper using smaller-diameter, second-growth spruce and fir logs.

The long fibers of New England's softwood spruce and fir produced high-quality paper. In the 1890s, investment capital poured into the northern New England wilderness to build paper mill towns in Millinocket and

Rumford, Maine. Wall Street investors required new corporations, such as Great Northern and International Paper, to acquire millions of acres of forestlands to assure the mills' wood supply. Nineteenth-century timber barons were eager to sell off their cut-over lands at bargain prices.

The great rivers of the region — the Connecticut, Androscoggin, Kennebec, and Penobscot, as well as the smaller Upper Ammonoosuc River, supplied waterpower to drive pulpwood to the mill, water for the papermaking process, and steam to power the mill. In 1892 the *Coös County Democrat* reported: "The Weston Lumber Co. have completed their road into the big bogs in Odell. They have raised the dam six feet and have the bushes nearly all cut on the bog, which will give them a pond two miles long and a half mile wide. A large body of water to hold up in the mountains."[3] A decade later the paper mill acquired the Nash Stream, and until a disastrous flood in 1969 washed out the dam's earthen abutment, the Nash Stream Bog assured adequate water supplies for the mill.

Prior to the advent of heavy logging machinery in the 1950s, logging was a labor-intensive, winter activity. The nineteenth-century sawmills and the twentieth-century paper mills established logging camps at strategic places in the forests. Old-time loggers and teamsters driving horse-drawn sleds used the snow and ice to move sawlogs, and later four-foot pulp logs, from forest to river's edge or to a railroad siding.

Loggers often toiled in temperatures twenty or more degrees below zero from before sunrise until after sunset, equipped only with axes and handsaws. They cut, moved, and piled wood by hand. Many loggers and horses were killed or maimed when a horse-drawn sled sluiced — went out of control on an icy downhill stretch. Loggers suffered injury in a variety of ways, especially from an ax, a falling tree, or a "widow maker" — a broken or dead branch hung up on a tree that, when dislodged, could crush the unsuspecting logger. In 1899, Thomas Gibbons, while peeling pulpwood, was killed "by a limb falling the distance of about 70 feet, striking him on the head, breaking in his skull. He was helped to his feet by one of his companions and walked a mile after the accident." The impoverished French Canadian died before the doctor arrived.[4]

A river driver in the Nash Stream was badly injured by dynamite in 1898. In 1909, Henry Downing "was assisting on blasting the ice in the [Nash] stream when the ice broke, letting him into the water. The current carried him under the ice several feet but he caught his arm around a log and held himself up until men cut through the ice and rescued him."[5]

Over time, the Groveton paper mill accumulated about ninety thousand acres of timberland in northern Vermont and New Hampshire. When he bought the mill in 1940, Old Jim Wemyss retained most of the managers, but he replaced the superintendent of the woods operation with his friend Lester Fogg, who insisted the new owner accompany him on a tour of Nash Stream. "We had a lot of land," Young Jim said. "They drove deep into Nash Stream, and [Fogg] walked him into the woods — in the snow. Father said, 'I'm not ready to go in the goddamn snow like this. I'm not dressed for this, Lester.' There was a dryer felt, which is off a paper machine, hung between two trees, and made kind of like a tepee. And in there was a horse, and there was a cot and a bucksaw, and a little stove. And he said, 'You see this man here? This is how he's working for you. To cut your wood. He lives with a horse.' Not just us; this was all over the country. 'Now,' he says, 'When somebody tells you to cut the price of wood to these people fifty cents a cord, you think about what you saw, and get down and figure out how to get the price of your paper up fifty cents. But don't take the money away from your woodsmen. You need them. You can't replace men like them. If you're going to treat these men like that, I'll work for you.' My father did almost the same thing to me when I joined the company."

Near the entrance to the Nash Stream watershed the paper mill maintained a company farm that raised cattle and horses for its logging operations. The company's logging camps boasted rudimentary bunkhouses, a cook shack, and shelters for horses, called "daigles." On Lester Fogg's advice, Old Jim phased out the camps during World War II. For the next couple of decades independent contractors operated logging camps. The contractors paid for equipment, insurance, wages, trucking, and sometimes road building.

Albert Cloutier, a young blacksmith, arrived from southern Quebec in 1948 to work in one of the camps. He did most of his work at night: "If I shoe the horse in the morning, they lost time. I figure, what the hell, I'm gonna shoe them, and everybody's happy. Every night somebody comes; we stayed in the blacksmith shop sometimes till nine o'clock at night. Because the guys keep talking; all young guys like me. They start work, get up about five o'clock. We eat about six thirty, six, and the guys go get the horse ready and go in the woods. [In the daytime] I make some ax handles, carving some few little things. I sold ax handles for twenty-five cents." Cloutier recalled that there were about a dozen horses in camp. Two men worked with one horse. One man would haul the logs to the log yard, where the other would cut them into four-foot lengths and pile them.

By the 1940s, trucks transported most of the pulpwood. John Rich started hauling pulpwood from Nash Stream when he was fifteen. "My father had trucks," Rich said. "I had a man with me; we loaded the pulp. There were piles along twitch roads. They'd get a road smoothened out in there in the winter, places you could never get into in the summer. That was a good job. I'd be the first one up there, about six o'clock. It was dark. Every morning it snowed. The air was all full of snow coming down — frost, sparkling away. It was pretty, really. Every morning you got an inch of fluff, anyways. Sometimes you got two feet." One year, he recalled, "we hauled across a beaver dam. Jesus, it was all right until it started thawing in the spring."

A "scaler," employed by the mill, measured each load of pulpwood delivered to the mill or to one of several piles along the Upper Ammonoosuc River. Most of the time, pulp drivers felt they were treated fairly by scalers. Herb Miles drove a truck in the late 1930s: "The scaler would be standing where you come out from the woods, or wherever you were hauling from. Run a stick up there. They could tell by looking at it. Four-foot sticks, three or four tier. The last of it, they had a scaler [at the mill] unloading it. He would scale it, and they would drive out to [the Red Dam a mile north of the mill] and dump it off and go back and get another load."

Occasionally, someone scammed the company, Miles remembered: "They had one fellow, he'd haul a load up through by the office, get a scale, and he'd go out and keep right on going and take it to Berlin and get a scale down there. They caught him after a while."

In the early 1950s mechanization revolutionized logging. One man, using a chainsaw and a skidder, could do the work of many old-time loggers and their increasingly obsolete horses. Gerard Labrecque remembered the early chainsaws: "When they first come out with a chainsaw — a chainsaw for two men. The blade was four feet long. On the end there was a handle in there. You could cut a big tree with that. My God, that was heavy. That's why you needed two men to saw." In the mid-1960s, huge chipping machines moved into the forest to turn whole trees into hardwood chips that the Groveton mill used for making its paperboard pulp and, after 1982, for feeding its boiler to generate the mill's electricity.

In springtime, the river crew would put up splashboards on the Red Dam and close the dam's gates most of the way. The impounded water moved pulpwood to the mill in the summer months and supplied clean water required to make steam and paper. In the fall, the river crew would remove the Red Dam's splashboards and install splashboards at the Brooklyn Dam next to the mill to hold water for the mill's papermaking operations during the winter months. The river crew removed the Brooklyn Dam's splashboards in the spring.

Armand Gaudette was head of the river crew for decades. He was notorious for his liberal use of dynamite, his inability to swim, his imperviousness to frigid working conditions, and his malapropisms. Puss Gagnon recalled: "One time, he was cutting some steel for something. [He said,] 'Jesus Christ, this steel's soft.' It ain't soft, it's all the same, for Christ's sake."

After returning from Vietnam in 1969, Bruce Blodgett was assigned to work on Gaudette's crew. "In the springtime that water's ice cold," Blodgett chuckled. "Gaudette would be working barehanded, while us other guys would have rubber-insulated gloves on, standing there freezing. He'd be almost in a T-shirt. Everybody else would be heavy jackets on. Kind of a tough guy."

John Rich enjoyed tormenting Gaudette: "We used to have a guy down in the wood room — Lionel Maltais from Stratford. That was one rugged boy. Armand had these big spikes. They must be about that long [a foot or more]; they spiked in cribbing out in the river. Maltais would take one of them old spikes, and he'd bend 'er. Then he'd flip 'er over, and he'd straighten 'er back out [laughs]. Armand says, 'By Jesus, I ought to be able to do that.' I said, 'You ain't got the guts to do that.' I twitted him all the time. He tried to bend it, and he couldn't do it. He'd get it in a vice with both hands. I said, 'That's cheating, Armand.'"

Many of the river men could not swim. "I was working one day for [Gaudette] up Red Dam," John Rich said. "Him and Everett Pierce got into a tussle about something in the house. He come running out, and Armand had stepped in the pail, and he was still trying to run with this pail on his foot. He went by me, and I gave him a nudge, and he went in. 'You son of a bitch, I can't swim.' I said, 'You'd better learn.' We passed him over the pole and pulled him over to the boom. Armand, he was quite a rig."

After ice-out, the river crews began to knock the piles of softwood into the river, often using dynamite to free up frozen piles. Men working in pairs on rafts used pick poles to direct the wood toward the mill. "In the spring, I worked on the river up there, tearing [the woodpiles] apart on a raft," Puss Gagnon said. "You stand on a raft, pull the wood out. When I first went up there, I was a little scared, but after, no, no. We used to even dynamite them piles. We'd take six sticks of dynamite, tie 'em on little sticks, and go out with the raft. Put them in the pulp pile. You'd find a hole in the wood, and you'd put 'em under the water. If it's on top of the water, it's too much open. I let a few go on top; I got scared of the sons of bitchin' things. But after you do it a while, it's not really that bad. I've been out there in the raft and the wood would come down — sink the raft right to the bottom of the river. You'd have to have the other guy come over and pick you out. That's what was the bad part. I never could swim a stroke." Puss developed a bad habit on the rafts: "I had a tendency to keep moving this foot ahead. Sooner or later I'd walk off the end of this fuckin' thing. Here I go. I knew I was going; I couldn't kind of swing my weight so to stay on the raft."

"We had a logjam at the Brooklyn Dam, and the guys were throwing dynamite at the ice," Jim Wemyss Jr. recalled with amusement. "[Snip Cushing] looked at me: 'Mr. Wemyss, they're nuts. That's not how you get the ice out of there.' I said, 'Well, Snip, how would you get it out of there?' 'Go over to the mill and get me some cutter stick.' They were bars about one and one-eighth inch square about eight feet long. 'Get me a couple of bottles of Old Overholt whiskey.' That's one-hundred-proof whiskey. 'And get me half a dozen sticks of dynamite and some caps and some twine.' 'OK.' He takes the dynamite and wraps it around the end of the stick and he sticks a cap in it, and he's got a cigarette. 'Give me that Old Overholt.' He takes a big swig. 'Would you like one, Jim?' I said, 'Not right now.' He said, 'Come on with me.' We walked out on the boom logs. 'Stand right behind me, and light that thing when I tell you to.' He shoved the dynamite right down under the corner of the logs. He said, 'The blast always goes [sideways], it doesn't go back this way.' BANG! Jesus Christ! The ice started to rumble. 'Give me another one of these.' In about ten minutes all the ice had blown out. Of course two or three more shots of Old Overholt."

The mill's 1920s in-house publication, *Gropaco News*, wrote: "When the 'Drive' is on, the river, filled with logs, has the appearance of a corduroy road; there is little or no water to be seen."[6] Strategic release of water from the Nash Bog Dam and the Red Dam flushed the pulpwood down to boom logs by the mill. If the wind blew the wood upstream, the river crew had to pull the wood down to the mill. Francis Roby, whose handshake was still bone-crunching in his mid-eighties, said: "You had to put a boom and pull [pulpwood] down with the boom. Just pull with a rope. You have a walkway on the edge of the river. There'd be one on each side. You'd pull that boom that you'd got in there — you got a rope on it and you'd pull it right down."

At the mill, crews with long pick poles pulled the four-foot logs out of the river and onto a conveyor belt that carried the logs up to the drum barker. Before shipping out to Vietnam in 1968, Pete Cardin worked on the crew: "I was eighteen years old. A skinny little kid. There was a couple of us that got hired at about that time. All just kids. Then you've got all these old-timers who'd been there forever. Of course, they're going to test the new kids to see if you're going to make it. You either make it or you don't. My hands were baby hands, and boy, there's a trick to pulling pulp out of the river. They use pick poles. You go out, and you stab a piece of pulp, and you use that piece of pulp to kind of haul in the rest of the pulp, and you have a big drag chain that's going, and you pull it into the trough and up the drag chain. You'd kind of throw it like a two-handed spear — *tsssh*. Then you'd just pull that one piece of pulp, and that would kind of catch onto others."

"There was always the initiation, and you had to end up in the river," Cardin laughed. "That river back then was pretty foul. Yes, it was pretty nasty. There was an awful lot of discharge in that river. You could throw something out on the river and it wouldn't splash; it would go *bloooopp*. There was always this head of beer, this head of foam. Nasty."

"You'd sweat. You wouldn't fall in purposely," old-timer Francis Roby remembered. "I fell in a couple of times. You'd miss a stick, and you'd go into the water. Them were the good days."

The conveyor took the pulpwood up to the drum barker, a violent spinning cylinder that removed the bark from the log. After the wood passed through the drum barker, a three-man crew culled the logs that retained some bark and dropped them onto a return conveyor so they could take another trip through the barker. "That was a man's job," Roby said with satisfaction. "That was a good job."

"[The barker] was probably ten to twelve feet in diameter, and it constantly rolled on these big rollers," Lolly LaPointe remembered. "Inside of it they had these baffles, and that would literally tear the bark off. That bark went out through some slats in there, and down into a chute and into a waiting truck underneath there. They'd haul that all away. It rotated on what they called trunions. They were huge steel things; they actually rolled the drum."

There was a reason, LaPointe explained, why the drum barker was a job for new hirees: "Everybody who worked at Groveton Papers started on the drum barker, it seemed like because it was a crazy job. . . . Nobody would stay there because it was really work-intensive and scary. It was really, really a scary job. When I first went there I didn't even know if I dared get out on that chain. It was just absolutely scary all the time. That wood would come at you at a tremendous rate. I'd never seen a pickaroon [an ax-handled tool with a perpendicular, slightly curved metal head for handling pulpwood]. I practically had to pry my fingers off that; I was so stiff and lame and not used to that type of work. After a few weeks you got toughened into it, and it went good after that." LaPointe bid into the stock prep department inside the mill as soon as he could.

The debarked wood continued on conveyors to woodpiles that contained as much as forty-five thousand cords of pulpwood. The wood yard crew built giant retaining walls along the railroad tracks as the piles grew in size and height. They were forever adding heavy conveyors as the pile grew. "They had these chutes about five feet long [and about four feet wide]. They were hardwood; there was irons on them. They probably weighed 250–300 pounds," John Rich said. "Most of them would take two guys, and they'd drag them up, one on each side with a pulp hook. [Lionel] Maltase would take it right on up there [alone]. That old wood was slippery, you know. Peeled pulp. He'd walk up through there. He was rugged. Very rugged." I asked Francis Roby what it was like working atop those woodpiles. "Nothing. Just like any other place," he replied. "You're getting closer to heaven, that's all."

The woodpiles supplied the mill throughout the winter. The tough birds on that crew were out in all kinds of weather feeding pulp logs by hand onto the conveyors to the wood room, where the debarked logs were fed into a giant chipper. The wood yard crew was notorious for its consumption of alcohol. Raymond Tetreault's first job was in the mill yard. "I kept getting laid off," he said. "I worked with these guys who were drinking. Every weekend they were drunk. They [his supervisors] sent me home. I told them, 'I'm not drinking.' He said, 'But you're with that crew, so you've got to go home.' That's why I bid out of there and went in the mill."

A REAL STEADY EDDIE

Don Noyes was one of the cast of characters who worked in the yard in all weather. He was mentally challenged, but his prodigious strength, coupled with his willingness to perform the most exhausting and unglamorous jobs, earned him the respect of his fellow workers. Pete Cardin was newly hired when he first encountered Noyes in 1968. "Everybody in Groveton knew Don," he remembered. "Don was strong as a bull. He was huge — big and round. He was a big stocky guy. He was kind of slow, but he was a real Steady Eddie. They'd always have him in these places that were the lousiest places to work. They were always moving conveyors around because the pulp pile would grow or it would shrink."

Cardin had been sent out to the woodpiles to relieve Noyes: "I came around this corner, and didn't see anybody, and all of a sudden I hear this *Wheeeee*. That was his nickname, 'Wheee.' That's what he'd say all the time, 'Wheee, what ya doin'? Lookin' for somebody?' And I'd say, 'Yes. I'm looking for you, I guess.' It scared the heck out of me because he kind of reminded me of a gnome of some sort, down underneath that conveyor system. He had a bucket or something he was sitting on. That big cigar, sitting on that bucket, crap falling all around."

Bruce Blodgett told of the time Noyes stood atop the woodpile, "and he dropped his pants and gave somebody the moon, and there was a woman that happened to take a picture at the same time that Don gave the moon. And she didn't have a very favorable comment to the mill when she got her pictures exposed. Don with his big old rear end."

Because of his mental challenges, Noyes was the butt of pranks and cruel jokes. One paper machine crew conned him into painting the machine tender's favorite bench green. This tender was furious because he couldn't sit on the wet bench. "There was still some of that paint left," Lawrence Benoit said. "They had the whole crew hold [Noyes] down, and [they] painted his ass green. He was a strong man."

Joan Breault witnessed times when Noyes walked past a paper machine and someone said, "'Come on, let's wash old ass.' He'd drop his pants right down and turn to them, and maybe they'd throw a bucket of water on his rear end, or hit him with a fire hose. And he'd do it every time. Most of these companies wouldn't bother with somebody like that, but the Wemyss [family] did. I guess they figured these people were valuable in their own way, and they had to make a living."

Pete Cardin admired Noyes and the other mentally challenged workers: "There were characters throughout the mill. Because back in the old days, people weren't hired as they are today; they would just hire people, and if they worked out, they worked out. They were judged by their ability to do the job. A lot of these people would be given the jobs that nobody else really wanted to do. They were valued because they could do the job. In this day and age, there really wouldn't be a job for that guy. Everybody is so much into being fearful of liability. It didn't seem to be an issue back then. It seems like everybody was looking out for each other, and they were all part of society up here, so therefore they deserved to work just like the rest of us.

"You wanted people to be able to pay their way. So how are they going to be able to pay their way unless you give them a job? And there was always a job. They were paid a good wage. They were part of the union, so they had all the benefits that everybody else had. So they were equal at that level. And it was satisfying work for them, and they felt they were part of the community, and they were. I think they had a lot of self-esteem because they were providing for themselves. They weren't asking anybody for anything; they were doing it for themselves, which was a good thing."

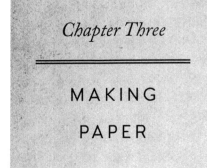

Chapter Three

MAKING

PAPER

NORTHERN NEW ENGLAND softwood paper has been highly valued for over a century because its fibers tend to be longer and stronger than hardwood fibers or softwoods grown in warmer climates. Wood is composed of cellulose, hemi-cellulose, and lignin, a natural glue that holds together the cellulose. Lignin is light brown, and, if not removed, contributes to the chemical degradation of paper.

The pulping process separates wood fibers to create pulp — cellulose fibers embedded in water. The Groveton mill relied on chemical pulping for its fine papers and tissue papers because this process produces pulp that is stronger and more bleachable. The yield from chemical pulp is only 40 to 50 percent of the wood used, while the yield from mechanical pulping is about 95 percent. Mechanical pulping grinds logs or chips, but in the process it damages fibers and does not remove lignin. Accordingly, it is commonly used for newsprint and lower-grade papers. It was not utilized in the Groveton mill.

Beginning in the 1950s, the Groveton mill began to use the semi-chemical process to produce hardwood pulp for its paperboard — the corrugated paper that gives cardboard its strength. Semi-chemical pulp is first chemically treated and cooked; afterward, it is mechanically ground.

Groveton's chemical process required a sulfuric acid solution, called "liquor," that was produced in the mill's two acid towers. As a young man in the late 1940s, Hadley Platt transported lime to the acid towers: "We used to load these big [lime] rocks into these little carts, put them on that elevator, and take them up to the top. An old guy was up on the top all the time. Us two young fellows would load this stuff by hand. Big chunks of rocks. They'd come in in them big open [railroad] cars. They had a couple of old guys that would throw them out of cars too. They didn't have no machines. They had to do it all by hand. [We were paid] about sixty-five, seventy cents an hour."

Sulfur chunks also arrived in railroad cars. Unloading the sulfur, Pete Cardin recalled, "was a horrible job. They would have boxcars with solid sulfur — chunk sulfur, and that would all have to be shoveled into a conveyor system and then put into a tank where they would melt the sulfur. Just nasty jobs. You work around that stuff all day — you know the dust and what have you."

The sulfur was cooked in a burner to produce sulfur dioxide. The crew had to monitor the mix of air and sulfur so that the process produced sulfur dioxide and not sulfuric acid. The hot sulfur dioxide gas flowed through cooling tubes to achieve the desired temperature as it entered the tower at its base. Water, introduced from above, trickled to the bottom of the tower, where it was collected as acid cooking liquor and piped to the digesters. Some of that water formed a heavy steam cloud that produced a foul sulfur smell.

Jim Wemyss explained how the acid towers could cause London fog in Groveton: "To make the liquor, we had Jenssen towers. You fill those [two] towers with lime rock, which I think was mined over in Vermont. The sulfurous gas passed up through the Jenssen towers from the bottom to the top, and by the time they'd got to the top, it was mostly absorbed with the water that trickled down over the lime rock. But a little wisp went out of the top of the Jenssen tower, and it seemed to have a specific gravity that made it attract to the ground rather than go off into the stratosphere. A cool morning, or an evening, especially in the fall, it came down like a fog. It didn't stay all day; it would be for a few hours. It would not be allowed today, I don't think."

Greg Cloutier, who grew up in Groveton in the 1950s and 1960s, recalled the evening discharge: "The acid towers would put the steam cloud out at night, and I remember it hung low over downtown. I knew it was important to get home before 9 p.m., the curfew, because the sulfur smell took over the town after that time. My parents' home on Riverside Drive didn't seem to get the smell."

Pulpwood entered the mill at the wood room, in the southwest corner of the mill. After the logs passed through the wood room's chipper, the chips were screened to remove sawdust and excessively large chips. The screened chips rode a conveyor to the top of the four-story digester building. There they were packed into one of the four digesters that cooked the chips at high pressures and temperatures in the sulfuric acid solution.

The digesters were like giant pressure cookers, fifty to sixty feet high and approximately eighteen feet in diameter. The digester crew loaded fifteen to eighteen cords of chips into a softwood digester and then added the acid solution and sodium carbonate (Na_2CO_3). Mill workers referred to sodium carbonate as "sody ash." It softened wood chips and controlled pH levels during the cooking. "Our job was to keep the sody ash mixed so you have some all the time," Gerard Labrecque explained. "We had to wear a mask all the time on account of the dust and the sody ash. We used to shovel it out of the boxcar. Put in the wheelbarrow and go and dump it in the tank. Then we used to put some water and mix it up and dump it in all the tanks. Sody ash would burn your eyes, your face. That's why we had to wear masks."

The digester crew bolted the top of the fully loaded digester tightly, and pumped in steam to cook the chips for about eight hours. Raymond Tetreault worked on the digesters for nearly forty years: "Towards the end, I was the cook. You put the steam to it after it was full. Then as it built pressure, you had to keep relieving it — like a pressure cooker. The same thing, only a pressure cooker had a button to let the steam out. Out there, we had to do that by hand."

"In the digester room, Stuart Nugent was the boss," Labrecque remembered. "He asked me to work overtime. Sometimes, too much overtime, I'm getting tired. 'Aw, you'll be all right,' he said. 'You'll get a break. You go behind the tank and have a nap.' You couldn't ask for any better boss [laughs]. I wasn't the only one to do that because the cook is the one that is still awake. Sometimes, we had a pretty good break. An hour or an hour and a half. He said, 'Go behind the tank there and have a nap.' I didn't say no."

After eight hours, the cook turned off the steam, and a helper climbed down three flights of stairs to open the valves at the base of the digester. Decades of climbing stairs took a physical toll on Raymond Tetreault. His wife, Lorraine, said: "Up and down those stairs — he had to have a knee replacement twice, I think. The third time, they put a rod in his leg."

Gerard Labrecque recalled the first time he blew a digester: "There were [five] of them digesters. At first I was kinda scared. 'Jesus Cripes, if I make a mistake and blow the wrong one, I could have killed a lot of people.' There was a pipe about that big [1.5 inches] from up there to downstairs. The cook said to rap on that pipe, and he said, 'I'll come to the pipe. You ask me which one it is. Make sure you blow the right one.' So I made sure I was going to blow the right one. Jeezum. That [smell] was pretty strong when you used to blow the digester."

Tetreault wryly observed: "We never had too much visitors in the digester room because it stunk so. It would take your breath right out of you. That was strong. We had a mask over our mouth and breathe through that way. The only time it was real bad was when you'd blow. While you're cooking it weren't too bad, unless you had a leak. If you had a leak in the head, well you had to stand it." Lolly LaPointe said, "When they blew a digester, I've seen times when you'd come out of that mill, and you'd want to walk on your hands and knees to try to get under that stuff so you could breathe. It would bring water right to your eyes." Roger Caron recalled: "I remember growing up, my father coming home with sulfur smell, and my mother always kept his clothes segregated and would wash them every day, immediately."

The pressure in the digester blew the chips and acid solution into blow pits. "When those digesters used to blow," Jim Wemyss marveled, "I mean, incredible. Ten-inch [pipe], two hundred and ten degrees, chips flying right out into this big blow tank." The softwood pulp in the blow tanks looked like beige mush. The blow pits were flooded with water to wash out some of the acids. "I went down and worked in the blow pits for a while [in the late 1940s]," Hadley Platt recalled. "I had to wash the stock with them old gents that were down in there. I was spare help. There was one old guy that used to talk to himself all the time, and when I'd think there was somebody there with him, he was all alone in one of the other blow pits. They were big old wooden pits where the stock was. They had these big hoses, and you'd reach in through a big wooden hole and wash it down. It was all old wood, and it was in really pretty bad shape. At times — if they blew a digester or something, [the smell] could make you really sick if you was down in the hole there."

From the blow pits the mush was pumped to the bleach room, where it was treated with bleaching chemicals, then washed and screened three times. First, chlorine, which reacts with lignin to form water-soluble compounds, was added. This solution removed chemicals and dissolved lignin. Next, in the "extraction stage," chlorine dioxide was added. A second series of washers and screens removed chlorinated and oxidized lignin. Finally, hypochlorite, the actual bleaching agent, was added to the mush to make the paper white. It removed most of the remaining lignin. A final series of washers and screens removed chemicals and dissolved lignin. The wastewater, containing toxic organochlorines, including carbon tetrachloride, chloroform, benzene, and dioxin, was dumped into the river until the pulp mill was shut down in April 1972.[1]

The bleached mush then went to the stock preparation department, often referred to as the "beater room." Lawrence LaPointe worked there for thirty years. Initially, he was given "the most menial job" of collecting and baling wastepaper pulled from the paper machines. The top jobs in the beater room were beater engineer and his first helper. The first helper mixed the vats for fine papers, using about 80 percent bleached virgin pulp and 20 percent re-pulped wastepaper. Then the first helper added the chemicals, the talc, the clay, the sizing, and dyes for colored paper runs.

LaPointe described the stock prep process: "A beater is a big tub with an agitator in the bottom; some of them had agitators on the side, or cutters. They would beat that paper right up and make slush out of it. You added water; then after it got to a certain consistency, you had to open a valve and start a pump. It would suck that stuff out. You'd direct it to the chest that you wanted it to go to. There was a tremendous amount of chests everywhere. Underneath that floor was basically chests in some areas. Big holding tanks with an agitator to keep that stuff circulating to keep the consistency the same."

The bleaching process and stock preparation were major sources of water pollution prior to the early 1970s. "On the night shift, if there was a color change to be done, you'd take and dump all these dyes," Bill Astle, son of a paper machine tender, said. "There would be this deep blue, deep red, and gold dyes. You'd flush out all of the trays, and it would go down into the sewer which was a straight pipe that went right into the river. If you were out there and shined a light on it, you could see it was just brilliant. It colored the entire river. The interesting thing is if that happened today, there would be people serving jail time. But that was considered very acceptable. There was raw sewage in the same river."

The stock was now ready for the paper machines — large, long machines that require staggering amounts of energy to operate. Channie Tilton, a former tour boss (pronounced "tower boss" by former Groveton mill workers), described a paper machine as "a giant, endless, dewatering machine." Foils, vacuums, wires, felt, and presses transformed the slushy stock that came from stock prep into a paper product with very little moisture.

Prior to the nineteenth century, paper was made one sheet at a time in presses that squeezed the water out of the stock. Around 1800, Fourdrinier paper machines were developed to make continuous sheets of paper that formed reels. Advances in steel making, engineering, and power generation led to the development of larger, wider, faster paper machines in the final two decades of the nineteenth century.

The top men on a paper machine crew — the machine tender and the back tender — are among the highest paid workers in the mill. Given the high pay scale, one would expect a long waiting list for these jobs, yet Joe Berube secured a job on a paper machine while still a teenager. *Why?* "That's a double-edged sword," he laughed. "Even though they were giving all these incentive payments, all this extra money, those jobs weren't user-friendly. These paper machines are man killers. I mean when I first went to work there, you saw guys with eyes missing, fingers missing, arms missing from these paper machines because they were a safety hazard to work around. I'm one of the fortunate few that worked there that long that still have all my appendages. That was not unusual to look around and see all these guys handicapped in some way from having worked on those machines, and a lot of them had not worked there that long."

Five crew members operated a paper machine. The fifth hand performed all sorts of menial tasks, including cleaning. He hauled away the substandard paper to the beater room when the crew was rethreading the machine. The fourth and third hands operated the dangerous rewinder, a machine that cut the reels produced on the paper machine to narrower rolls that were sent to the finishing rooms.

The back tender, never referred to as the second hand, made the reel of paper coming off the machine at the "dry end." He threaded the paper down the machine while it was running. Many men lost fingers on this job. In later years the mill installed a rope — a much safer method to thread a machine. The machine tender was the head of the crew, and he operated the paper machine controls at the "wet end." If things were running well, Channie Tilton observed, "there was not a lot to do."

The tour boss was the shift supervisor, and, along with the beater engineer, he ran the papermaking process. He had to check on quality and to make certain the product met specifications. Was the paper curly? Was it too dry or too damp?

The stock preparation department pumped the 4 percent solution of water and pulp to the machine chest, a big holding tank often referred to as the "4 percent chest." Joe Berube said: "It looks almost like cream of wheat," and it was heated to about 125° to help with drainage on the "wire." The stock was pumped up to the "stuff box" roughly thirty feet above the machine. It was then gravity fed into a huge fan pump where additional chemicals were added.

The fan pump delivered the stock to the head box that spread it evenly onto a thirty-foot-long moving screen called the "forming fabric" or "wire." "It's just a big screen, and it's made out of monofilament — Dacron in both directions," Berube explained. "It's like a regular fabric, only it's a coarser weave. It's real flimsy if you ever took it off. Those run about fifteen thousand bucks." *How long do they last?* "Typically three months, if you're lucky. If you're lucky. And it's a major operation to change one. You have to get two complete machine crews, and it takes about three hours. You have to completely dismantle the wet end of the paper machine. You've got to get everything super clean. If you punch a hole in that thing, say the size of that ballpoint pen, you've ruined fifteen thousand dollars worth of equipment. So it's pretty sensitive."

The wire was porous, and all along its thirty-foot length, water was continuously draining out of the mushy stock. Foil blades and vacuum boxes under the wire sucked out as much as 60 percent of the water by the time the sheet reached the end of the wire. Dave Miles described one of the occupational hazards of a machine tender: "It's always wet up there. It got so, when I was running Number 1 [paper machine], between [my feet] and my toes would all bleed. I went to the doctor about it, and he said it was because of the dampness. I'd come home and take my shoes off, and my socks would be all blood. That's one reason why, when I got onto [back tender on Number] 6, I was comfortable. Shortly after that, my toes all healed up because it was so much dryer. My wife could tell you I threw away more socks."

At the end of the wire a "cooch roll" vacuumed more water, reducing the amount of moisture to about 15 percent. The sheet passed from there onto a quarter-inch-thick felt. "In the old days they used to be made out of real fine, virgin wool," Berube said. The felts took the sheet through a squeeze press that Berube compared to "old wringer washing machines" and fed it onto the first press, where a vacuum roll under the felt sucked more water out. A second press, with a second felt, removed more water. A third press, called a "smoothing press," was used on some, but not all, grades of paper. It added smoothness to the paper and helped determine the caliper (thickness) of the paper.

The wet end of Number 3 paper machine in 1955. A fine-papers machine for most of its active life, it made paperboard from 1950 to 1967. From a 1955 Vanity Fair sales catalog. (Courtesy GREAT)

Dryers on Number 3 paper machine. From a 1955 Vanity Fair sales catalog. (Courtesy GREAT)

After the three presses, the sheet of paper entered the drying sections. The main section on Number 3 paper machine consisted of thirty-six big round drums. Steam was pumped into the dryers at about 125 pounds of pressure from both top and bottom. The first of these dryers applied low heat, and each subsequent dryer gradually increased the temperature. "You don't want it too hot near the wet end," Berube explained, "[because] it will set what they call a curl in your sheet. You want to keep your sheet flat." The sheet of paper retained only about 2 percent of moisture when it emerged from the first set of dryers. It entered the size press, where starch and other chemicals called "fillers" were added; they gave the final sheet its special surface properties. In the size press the sheet regained considerable moisture, most of which was then removed in the ten after-section dryers.

Finally, the sheet, containing about 5 percent moisture, went through a vertical set of rollers called the calender stack at the dry end of the machine. Calenders applied pressure to fix the caliper, or thickness, and smoothness of the paper. Berube cautioned, "There is a problem running too much calender pressure. That's a whole other science altogether. Sometimes you get calender marks and what they call stack veins that leaves little veins in your sheet, plus you can run into real structure problems: corrugations, ridges, stuff like that. If you get too bad of a corrugation or ridge in a reel, you have to throw the paper out."

"The back tender was in charge of building the reel," Dave Miles said. "Make sure you've got a good reel, so it would go out the door, rather than a bad reel and have to be cut up and sent back to the beater room. You had to keep your eye on it all the time. If you got hot spots in here, the reel would go soft. You'd be feeling along here and you could tell when it was soft just by tapping it — an experienced back tender. A lot of people would come into the mill on tours, they'd come over [and touch the reel and recoil from the heat]. Once you got used to it, your hands could stand that, but if you weren't used to it, it was hot on your hand."

A reel of paper on Number 3 was usually five or six feet in diameter and weighed five tons. To remove a full reel and start a new one while the paper machine continued to churn out paper, the crew at the dry end brought an empty reel down and kicked out the full one; the fifth hand cut the sheet, and the back tender used an air hose underneath the new reel to blow the

Joe Berube at the controls of the dry end of Number 3 paper machine. Raymond LeClere is testing for hot spots on the reel. Photo ca. 1983. (Courtesy GREAT)

paper onto it. Berube recalled that when he started on Numbers 1 and 2 paper machines in 1964, "a guy would be there with a gallon pail of water, and he would throw it in behind this reel at the same time that they kicked the existing reel out and the water would make [the paper] stick on this [empty] spool. That's the way the old-timers used to do it."

What happened if your timing was off? "You'd have a mess." *You'd shut down the machine?* "No, not necessarily. You'd keep trying till you'd get it on there. Those old machines didn't go that fast. It got pretty dicey sometimes. If you had an experienced crew, it wasn't a big deal. If you had a bunch of green people, it could be a problem."

Whenever paper machine crews changed an order, or when there was a tear in the sheet, a "break," the back tender would have to rethread the paper through all the presses and dryers and back onto the reel. Joe Berube described the process: "A lot of your breaks would be in the midsection where the size press is. This is like liquid cornstarch. It's a real watery solution, but it's one hundred and forty degrees and it's got pipes the whole width of the sheet all the way across, top and bottom. You're actually gaining about ten pounds of weight with this cornstarch, and it sealed both sides of your sheet so it gives it a lot smoother sheet. A lot of your breaks would occur right here. Either you'd lose your starch here, or you'd have a hole come down, and it would hit that starch and pop it and break it there. And so, you'd have to cut a narrow strip of paper, and your back tender would come along, and he'd have to thread that through, back over the paper machine. You'd add right onto the reel. You'd take a lumber crayon, and you'd mark it on the side of the reel where the break was. After you took the reel off the machine, the rewinder would stop there, and he'd cut out any bad paper, skin it out, take it off, and make a splice. They had this two-edged double-thick splicing tape so there wasn't any actual bad paper there by the time he got through. You'd splice it and flag it, so that when this was taken out to the finishing room, they would stop it where the splice was and kick that splice out, and they'd have good paper."

Joan Breault worked in the tissue finishing room in the 1950s: "There was a big open doorway right into the dry end of Number 3 paper machine. We could see right down the length of the machine. Charlie Allin from Lancaster was the back tender. He threaded it. I can remember seeing him taking a tail and going. They alternated hands putting it through the different rolls. Guiding it through. And the rolls were running. Charlie made it look so easy, and you knew it wasn't. He was fabulous on the machines."

When the sheet failed to thread through the paper machine, a disaster referred to as "haying," the entire crew had to pull the balled-up paper onto the machine room floor. "I've seen many times, we would hay so bad, we'd have to shut the machine down — we had no place to pull the paper," Dave Miles said. "The whole place was full of loose broke. Everybody worked when that went down." *How often would you have a break on an eight-hour shift?* "If you had a good day," Berube answered, "you didn't have any breaks. It would depend on what type of paper you were running."

When a paper machine was making unsellable paper, the mill was not making money. The crews dropped everything to fix the problem in the shortest time possible. "The amazing thing was that that culture in that mill was a culture of urgency," Pete Cardin explained. "A sense of urgency. Everybody understood it; when a paper machine went down, as soon as it went down, started to hay, we had a sheet break; as soon as that happened, if you weren't moving, I mean somebody was going to kick your butt, and it was going to be one of the other guys that you were working with because our job was to get this thing back on the iron as fast as we can. So guys would run *tssk, tssk, tssk.* Everybody knew exactly what they were going for; everybody had their role to play. You don't think, you just do. Put the sheet on, get it down. There's a lot of whistling and screaming. It's pretty cool. Get the sheet down, get it on the reel; what a sense of accomplishment. We've done it in, 'Oh, man, what was that down to?' 'Five minutes.' 'Oh, all right!' That sense of urgency is for the company. We were smart enough to understand that without that machine, without it running, we don't have a job. So it was a good culture that way; it was a great culture."

Working for decades on a paper machine took its toll on crew members' health. Paper machines are brutally hot, especially the dryers. Lolly LaPointe said: "Back when they had the older paper machines, it was just horrible hot in the summertime, comfortable in the winter. Then they started enclosing the paper machines and add the huge fan that would draw the heat out. That worked pretty good. It was hot in the summer, and not too bad in the winter."

"It was not unusual to go in there at a hundred degrees," Joe Berube recalled. "And if you had to work up on top of the hood to install new wet-felts, sometimes it was as much as a hundred forty up there. That's warm. Probably the last ten years that I worked there at my wet end station, we had an air-conditioned office at the end of the machine there because we also had a computer in there. They wanted to protect the computer probably, more than us."

Paper machine operators invariably suffered serious hearing loss. "My hearing ain't good," Thurman Blodgett said. "'You shoulda wore earplugs.' 'I'll be all right today; I don't need them today.' That's just the way it went." By the time the Occupational Safety and Health Administration (OSHA) mandated ear protection, Ted Caouette recalled, "I suppose I'd lost most of my hearing anyway. I have a difficult time hearing a lot of things. My wife will say, 'Listen to the birds this morning.' I cannot hear any noise whatsoever. But different pitches I can hear."

"My knees were going, and I couldn't have kept going on that cement floor,"

Dave Miles, a veteran of four decades on paper machines, said. "They're hell on your knees and feet. My knees got so bad, and they had a job come up taking care of the dock, sweeping floors out there and running the compactor out there, and I got that. I'm guessing probably the last four or five years that's what I did. I think I went from sixteen or seventeen [dollars an hour] down to eleven or twelve, but it kept me going until I got to sixty-two. So I was able to get my time in."

The harsh working conditions frequently provoked zany behavior, and paper machine crews were notorious for playing pranks. Fifth hands, lowest in the pecking order, were the target of many initiation rites. However, everyone was a potential victim, and woe to the fellow caught catnapping. Anyone might bite into a bologna sandwich and discover a slice of red rubber had been substituted by some clever wag.

"When I first went on the paper machine [in 1952], they were getting wrinkles on a sheet," Lawrence Benoit recalled. "One of the guys said, 'We've got to send somebody up to Number 3 to get that paper stretcher.' I went up there, and I says, 'I've got to get a paper stretcher.' 'Oh, yeah, it's over here.' Christ, I looked at this thing, and the damn shaft must have been that big and probably from here to the wall. 'How the hell am I going to get that on the cart?' A guy says, 'I'll help you.' We picked up on that shaft, and I wheeled it all the way down there. Bill Jewell was down there. 'What the hell are them guys doing up there? This ain't the right one. This is a small one. I've gotta have a big one.' They sent me all the way back up there. They had it all planned. Right beside that small one, there was another one. Here I am wheeling it back down, and here comes Opie Veazey, a tour boss. He says, 'What the hell are you doing, Benoit?' 'They want this paper stretcher.' He knew they were playing a joke on me. He said, 'Wheel it over there, we'll put it on in a minute.' It never went on."

During a public presentation of mill stories, Joe Berube and Dave Miles regaled the audience with tales of pranks. *When did you find time to make paper?* "The work was so disastrous that you had to do something," Berube replied as the audience erupted in laughter. Miles added: "Like Joe said, it kept us sane working on those machines. When the days were bad, they were very bad. You'd bring your lunch in, and some days you'd bring it back home."

Nevertheless, the danger and stress fostered an esprit de corps comparable to bonds forged in wartime. "I started on old Number 1. [It] was 1800s technology. It was all by hand, and it was a real art. It was craftsmanship in making paper. There wasn't much for instrumentation; it was all knowing," Pete Cardin said. "These guys could see it; they could hear it, sense it, feel it. They knew how to make little adjustments. There was an awful lot of pride in it. To get it just the way they wanted, there was an art to it. As a fifth or fourth hand, no way did I have a right to ask what was going on here. There's no guarantee I'm going to be there that long. Why would he want to waste his precious time and his knowledge on me? If you get up to third hand, and they knew you were working into a back tender slot, then they'd start bringing you more and more into the Brotherhood — the Brotherhood of the Papermakers."

As in war, the Brotherhood suffered grievous injury and even death. The most dangerous job on the paper machine crew was operating the rewinder at the dry end of the machine. The rewinder trimmed off rough edges and cut the reel down to several smaller dimensions for the finishing room. Joe Berube recalled the old rewinders: "They had these old cam machine winders when I first got there, and those were man killers. Dick Sheltry was a third hand [in 1943], and he was feeling for wrinkles on the drum. You used to have to have this spreader bar underneath the rewinder. He was feeling the drum for wrinkles because sometimes they would wrinkle when you're first starting the rewinder up. He was going slow, and he was trying to adjust the spreader bar, and his hand got caught in that reel, and he couldn't get it out. Two guys jumped on him to hold him, and it yanked his arm right out of his socket. When I came to work there, he was a supervisor in the stockroom."

"Another accident happened while I was there on a Manchester rewinder," Berube continued. "I had just come in and relieved the crew that this guy had worked on, and there was blood all over the floor, all over the rewinder. He caught his hand in the reel there on that rewinder, and they got him out all right. He still kept his arm, but he lost most of his hand and everything on it. I don't know how many operations they done on him. That was a mess. We had to come in and clean that up after they took him out."

Dave Miles and Lawrence Benoit had been working only a couple of years as fourth or fifth hands on old Number 1 and Number 2 machines when they experienced the ultimate horror in a paper mill on May 28, 1955. The two machines stood side by side, and when one crew was having trouble and the other machine was perking along, the latter crew lent a hand. Following some repair work on Number 2, its crew was struggling to get it to work properly. Amie Bean, a well-respected machine tender on Number 1, was trying to tighten up the paper on Number 2 when he slipped and fell and was pulled into the machine between the great dryer roll and the smaller felt roll.

Benoit said: "I was right from me to you when he went in there. Horrible. When he hit that thing, it sounded like somebody took a sledgehammer and hit that dryer. All it was was his feet sticking out. Evidentially, the roll was too high, so you're reaching down too far, and it caught his hand and hauled him right in. Stopped that machine dead. The dryers were still going, but it shut the felt right down. There was so much pressure with him in. It was awful. I'll never forget that. We got a great big pipe wrench, and we tried to back up the dryers, but we couldn't do it because back then they had just Babbitt bearings and stuff. And the weight was tremendous. They got the millwrights down there as fast as they could. They took the roll out, and that dropped the thing down and then slacked the felt off, and then pulled him out that way. They claim he died on the way to the hospital; I think he was dead before that. There was blood all over the felt. Wemyss was mad because they made him cut the felt off. Of course it was big money for a felt. After that, I went down to clean the mess up. Part of his ear was laying in the pit. I remember that."

"It was horrifying," Dave Miles shuddered. "I didn't eat for a few days afterwards. We thought he was still alive. We found out afterwards it was just, what do you call it? Nerves, I guess it was. I think we shut down for a day. It was horrifying."

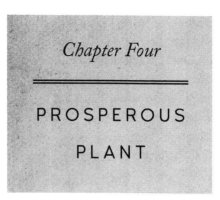

Chapter Four

PROSPEROUS

PLANT

WILLIAM THOITS and James Sivret of Northumberland and Pearson G. Evans of Gorham announced in April 1891 plans to construct a paper mill that used the new chemical process to make pulp out of wood chips. They acquired land along the banks of the Upper Ammonoosuc River from the Weston Sawmill on May 12, 1891, and additional land from the Soule Sawmill on May 14. Two weeks later, they broke ground for the new pulp mill.

"The foundation of the pulp and paper mill is approaching completion," the *Democrat* reported in a lengthy account buried in the Locals column that July. The office and a fifty-by-twenty-foot machine shop had been completed. The north wing of the mill, 197 feet and six inches long and 62 feet wide, would be one story tall and house two paper machines. A small building joined the north and south wings. The south wing, measuring 283 by 56 feet, would house the four-story pulp mill on the west end and the boiler room on the east end. To minimize the threat of fire, the boiler room would be built of brick, covered by an iron roof. The mill planned to install four 150-horsepower boilers, with room to add three additional boilers. Two engines north of the boiler room would power the machines and illuminate the mill. Once running, the mill expected to employ seventy-five men. The pulp mill intended to use waste wood from the neighboring sawmills and four-foot pulp logs. The Concord and Montreal Railroad was laying tracks to enter the building from the west between the north and south wings. Additional railroad tracks would run between the office and the north wing.[1]

The following week, four masons were adding 5 feet a day to the planned 125-foot smokestack. On July 23, Thoits, Sivret, and Evans sold the mill property to Groveton Mills (which they controlled), and, that same day, the new corporation took out a $25,000 mortgage on the mill from the Norway Savings Bank in Norway, Maine. In mid-August, the Locals column reported that the mill was making progress, but it was not expected to make paper until cold weather. In mid-September, the chimney was completed; the exteriors of the buildings were nearing completion, and the engine rooms were almost ready for the installation of the boilers. On September 16, the Locals noted "a man named Wells" fell thirty-two feet in the pulp mill and broke an arm and suffered a serious back injury.[2] This is the earliest known report of an injury at the mill.

Number 1 paper machine was installed during October and November. It made a sheet five feet wide and produced seventy-five feet of paper a minute. The *Democrat* crowed on November 25: "They have one of the largest and finest machines ever built." The mill's new chime whistle sounded for the first time on November 21, and on December 23, the *Democrat* reported: "The paper mill is now in operation and some very fine paper is being produced."

Early in the new year, Groveton Mills secured a second $25,000 mortgage from Norway Savings at 6.5 percent interest, due in one year. The paper machine was shut down for a few days of changes and repairs early in February; it restarted on February 12. The mill was using waste wood from sawmills to fuel the boilers and, eventually, the pulp mill.[3]

The Locals correspondent reported on March 23, 1892, that the mill had been shut down for the past week. "It is hoped," Locals added, "that it will soon be running again with an increased force." Ominously, an April 6 report informed readers that the mill had been running for two days "to run out some partly run stock." From May to October, there were periodic, hopeful reports that the idle mill was expected to start up again soon. In July, Locals assured its readers: "This time it will have money enough behind to keep it moving."[4] In October there was welcome news that the mill expected to add two hundred men to the workforce.

There was no further mention of the Groveton mill in the *Democrat* for nearly three years. The Coös County Registry of Deeds suggests an explanation for the silence. On October 3, 1893, Norway Savings Bank filed for foreclosure on the long-idle paper mill. Foreclosure was granted on January 27, 1894, and Groveton Mills, quiet since early 1892, was defunct.

The July 24, 1895, issue reported that John Mitchell, superintendent of Odell Manufacturing Company — the new name for the Groveton paper mill — and C. C. Wilson and wife had lodged at the Melcher House for a few days. A week later, the Groveton Locals columnist reported good news:

"Paper making is progressing finely at the Odell."[5] Odell's books from around July 1895 reported that E. M. McCarthy, who was general manager of construction, earned $3 a day, and a regular mill worker earned 75 cents a day and took home $21.38 a month for 28.5 days' work![6]

Five Maine investors, George B. Bearce and John D. Clifford of Lewiston, Charles Wilson and Samuel R. Bearce of Auburn, and Frank Purrington of Mechanic Falls, had paid Norway Savings $35,189.14 for the mill on July 16, 1895. This sum represented the unpaid portion of the two $25,000 mortgages taken in the mill's first year. Four months later the five men sold the mill to the Odell Manufacturing Company for $75,000. They, of course, were the officers and owners of Odell Manufacturing. In 1897 another prominent Lewiston businessman, Willard Munroe, joined the Odell Manufacturing Company as treasurer. Munroe's association with the mill would continue until his death in 1938. For the final two decades of his life, "Willie" Munroe was the dominant mill owner.

In the fall of 1895, construction of Odell's sulfite mill commenced under the direction of E. L. Savage. The following May, the Locals correspondent reported the new mill owners were spending $125,000 to expand the mill. Two new digesters were nearly ready for operation, and a second paper machine, costing about $40,000 and manufactured by Bagley and Sewell of Watertown, New York, would begin to make 106-inch-wide rolls of paper by July 1. Three new 150-horsepower boilers would increase the mill's steam capacity to 1,000 horsepower. A two-story repair shop, measuring thirty-seven by sixty-five feet, would soon be built. Three "large engines," capable of 350, 110, and 100 horsepower, would power the additions. When completed, the pulp mill would produce thirty tons of dry pulp a day, and the paper machines and finishing room were expected to turn out twenty to thirty tons of paper daily. The mill employed 120.[7]

By June 1896, the expanding mill's 160 employees had broken records for paper production with thirty-five tons, "more last month than any month since the mill started." The report continued: "Everything about the mill has the appearance of thrift and industry." The new machine shop had been completed, and work had begun on the wood room, where machinery would be installed to chip pulpwood. A storehouse for lime and paper, detached from the mill building for purposes of fire safety, was completed.[8]

Odell Manufacturing Company paper mill, ca. 1906. The digesters are in the tallest building. (George Vervaris Collection, courtesy GREAT)

The July 22, 1896, *Democrat* reported the pulp mill had started up successfully; unfortunately, "Quite a serious accident occurred at the Odell Mill Saturday [July 18]. Geo. Parks, foreman in the beater room, had his arm severed near the wrist by contact with machinery."[9] This is the first known report of a serious accident inside the mill.

The rate of injuries and deaths in industrial America before about 1920 was appalling. Eventually, more enlightened safety procedures, shorter working hours, the rise of labor unions, and safer machine design dramatically reduced the accident rate. In the fifteen years between 1896 and 1910, there were literally scores of *reported* injuries due to falls from high places, flying machinery, falling lumber, burns from fires and burst pipes, railroad yard accidents, and, of course, from operating the machines in the mill. Routinely, Groveton mill workers — mostly men — lost fingers and suffered burns. All too often they suffered head wounds, crushed or amputated hands and feet, and serious cuts from finishing-room cutting machines.

Of the twelve deaths at the mill recorded by the local press between 1901 and 1960, six occurred in the decade ending in 1910: Benjamin Mountain, a wood room worker, succumbed five days after being caught by a screw pulley and "hurled with great rapidity around the shaft" in January 1901.[10] George Taylor died in an unknown accident six months later.[11] George Smith was killed while threading the calender on Number 2 paper machine in March 1907.[12] Sixteen-year-old Albert Moulton, working by the Brooklyn Dam, apparently fell asleep and rolled into the river in October 1907.[13] Edmund Gardner, also a teenager, was coupling cars in the railroad yard in March 1910. His foot was caught "in the frogs of the switch," and the car severed his leg, leading to his death.[14] Frank Tibbetts, a sixty-year-old oiler, said to work in the mill 365 days a year, died mysteriously: "It is supposed that in some way Mr. Tibbetts fell upon a belt which carried him over a pulley, breaking his neck, one arm, several ribs, and crushing his skull."[15]

And then there is the sad case of Billie Downing. In August 1897, he lost his third finger in the mill. There was no report on how he had lost the other two digits. Late in 1905, his foot was caught in machinery and two toes were amputated. Three months later, his hand was mangled in machinery. "He seems to be fated," the Locals correspondent concluded.[16]

On May 19, 1897, the mill made 26.5 tons of paper, a new one-day record.[17] In late August, nineteenth-century Groveton's greatest engineer, Charles Richardson, and his work crew raised the mill's new eight-ton smokestack. An 1898 profile of Richardson noted that, during the previous thirty-five years, he had constructed dams, bridges, and mills, raised thirty-four smokestacks, demolished twelve smokestacks, and built the four-hundred-foot-long Bethel (Maine) Bridge. Owing to his careful practices, his work crews had suffered no accidents in all those years.[18]

In April 1898, the paper mill announced it would build several houses on lots on the Heights, north of the tracks and mill. The Locals correspondent opined: "This will make it lively for Groveton and looks as if they [the new mill owners] mean to have a permanent business."[19] By early May, the Groveton Land Heights Company had laid out streets on the hill. In October, the mill's plans to erect a large building between the coal sheds and the machine shop provoked the Locals correspondent to complain: "Mr. Wells of Lewiston, Maine has the contract to build the new building for the Odell Mfg. Co., while several of our home carpenters are idle."[20]

In October 1898, the pulp mill produced forty-eight tons of sulfite pulp a day. Fifty two-horse wagons were making two to four trips a day to deliver four-foot pulpwood logs to the mill. In the fall of 1899, the mill built an addition for two new boilers to augment the seven already in operation. "Quite a good many changes have been made recently by the company," the Locals correspondent cheerfully reported, "and everything is running in apple pie order. The company have the reputation of making the best paper and pulp in the northern country, and for the past two years, they have been unable to fill their orders; and at the present time are weeks behind with them, which speaks in high terms of their management."[21]

As the new owners pumped substantial capital into the paper mill, the village of Groveton boomed. At a contentious town meeting in March 1895, residents voted $600 to pay for street lighting, and they approved a proposal to establish a high school. In September, water pipes were laid the length of Main Street. A Village Improvement Society raised money for a public library, a town clock, and a drinking fountain. The covered bridge over the Upper Ammonoosuc was completed in the spring of 1896. Twenty trains a day roared in and out of Groveton. On State Street, Lowe's Opera House, with a seating capacity of twelve hundred, celebrated its gala opening on May 5, 1897. Locals reported: "The hall is tastefully frescoed in shades of pale pink, green, and cream."[22] Four large town clocks, which would be landmarks for the next seventy years, were installed in the Opera House tower in July.

That month, the Groveton Tavern, under the management of H. S. Goodwin, opened for business on the southwest corner of the intersection of State and Main Streets. The new hotel advertised the telephone installed in its office. In the fall, work began on a Catholic church on State Street opposite the Opera House. Burt May's Billiard Parlor opened on November 9 in his new State Street building; he rented apartments on the second and third floors. Soon he was advertising: "Smoke the 'Odell' 5¢ cigar at May's Casino only."[23]

Groveton exhibited some of the characteristics of a frontier town. In October 1897 the Chinese laundryman, John Cheng, became so exasperated by taunts from kids that he fired a shot at them, grazing the head of one. A year later, Locals jocularly reported on the rough treatment accorded a recent visitor: "A young darkey from Berlin struck town last week, causing considerable disturbance. He called into the store of C. T. McNally's, and on being ordered out by Elbert, refused to go, but a little later decided he would, but in the melee some way Elbert got his thumb mixed up with Mr. Nig's mouth, and consequently Bert is carrying it done up. Elbert had the darkey pulled in and taken before Judge Curtis the next day, who decided that the darkey gentleman was looking for some place to spend the winter; so gave the darkey man until noon to leave town, which he did. Soon after he turned up

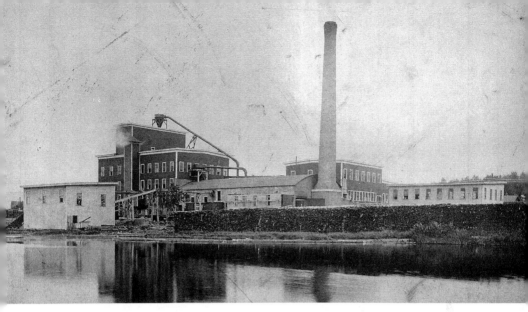

View from the Upper Ammonoosuc River of the Odell Manufacturing Company paper mill before the 1907–1908 additions. (Courtesy GREAT)

in Gorham where he takes a stick of wood and goes at some one there and gets another night's lodging. Elbert has one satisfaction; he has but one black eye, while the darkey went away with two."[24]

"About 100 woodsmen came into town Saturday night [December 23, 1899] to spend Christmas and to do the town," Locals reported, "but some of them got done before they got fairly started and decided to return to their camps which they did at once." Mill workers could also be rowdy, as Locals noted: "The paper mill was shut down for Christmas, and so were the bars. Too bad, wasn't it, boys? We will try not to have too many shutdowns at once hereafter."[25]

A special report to the *Democrat*, titled "Prosperous Plant," described operations at the Odell mill in early 1904. Ten of the mill's furnaces burned coal and generated about one thousand horsepower. The mill consumed two railroad carloads of coal a day, approximately fifty-eight tons, at an annual cost of $200,000. A wood-burning furnace required nine cords a day.

Odell Manufacturing had recently filled in a "foul smelling swamp and muck hole" for its new wood yard. Fifteen railroad cars delivered about 165 cords of pulpwood a day. A five-man crew threw the logs onto a five-hundred-foot-long, forty-foot-high "carrier" with an endless cable, run by a twenty-five horsepower engine that "catches the wood as it is thrown from the cars into the trough and carries it to the several openings at the top where it is dumped from the sides."

The glowing report on the status of the mill concluded: "The employees as a whole are very well satisfied and have recently received an increase in pay. They are working under amiable superintendents, and the output from this mill is something immense. Their products are shipped to nearly every state in the union, some even going to California. A corporation like the Odell Manufacturing company is a great benefit to the town and Groveton should be proud of it."[26]

Relations between the amiable superintendents and satisfied workers deteriorated over the following year. Prior to June 1904, the night shift had worked thirteen hours a day, six days a week, including Saturday nights and into Sunday mornings. That month the Saturday night–Sunday morning shift was eliminated. When management attempted to reinstate the old hours, fifty papermakers declared a strike on January 7, 1905, claiming that this was "more than they could endure." "Townsman," a sympathizer with the strikers, wrote to the *Democrat*: "Men that are use [*sic*] to taking charge of laborers should have tact enough to be leaders of men, instead of drivers. I have had experience enough in taking charge of men to know that if you treat them like men they will be men. You undertake to drive them and you will soon find where you are at."[27]

William Hamilton, vice president of the Paper Union, addressed a large and enthusiastic crowd at Forbush Hall on State Street on January 15. He urged workers to organize, because machines had made it impossible for artisans to compete. A cobbler, he explained, could make one shoe while a machine turns out thirty. Since workers have only their labor to sell, they must join together to assure that they receive the highest price for that labor.

Work at the mill resumed on January 16, and the labor problems appeared to have been resolved by the hiring of "non-union" men to fill the "vacancies." "For the past ten days," the *Democrat* reported on January 25, "new families have been moving into town to replace the union men that went out and refused to return. A large number of men have given up their [union] cards and returned to their old posts. It is understood that in a few cases the company

The finishing room in 1905. Are these women strikers, replacements, or wives of officers? (Courtesy GREAT)

has refused to take back some of the old help. A large number of girls went out with the old hands and their places are filled by townswomen, in several instances, wives of the officers have stepped in to help out. The non-union [should read "union"] men deserve credit for conducting their affairs in a quiet manner and making no attempt to interfere with the new men that have been engaged to fill their former jobs."

Five weeks into the strike, Hamilton again wrote to the *Democrat*: "Those who have never worked tour work in a paper or pulp mill, and do not know anything of its hardships, the demoralizing effects, physically, morally and mentally, of working thirteen hours a night, six and seven nights a week, are not expected to sympathize very strongly with the men, but they would if they ever had gone through the experience several months or years." Hamilton acknowledged the worries and pressures mill owners and managers suffered, but added: "The paper makers have had the sixty-five hour per week system, or the 'Saturday night off' for six months previous to the trouble. This 'Saturday night off' is something which all paper makers tour workers, very much desire, and are naturally sensitive on this point, especially when a move is being made to deprive them of it. Even the offer of extra pay is little inducement, for the benefits in the way of rest, health, and opportunities are of more value to the tour worker than a money consideration. It is because of this hardship of long hours night work in paper and pulp mills, that many such concerns throughout the country are adopting the three tour system, or eight hours per day."[28] There were no further reports on the strike in the region's only newspaper.

Groveton's economy continued to boom. Fred Taylor opened a grocery store on May 19, 1906, which remained in business until 1960. Construction on the town's sewer system began that summer. The Locals correspondent noted: "The new sewer is progressing finely. One gets quite an idea of Italy by going down West street and going through their quarters. So far they are a very quiet and orderly lot of men."[29] With the arrival of cold weather at the end of October, the sewer construction ceased, and the Italian laborers returned to Lewiston, Maine.

For a decade, the fledgling Groveton paper mill shared the Upper Ammonoosuc River and the forests of the surrounding landscape with the Soule and Weston sawmills. After 1905, Odell Manufacturing operated alone. Weston never recovered from a boiler explosion in 1901, and it sold off all its Northumberland assets to Odell Manufacturing on August 22, 1904. Soule Lumber did the same in a series of three transactions between October 14, 1905, and October 14, 1907. Henceforth, the Odell mill would face no significant local competition for the price of labor or wood fiber. The mill dominated the regional economy thereafter.

In the summer of 1907 the Odell mill purchased a new paper machine from Pusey and Jones. Number 3 paper machine, reputedly the largest in the world, required the construction of a new building that doubled the mill's size and also included a new beater room, boiler house, turbine room, and finishing room. A century later, Number 3 produced the last reel of paper ever made in Groveton.

A barefoot crew on Number 3 paper machine. It seems incredible that men would work in such a dangerous and toxic environment barefoot. (Courtesy Jim Emerson)

Some of the Italians who had come to Groveton to build the town sewer remained in town working at the expanding mill. The *Democrat* reported early in 1908: "Much excitement has been caused this week by disturbances among the Italians employed on the Odell Mill addition. There have been reports of highway robberies of a sensational character, escapes, arrests and police court hearings, but nothing has developed. If there is any truth in the claims made action has been stalled by the refusal of parties to make complaint. It is rather a mixed-up mess requiring the services of Sherlock Holmes."[30]

That April, several of the Italian workers, having spent a Sunday at a local "resort," were walking along West Street. Vito Ratta purportedly had developed a romantic interest in the seventeen-year-old daughter of his landlady. As Ratta and his companions passed the house, they began arguing. The young lady attempted to persuade him to return to his lodgings with her. He refused, and a moment later Ambrozio Chiaravattati reputedly shot him with a revolver. The assailant vanished, and the victim succumbed to his wound the following day.[31] There were no further reports on this tragedy in the *Democrat*.

On November 26, 1909, the *Groveton Advertiser* published its first issue.

For the next decade, both the *Advertiser* and the *Democrat* would chronicle the doings of Groveton in a haphazard way. Neither paper regularly offered feature articles, and most news from that era must be gleaned from the columns of the Locals. The March 11, 1910, issue of the *Advertiser* contained this suggestive classified ad: "Notice: We will be in Groveton every Tuesday preceding the Odell Manufacturing Co. payday, where we will be pleased to transact legal business at reasonable rates. We make a specialty of collections. ...No collection, no charge. We will be located temporarily at the police court in the office of Wm. Hayes. [Signed] Libby and Coulombe, attorneys at law, Gorham, N.H." One can imagine the games of cat-and-mouse between mill workers and collection agents.

In 1912, the prospering mill replaced the original Number 1 paper machine, installed in 1891, with a J. H. Horne and Sons paper machine, which, despite its relative youth, would be named "Number 1 Paper Machine." The new machine produced a sheet 106 inches wide and was almost identical to Number 2 machine. Both were 205 feet long and 13 feet wide; they produced approximately eighteen tons of paper a day, at a rate of between two hundred to four hundred feet per minute. Number 3 machine, by contrast, was capable of over one thousand feet a minute. In 1913, Odell installed a bleach plant that enabled it to turn out white paper. The bleach plant would be rebuilt in 1919 when the acid tower was added, and again in 1928.

Groveton's numerous saloons stirred controversy as far away as Franklin, New Hampshire, in the autumn of 1913. A temperance man from that downstate town alleged that since a saloon license went into effect on May 1, "Groveton has become a plague spot." He claimed that men were found passed out along streets and in the yards of respectable citizens. Lancaster teetotalers also condemned the public drunkenness in the mill town. The *Groveton Advertiser* admitted that Groveton had a drinking problem, but noted that most of those arrested in Groveton hailed from Lancaster. It accused Lancastrians of hypocrisy: while censuring Groveton's saloons, "Lancaster people like our money, taint and all," as evidenced by the swarms of creditors in Groveton every payday.[32]

Chapter Five

RATVILLE, NH

"CONDITIONS ARE QUIETER at Groveton than they have been for some time," the *Democrat* reported in July 1917. "One carload of strike-breakers has left town and Charles Kelley of Colebrook has been appointed superintendent of police. This combination has worked to stop some of the disorder that was creeping out at intervals.... There have been occasional records of assault that resulted in police hearings. In one instance a shot was fired and the offender was held for aggravated assault to await the grand jury."[1]

The longest strike in the Groveton paper mill's history had begun on May 10, 1917, five weeks after the United States entered World War I. Four hundred and fifty striking mill workers, members of Local No. 41 of the International Brotherhood of Paper Makers and Local 61 of the Pulp Sulphite Workers and Mill Workers Union, shut down the Odell mill. The *Advertiser*'s correspondent predicted a short strike. A week into the strike Odell agreed to two of the strikers' three major demands: wage increases and an eight-hour workday of three shifts to replace the eleven-hour day shift and thirteen-hour night shift. Willard Munroe, co-owner and manager of the mill, who had moved his family from Maine to Groveton when the strike began, refused to recognize the union, vowed to keep the mill closed for a year rather than yield, and imported Boston police officers to guard the mill and village.[2]

The union blamed the strike on management's refusal "to do business with their employees as men.... These men had been working for the Odell Co. eleven and thirteen hours for years at starvation wages."[3] In the first week of the strike, one hundred mill workers and their families left town for work in Fraser's Madawaska paper mill in far northern Maine.

While strikers, led by a band, paraded around town to honor a visiting union leader, the mill began to import strikebreakers. The *Paper Makers Journal*, published by the United Brotherhood of Paper Makers, alleged that Odell had brought in a number of carpenters from Lewiston, Maine, who were members of the United Brotherhood of Carpenters and Joiners, "under the protection of imported gun-men and so-called detectives."[4] The strikers were furious Odell had granted raises and an eight-hour workday to scabs after denying them to longtime workers.[5]

Mickey King's grandfather told him about the strike: "There was this woman, Mrs. Lavoie; she was very outspoken about the scabs. I guess she had gone to church with a buggy, and someone had said something, and she hollered, 'You scab.' And she took the horsewhip to him, sitting in the buggy. She didn't get him real good, but it made them angry. She was hanging out clothes, and they shot at her a couple of times."

On August 19, an arsonist burned one of the mill's barns on the meadow near the B&M Railroad bridge, below the Weston Dam, downstream of the mill. Four days later, the Associated Mutual Insurance Cos. sent H. B. McClune to survey the entire mill. (A framed copy of McClune's handsome and informative floor plan hung in the mill's office for decades.) At the end of August, James Prosser, a foreman in the fire room, was electrocuted in the coal yard. He left a widow and seven children.

Berlin mill workers brought their traditional Labor Day parade to Groveton, where "one of the largest holiday crowds ever seen" marched around town, enjoyed baseball games, speeches, a picnic, an evening band concert, a speech by Berlin's mayor, and "a dance under union auspices in the Opera House." The union reported that proceeds from the Labor Day parade had paid off all bills and netted a surplus of $104.36 that went to the strike fund. The *Advertiser*'s sympathetic report of the Labor Day festivities concluded: "Considering the feeling caused by the strike situation the day was remarkably free from disorder." Nevertheless, it reported Everett Mayhew was stabbed in the left shoulder by a strikebreaker, and two or three other men were arrested "for minor offenses, or no offense at all, according to different views of the case." The following morning while waiting for a train, Lee Whitcomb was hit in the face.[6]

In early October, the *Advertiser* reported that Numbers 1 and 2 paper machines were running twenty-four hours a day, while Number 3 was operating ten hours a day. The pulp mill was cooking sixteen hours a day, and all departments outside the mill were working overtime. The old blacksmith shop near the B&M tracks on Main Street, recently used by the mill as a mess hall for its scab force, was damaged by fire on October 21. Firemen were forced

The shipping department crew in 1914 when the mill was prospering. (Courtesy Doug White)

to break into the locked firehouse because, the *Advertiser* surmised, the key had been stolen. A second fire in the same location occurred later that day.

Throughout the fall and winter, strikers and management traded barbs. The union accused the mill of blacklisting strikers trying to find work in other mills in northern New England. In December the *Paper Makers Journal* gleefully reported: "After a desperate struggle all summer, they failed to get the whole supply of logs from the river, and at present there is over ten thousand cords frozen solid in the upper river awaiting the spring freshet which will clean everything in the onward rush for the great waters of the Connecticut." The following month, the union reported that the mill was suffering from a "scarcity of fuel as well as a scarcity of labor. What the management of the Company at Groveton expects to achieve by continuing the strike is beyond common sense reasoning."[7]

Management charged the union with bad-faith bargaining and misuse of funds, while the union blasted the mill for buying up all available firewood and refusing to sell to non-employees. Early in December, the *Advertiser* reported that three families had moved to Groveton from Troy, New York, and that more than a dozen other families had moved to town in the preceding month to work at the mill. Three days before Christmas, an early morning fire in the mill's stockroom caused $100,000 in losses. The 120-by-50-foot building was separated from the rest of the mill by a brick firewall.

The strike continued into 1918. Insufficient shipments of coal, presumably due to the war effort, forced the mill to operate only part time in early February. In March, E. H. Macloon, an executive with the Groveton Power and Light Company and chairman of the local Public Safety Committee, expelled Alfred Deering, who was accused of being an organizer for the IWW, the radical International Workers of the World union.

"There has been no change in the general strike situation," the Groveton correspondent reported in the *Paper Makers Journal* in March. "The company are as hard up for help as they were last summer and the mill is in a desperate condition, in the machine room it looks like a junk shop, and from all reports they are junking the best part of it. The boiler room reminds one of a submarined fishing schooner where there had at one time, some human being lived and worked but at present they are all dead ones." The correspondent claimed the pulp mill was in worse shape than even IWW saboteurs could have made it. Two digesters were "entirely out of business," and the acid room was in terrible shape.[8]

The union reported that there was scant activity at the mill during the spring, and in August 1918, a union report from "Ratville, NH" noted that most strikers had found other work, and that the "large machine," Number 3, had not been in operation for eight weeks. Thereafter, the strike continued, albeit at a low key. The *Paper Makers Journal* reported in September 1919, "At the present time we have no expenses, but the strike is still on." Sometime before June 20, 1920, the strike had been called off.[9]

The mill owners never achieved the sort of control over the lives of their employees owners of classic company towns achieved, but Odell's managers took several steps designed to weaken the threat of a well-organized labor force. Odell had been operating a company store in the old Soule store since about 1907. The October 1917 issue of the *Paper Makers Journal* reported: "The Company here has a soup house for their Boston rats, where they are fed like cattle and housed on the same plan the company hogs are, every hog for himself. . . . We call them the union scabs from Kennebec."[10] The following year, the mill constructed single-family houses on Odell Park for employees to rent.

Bitterness over the strike festered for decades. Jim Wemyss Jr. encountered it in the late 1940s: "I can only tell you one thing. It was like the Civil War in the United States. Brothers against brothers, and sisters against sisters, and mothers against their daughters. It did a terrible thing to this town because some were mad that the mill was on strike, and some wanted the mill on strike. It's a town here. Just one town. They never got over that. I even had that thrown at me twenty-five years later. That's when Willie Munroe became famous."

In 1900, Willard Munroe and a group of United States and Canadian investors had formed the Brompton Pulp and Paper Company that owned mills in Vermont, New Hampshire, and the Sherbrooke, Quebec, area. Groveton's Odell mill operated independently until it merged with Brompton on January 9, 1919, possibly as part of its strategy to defeat the union and end the strike. Brompton promptly changed the mill's name to the Groveton Paper Company, and the company store was renamed "Groveton Paper Company Inc. Store."

Despite an infusion of Brompton's capital, the mill's fortunes did not immediately improve. The United States economy, and the paper industry in particular, were in a postwar recession that would persist throughout 1921. Construction of a new acid tower for the bleach plant suffered a setback when one of its elevators fell about eighty feet on May 13, 1919. The man riding on it was badly shaken, but he escaped serious injury. A lightning fire on June 16 destroyed the mill's power plant on the site of the old Weston Sawmill. It was immediately rebuilt. An estimated crowd of three thousand to five thousand peacefully celebrated Labor Day 1919. A week later, the top of one of the mill's smokestacks blew over in a heavy rainstorm.

Around 7:30 a.m. on May 21, 1920, a fire broke out in the approximately ten-thousand-cord pile of pulpwood. Within an hour, the top of the pile was "a mass of flames." Eight buildings nearby caught fire and appeared headed for destruction despite efforts by local citizens and the fire departments of Groveton, Lancaster, and Berlin. Around noon, a heavy rain began to fall, allowing the firemen to turn their attention from the buildings to the pulp pile. Half the pulpwood was destroyed, and damages were assessed at $150,000.[11]

That summer, Brompton's Groveton paper mill launched a biweekly newspaper for its employees called the *Gropaco News*. It featured insider jokes about the antics of various employees, information about the company's

Eleven ironworkers who built the enclosed structural steel passageway that housed
the conveyor that transported wood chips from the wood room to the digesters in 1920:
who were these men? What stories they could tell. (George Vervaris Collection,
courtesy GREAT)

finances, photographs showing the progress of mill construction projects,
news of mill paper production, accident reports, articles on how to make
paper, and photographs of mill employees. In its Christmas 1920 issue, mill
general manager J. W. Bothwell wrote: "Despite the depressed condition of
business throughout the country, our company believes that business will
improve in the near future.... Our company is working and will continue to
work, for the best interests of the community as a whole, as well as for itself.
Our interests cannot be divided. As I said to you some time ago; what is
good for our Company is good for Groveton and what is good for Groveton
is good for us."[12]

The following spring, while paper mill workers throughout the country
suffered wage cuts of 10 to 15 percent, the *Gropaco News* continued to exude

confidence that Groveton would remain busy and prosperous. The new owners were investing large amounts of money to build a new wood room, a new boiler house, and a new generator building. The contractor for the brickwork and these new structures, U. G. Houston, had worked on the smaller brick chimney in 1891 and had superintended the construction of the 1908 brick chimney. He had also overseen the brickwork on the digester house, the screen room, the filter house, Number 1 finishing room, Number 3 boiler house, and the Brooklyn power plant that had been completed in March 1919. "Quite a record," the *Gropaco News* observed.[13]

The mill also installed a new drum barker that could debark 175 cords of pulpwood in eighteen hours. Some woodsmen continued to spend the warmer months of the year peeling pulpwood and swatting blackflies and mosquitoes, but, increasingly, the mill purchased cheaper unpeeled pulpwood that it fed to the new barker.

Willard Munroe and Charles Wilson bought back the Groveton Paper Company mill and its timberlands and hydropower from Brompton in 1927. The mill was running all three paper machines and employed 400. Formerly it had employed as many as 550, but mechanization had eliminated 150 jobs from the labor pool. The mill used ten to twelve million gallons of water a day to make paper and steam.[14]

Throughout the Depression, the Groveton mill struggled to survive. It failed to pay its 1932 property tax bill of $31,005.82. Its 1933 bill also went unpaid. By 1934, it was able to scrape together the wherewithal to pay off its 1932 tax bill, and for the remainder of the decade the mill avoided foreclosure, but it remained two years in arrears. The much larger Brown Company, located in Berlin, twenty-five miles to the east, filed for bankruptcy in 1935.

Number 3 paper machine had been shut down owing to lack of orders in the early years of the Depression. Although business improved enough by November 1936 to keep two paper machines running, Number 3 did not restart. Shirley Perkins Brown recalled that throughout the 1930s, the mill ran sporadically: "[My father] was working probably four or five hours a day, maybe two or three days a week. The mill was in pretty bad shape. They were trying to give the older workers time, but it really wasn't enough to survive on. They probably never worked more than fifteen hours a week."

"Willie" Munroe attempted to mitigate the crisis by adding a fourth six-hour shift to employ more workers, albeit at reduced hours. John Rich recalled: "I've heard some of the old-timers talk about it. They thought it was a great thing. Everybody got a little money. I've never heard anybody say but what he was an awful nice man."

On February 25, 1935, workers detected a gas leak in the boiler room. They put up a fourteen-foot ladder to the twelve-foot-high economizer stack, and Ray Kimball, forty-six, climbed up to turn the damper. Tragically, he was overcome by gas, and he fell from the ladder to his death.[15] Franklin "Honey" Beaton, a star outfielder on the town baseball team, suffered body burns and gas poisoning. Edgar Vancure carried the unconscious man to a window; Vancure suffered severe burns when a hot pipe fell on him. On November 5, 1936, another leak, most likely chlorine gas, overcame several mill workers. The Democrat reported that Truman Tickey and Merle McKean were injured. A couple of weeks later, the Locals noted that Arthur Pinaud was receiving treatment in Stewartstown Hospital after being gassed at the mill.[16]

On December 7, 1936, Willard Munroe agreed to a 10 percent wage increase. Recently business had improved, and the four hundred mill employees had requested a 20 percent raise. "It was hinted that the machines would not be started on Monday if the wage increase was not granted," the Democrat reported. Under the new agreement, the minimum men's wage would be forty-three cents an hour, and the minimum women's wage was raised to thirty-six cents. Paper machine tenders, the highest-paid union jobs, would earn eighty-eight cents an hour. Workers would receive time and a quarter for overtime and time and a half for Sundays and holidays.[17]

In the fall of 1937, the mill shut down for repairs to the Brooklyn Dam (the rebuilt Soule Dam), and a week later, the pulp mill shut down for repairs for a couple of days. In mid-November the mill was idled because of "slackness of orders." The Locals correspondent added, "All trust it will not be for long."[18] The mill closed for a week after Christmas 1937, and in February 1938, the Democrat reported that one out of ten residents of Coös County was receiving some form of relief.[19] Orders were again slack in early April, and only Number 2 paper machine was operating, while "much repair work is being done."[20]

Charles C. Wilson, one of the purchasers of the mill in 1895, died in Lewiston, Maine, on August 28, 1935, leaving Willard Munroe Sr. as the last of the original Odell Manufacturing Company owners.[21] Munroe's health was failing, and in the winter of 1937 the Locals column carried regular updates on his condition. He died in Maine on June 16, 1938, at the age of seventy-eight. His brother Horace and son Willard N. Munroe Jr. continued to run the mill.

SHIRLEY PERKINS BROWN:
THE BEST YEARS OF OUR LIVES

Shirley Brown was born in 1927 in Madawaska, Maine, where her father, John Perkins, had moved soon after the outbreak of the 1917 strike. The family returned to Groveton in the early 1930s, and her father worked in the stock prep department.

A chlorine gas leak at the mill in the mid-1930s destroyed her father's health: "My father was a beater engineer. Chlorine came into town in the big tankers, and one of those tankers sprung a leak. I've heard two versions of this. They evacuated everybody from the mill, and they needed two volunteers to turn the pipes off on this big tanker. Then the other story was he was in the beater room cleaning it, and they didn't know that he was there. From that time, he became disabled. It burned all the tissues in his lungs and everything. He was guaranteed a lifetime job. They gave him a thousand dollars settlement, which in those days was just incredible. His lifetime job was in the water room, which is in the subterranean part of the mill, and he wore a gas mask to work because the tissues in his lungs were all burned out. Practically all of our life was taking him to the Veterans Hospital in White River and taking him home for a little while. He was an invalid; he died when he was fifty-nine. I was probably about six or seven [when the accident occurred]. I can remember they didn't even take him to the hospital. He was unconscious, and they brought him home. During those times, there was no insurance, so if you got hurt in the mills, you were on your own."

Following her husband's accident, Lyse Perkins was forced to take a job at the mill. "That's when [my mother] started working for women's rights, because the women weren't paid equal to the men," Shirley said. "She was instrumental in getting the things for women that worked in the mill — benefits. We never realized what an important role she played in the mill. We were probably fourteen or fifteen, and she'd be going on these conventions and winning all these awards for her work, and still working in the mill. She worked with an ulcer on her leg. Her leg was bandaged all the time."

Despite the hard times, Shirley recalled the simple pleasures of a Groveton childhood in the Depression: "Most of the people that worked in the mill lived in company houses. There weren't that many privately owned houses. The farmers lived a lot better than the people in town. The Depression was so bad, we knew what it was to be hungry; we knew what it was to be cold. The Legion in town took care of an awful lot of people in this town during that time. They bought food. At Christmastime, I used to hate it because we knew we were going to get a long-legged union suit [underwear] full of apples and oranges. I think if it hadn't have been for the Legion, a lot of people in this town wouldn't have survived because they took care of people who were really having a hard time. I never knew we were poor. My older brothers and sisters said they never knew we were poor until they went to school."

During the Depression a relief truck came to Groveton once a month. "That would be a big truck with boxes of canned goods and food, and the necessities, probably, toilet paper, hygiene and stuff. I always dreaded seeing the relief truck come to town. Nothing was handed out. They'd throw it out of the truck. Whoever caught it, got it. It was awful. Once, the truck was empty; they had one box of prunes left, and the guy hollered, 'Who catches it, it's theirs.' I saw my mother and another woman rolling in the dirt over that. Fighting over that box of prunes."

In a scene out of Dickens, children scrounged for coal cinders to heat their homes: "When you used to walk downtown, you'd get home, and you'd look yourself in the mirror, and you could see in your eyes and mouth, that everything was black and sooty [from the coal burned in the mill]," Shirley remembered. "Also, the trains burned coal, and then every once in a while, they would empty the coal tank onto the tracks. We would go out after we got home from school [with] big pails. We'd walk the tracks and pick up the coal cinderblocks. People would put those in their furnace. A lot of times there would still be gas left in the coal. They would blow up." "And it would come through the grate and all over the furniture," her sister Patricia Woodward added.

Poverty carried a stigma. Shirley recalled a time she brought one of her Christmas presents into school: "Going back to school in January, after the

Christmas vacation, I brought an orange to school. Oh, my God, I was so excited, 'I've got an orange for lunch.' The principal said to me, 'Where did you get that orange?' 'I got it for Christmas.' She said, 'You did not; you stole it.' She took the orange away from me and gave it to her granddaughter who was in the same class as me."

Another time, Shirley and her older sister were accused of stealing: "When we went to school, it was almost an attitude, 'If you were poor, you were stupid.' It's bringing back a lot of bad memories. Some money came up missing in the school. I was in the second grade, and one of my older sisters was in the fourth or fifth grade. Anyway, instead of questioning any of the kids, they took my sister and I and undressed us because we might have the money in our bloomers. It was a nightmare, and all of the kids were calling us 'dirty thieves.' A couple of weeks later, they discovered that the doctor's son had stolen the ten dollars. They didn't do a thing because he was a status — the doctor's son. My older sister, it hurt her so much more than it did me because I really didn't realize quite what was going on."

"It was a hard time for kids to grow up," Shirley reflected, "but we had a lot of fun. My dad, as sick as he was, during the winter, we would skate on the river, and he would have this — I think it must have been a bamboo fishing pole. He would pull that and we would be all hanging on and screeching and yelling and having fun. We played games. Kids talked to each other then. Strange as it was, we were happy. We made our own happiness. We had a ball. It was the best years of our lives."

The Groveton Paper Company shortly before James C. Wemyss Sr. purchased it in August 1940. He immediately changed the name to "Groveton Papers." (Courtesy Greg Cloutier)

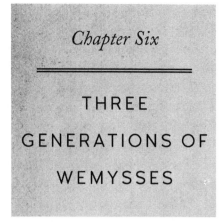

Chapter Six

THREE GENERATIONS OF WEMYSSES

JAMES C. WEMYSS JR. fondly recalled an August 1940 trip to Groton with his father, James C. Wemyss Sr.: "I was out of school. [Father] said, 'Come on, I'll take you to look at a paper mill over at Groton.' He and I drove over. We spent the night in the company house, which is now the [Passumpsic] bank. It was staffed with a lady. She cooked something for us to eat. I was only about fourteen. He said, 'Let's go down and walk through that paper mill.' So we walked through it, and he said, 'What do you think of it?' I said, 'Gee, I wish we could buy that.' He said, 'I just did' [*laughs*]. I said, 'Oh, that's good.'"

Rumors of the impending sale had been swirling around the North Country during the summer of 1940. Logger Cy Hessenauer recorded in his diary: "Aug. 13 (Tuesday): Looked like rain again and this time did. At noon it began. Phil and I went to town in PM. . . . Mill down. Everyone talking about the change in ownership. . . . Aug. 18: This new week will mark a landmark in Groton history. The mill under new management. Many men layed off. 270 out of woods alone."[1]

The sale of the mill was completed on August 14, 1940. Old Jim immediately changed the mill's name from Groton *Paper* to Groton *Papers*. The Wemyss family assumed responsibility for the mill's debts, which included two years of back property taxes owed to the Township of Northumberland and loans totaling $570,000 from Coös County that had been guaranteed by the State of New Hampshire. Old Jim Wemyss secured an additional loan of $180,000 to make necessary capital improvements to modernize and expand mill capacity.[2] The Wemyss family purchased roughly ninety thousand acres of timberland in New Hampshire and Vermont, including the forty-thousand-acre Nash Stream watershed, as well as nearly two hundred buildings and houses in Groton. "We owned most of the town," Jim Jr. said.

The elder Wemyss made a good first impression on Puss Gagnon, the recently hired fifteen-year-old. "I first started for Old Willie Munroe," Puss told me. "One week or two, then Wemyss bought it. We went from forty-eight cents an hour to fifty-one cents an hour. We thought he was a hell of a nice fellow."

Jim Wemyss Sr.'s father, James Strembeck Wemyss, patriarch of the family paper business, opposed his son's decision to buy Groveton Paper Company. Grandfather Wemyss had purchased an idle newsprint mill in Northumberland village on August 23, 1923. He converted it to a tissue mill. For seventeen years, he observed the struggles of Groveton Paper, three and a half miles to the north. Decades later, Jim Wemyss Jr. explained his grandfather's thinking: "It was a mess, and he said, 'It's been a mess for many years, and it's still gonna be a mess.'"

James S. Wemyss had gone into the toilet paper business in 1909 because, he told his grandson, "I didn't want to sell grand pianos. You only sell one to one family maybe in a lifetime. I want to get a business where they use my product every day of the week." In 1910 he paid a struggling Virginia business $5,000 for the right to call his tissue line "Vanity Fair." His first mill was on Town Creek, just across from the Brooklyn Bridge, next to a slaughterhouse. "My grandfather used to tell me it was not the cleanest water," Jim Wemyss chuckled. Around 1914, James S. Wemyss acquired a small mill in Pittston, Pennsylvania, in the Wyoming Valley, and another small mill in Troy, New York.

J. S. Wemyss renamed the Northumberland mill "Wyoming Valley Paper Mill." When the Town Creek mill was destroyed by fire in 1926, he shifted tissue-making operations to Northumberland. He and his twenty-three-year-old son replaced the existing dam with a new dam, and they constructed a hydroelectric power plant to run the mill. Jim Jr. wryly described his father's first job in Northumberland — to keep the dam builder, Mr. Harriman, sober: "[Harriman] drank Spirits of Oneida and Brown's Relief. [Father] said, 'The only reason I knew he was drinking Brown's Relief or Spirits of Oneida, I'd walk up to him and say, "Stick out your tongue."' If his tongue was purple, [Father] said, 'You're drinking.'" Jim Sr. also discovered the pleasure of heaving sticks of dynamite out of a Stutz Bearcat. "He liked to hear the noise, I guess," his son suggested. "Grandfather didn't like the idea of him throwing dynamite out of the car, so he took him back to New York. Said he was getting bad training up here."

In 1926, J. S. Wemyss took out a $100,000 mortgage on the Wyoming Valley mill and added a second tissue machine. He pulled nearly all his money out of the stock market just before the crash in October 1929 and paid off the 1926 mortgage. While other paper mills in the United States shut down or ran only sporadically, the Wyoming Valley mill kept running full tilt, producing toilet paper, napkins, paper towels, grass for Easter baskets, paper for wrapping fancy shirts, wax paper, and even paper to line coffins.

Grandfather Wemyss added two small, used tissue machines in 1929 and 1930 that produced about three hundred feet of tissue a minute. Jim Jr. marveled: "If OSHA could have seen that plant! You know how they controlled the speed of the paper machines? They had a wooden vat full of saltwater, and they had a little wheel up here with a winch, and they had these induction motors [that] drove the paper machine. As they lowered the celluloids into the saltwater, it put more resistance up on the motors and it would slow down. If you wanted to go fast, you pulled [them] up out of the water and it would go a little faster."

In 1933, J. S. Wemyss replaced the finishing room he had built in 1927 with a two-story concrete-and-steel finishing room that was 150 by 100 feet. It contained a printing plant to produce wrappers for the company's new line of napkins, towels, and waxed paper products. The mill used between twenty and forty tons of sulfite and ground wood pulp a day. Most of the longer-fiber sulfite pulp was acquired from the Groveton and Berlin mills. A Wemyss-owned mill in Danville, Quebec, provided the shorter-fiber ground wood.[3] Joan Breault remembered the Northumberland mill also used rags: "They had sidings in there towards the paper machine, and people would go over there because they had boxcars of cotton clothes come in to put in the paper machine. People got a lot of clothes out of that."

Jim Wemyss recalled the mill's worst month: "It was in February of '35 or '34, and [Grandfather] said, 'You know, Jim, we made $234 last month. We didn't lose any money. But if I have another month like this, I'm going to shut it down. I can do better with my income on my money. I hate like heck to put a lot of people out of work, but this is an awful lot of work for just $230.' Right after that, business changed and he started making considerably more money. That's how close it came. Berlin was practically shut down. Groveton had one little machine slobbering along."

The Wyoming Valley mill employed 350 in the mid-1930s. When unemployed men asked J. S. Wemyss for a job, his grandson recalled, "He'd say, 'I'll pay you a dollar a day. Here's a bucket of paint and a brush.' But with that dollar a day, they could buy a loaf of bread for five cents, or a dozen eggs for 25 cents. At least they were able to eat. That's the way he felt, anyhow. 'Paint it red.'"

"Times were tough," Herb Miles asserted. "If it hadn't been for the Wemysses, there'd have been a lot of hungry people around this area. People who didn't see it, don't realize it. People were hungry."

Jim Wemyss Jr. was born in November 1925. He lived with his grandfather in Lancaster when he was ten. The youngster often heard his grandfather preach economic diversification and avoidance of debt. If a mill produced only newsprint or bond paper, and the market was poor, "you're shut down." "My grandfather would never leave his office at night until all the bills were paid, unless there was one in dispute," Jim Jr. recalled. "He would not go to bed owing money to anybody. Never had a mortgage. [Actually, he took out a mortgage in 1926.] Never borrowed money. Didn't have any life insurance either. He said, 'That's a dead business. You have to die to win. I don't like it.' He knew everything [that] was going on. He taught my father the same thing, and I guess I must have learned something myself."

Grandfather Wemyss, a tough, paternalistic capitalist, was no friend of organized labor. A *Coös County Democrat* headline proclaimed on October 18, 1939: "Police Guard Paper Mill: The Wyoming Valley Mill Takes Action to Prevent Possible Harm from Outsiders." The outsiders, it turned out, were six strikers from a mill in Gouverneur, New York, that the Wemyss family had owned since 1935. Fearing the strikers intended to sabotage operations at Northumberland, J. S. Wemyss called on Groveton's selectmen and police to protect his mill. State troopers, along with Groveton and Berlin police, discovered that "the delegation from Gouverneur had no intention of molesting private property." Instead, they hoped to persuade the mill's workers to organize a papermakers union affiliated with the American Federation of Labor (AFL). The *Democrat's* unsigned news story opined: "It is not believed that any great number will be ready to join a union. The present wage scale is higher than is paid in similar mills operating under similar conditions. A five percent increase in wages recently went into effect, and another increase becomes effective automatically." Since wages were in the twenty-five-cents-an hour range, the raises were a penny or two an hour. Workers voted against organizing a union in mid-November.[4]

Walter Wemyss, a nephew of J. S. Wemyss, managed the Northumberland mill. At Christmastime 1940, Wyoming Valley workers gave both men large sterling silver cocktail sets. The engraving on Grandfather Wemyss's gift read, "To a Fine Boss." The boss was moved to give all Wyoming Valley employees a Christmas bonus of an extra week's pay.[5]

The goodwill did not survive the year. Two hundred men and one hundred women briefly struck Wyoming Valley on September 30, 1941. Walter Wemyss negotiated an increase for the hourly workers and an adjustment in the piece rate paid to the women in the finishing room.[6] The strike so embittered J. S. Wemyss that he turned his back on the mill. Jim Wemyss Jr. said, "My grandfather's parting words to me [were], 'Jim, don't do any more in this mill. We took everybody for work during the Depression,' and they gave him the cocktail shakers, and thanked him for all these wonderful things, and then they went on strike with the union. He said, 'That's my thank you. I'll walk away.' And he walked away. He gave it to me, but he said, 'I would advise you not to put any more money in this mill. Period.' And I didn't. That was good advice from a smart man." By 1941, the Wemyss family was putting its money into the Groveton mill.

Even though Grandfather Wemyss opposed the purchase of the failing Groveton mill, he put up the capital to acquire it. Young Jim acknowledged that this was one occasion when his grandfather misjudged an opportunity: "My grandfather was an executive. He was not a mill man. I don't want to demean him, but I don't ever remember him being that involved in his paper mills. He was involved in the executive area and sales. My grandfather didn't really understand them, as large as they were getting. He was used to smaller, one- and two-machine mills. Father had the foresight to look ahead to see what the hell was going on in the industry."

The Groveton mill was more dead than alive when Old Jim bought it. Len Fournier remembered the mill was "mostly all wooden floors" and infested with rats: "I don't mean that they bothered us, but you would see them. You couldn't leave your dinner pail around. They'd hide under the wooden floors. Eventually they got a man in to go around and put out poison."

James Strembeck
Wemyss in a top hat
and his wife, Margaret
Campbell Wemyss,
in the white hat, exiting
a family wedding in the
1940s. (Courtesy Jim
Wemyss)

Jim Wemyss believed his father was "the only man that could have bought it and run it. He knew what to do. The people before it were clowns. It took a helluva lot of work." The Groveton mill was antiquated: "The Number 3 [paper machine] was driven by a big Ball steam engine. [Numbers] 1 and 2 had great big flywheels on them, big pistons, something you'd see driving a Mississippi River boat. I'm not kidding. *Schuuuh. Schuuuh. Schuuuh.* Pistons going back and forth, and steam only ran four hundred feet a minute. They had no safety devices like rope drives. The men took the paper down between the dryers with their hands, and a lot of people got injured."

"You don't realize how tough it was when my father took this mill over in 1940," Young Jim declared. "Nothing had been done to it for ten or fifteen years. With his genius, and I mean genius, [he] got that mill to run and made a success out of it. His father didn't think he could do it. Just incredible what he did. I'm going to compliment him, but I argued with him all the time [*laughs*]. He was a very smart man."

Herb Miles, an electrician at the mill for thirty-six years, recalled that almost immediately the mill and the town came back to life: "It run steady all during the war. Guys had gone into the army and into the military, so they were shorthanded. Some guys, Mr. Wemyss told them they could stay there twenty-four hours a night — for example mechanics and millwrights — to keep stuff running, and be there if something broke down; they could repair it, keep it running." Cy Hessenauer, a boss in a logging camp, complained in his diary that it was impossible to find men willing to work in the woods: "September 23, 1940: Phil not here. Wants to get in mill very badly." On January 15, 1941, Hessenauer wrote: "Ray went tonight. Mill takes them as fast as I can get them."[7]

Old Jim understood that for the mill to survive he had to immediately restart the long-idle Number 3 paper machine. His son recalled: "He said, 'If Number 3 doesn't run, this mill can't exist. Gotta get it going immediately.' It had been shut down [around] 1932. They had not taken the water out of the dryers properly. The dryers were a little bit out of round. The machine could never run over 550 feet a minute because of that. It would snap the paper off."

Old Jim also had to rebuild the mill's customer base. His son remembered: "The mill had no sales organization to speak of. These people [the Munroes] didn't know anything about running a mill. My father did not want to sell to jobbers at a low price. So Father said, 'Who are these jobbers selling to? That's who we're going to sell to. We're going direct.' Right around the jobbers to the [mimeograph] machinery manufacturers. We didn't make any friends doing it, but we made friends with the machinery dealers because we said: 'What would you like? We'll make it specially for you.' We became very successful at that."

Jim Sr. understood that he could not revive the Groveton mill's fortunes if he provoked a fight with the two locals that represented the mill workers. Following three days of "friendly negotiations," Wemyss granted workers wage increases of five to seven cents per hour effective July 1, 1941. The agreement also protected seniority rights, permitted arbitration of disputes, and promised no strikes or lockouts.[8]

World War II had begun in Europe on September 1, 1939. By the time the United States entered the war twenty-seven months later, the transition to a wartime economy was well under way. The first draftees were called to military service in the fall of 1940, and four Groveton boys were on duty at Pearl Harbor on December 7, 1941. The war effort created unprecedented demand for paper, and this played an important role in the revival of the mill.

Three hundred sixty-two residents of Northumberland Township entered military service. Shirley Brown recalled, "It was a town of basically females." To make up for its depleted workforce, the mill hired women, French Canadians not in the Canadian army, very old men, and mentally challenged workers. "We hired anything that could stand up," Jim Wemyss Jr. quipped. "The digester plant was run by men all in their sixties and seventies."

Ruby Sargent filled in at a man's job in the wood room, where she and another woman pulled pulpwood from the wood room pond onto a conveyor belt that fed the chipper. Jerome Cote retired in 1945 at age ninety-one, after working at the mill for twenty-three years.[9] The wartime labor shortage was not the only reason old men continued to work at the mill; there was no decent pension system. Channie Tilton remembered an uncle who received a forty-seven-dollar-a-month pension — a dollar for each year he had worked at the mill.

Fifteen-year-old Raymond Jackson was hired in the summer of 1941: "I was going to school then. My father had been hurt in an accident [in May 1941], so I had to take over and be responsible for the family. He was out cutting some wood for himself. It came down in the 1938 hurricane. He cut the tree, and it kicked back, and it broke his ankle and his leg real bad. I had to get permission from the superintendent of the schools to work for the summer."

Jackson's first job was as fireman in the boiler room: "They cleaned these ashes, made sure the coal was going down the chutes. A big hopper overhead. It got to the boiler, the stoker part of the boiler, and that's where it stopped until you wanted it to go again. It was a good job." That fall, when school resumed, Jackson said: "I tried to stay on and work because we needed the money. I was allowed to work there and work through to the next summer again. Then I got to be old enough so that I could work on my own. I went to work at four o'clock in the afternoon from school, and then I'd work till ten or eleven o'clock. Then the same thing over the next day." Jackson worked full time at the mill the last two years of high school and graduated with his class in 1943. It had been a challenge, but he said, "It was to benefit my parents."

The war disrupted normal economic activity. In December 1943, there was a national shortage of coal, the primary power source for the mill. Pulpwood was also scarce. Groveton's mill was able to keep running, but in June 1943, the Brown Company in Berlin had shut down operations when it ran out of pulpwood. Wartime price controls, designed to prevent price gouging and profiteering, applied to existing, but not new, products. Old Jim responded with creativity. "Father started making things like 'Drug Bond,'" Jim Wemyss recalled. "Don't ask me where he got the name. There was no price control on Drug Bond; maybe instead of getting five cents, he made seven cents, which made the mill quite profitable. Then we started making butcher's paper, and there was no — to my knowledge — price controls on that."

Some things were beyond the senior Wemyss's control. "My father was taking us all out; we were young kids back in the '40s," Jim Jr. remembered. "We were running green butcher's paper down on Number 3 paper machine. He had on a brand-new gabardine suit. He was a very prestigious-looking guy when he was dressed up. Something was wrong with the pump in the cellar, and he went down in the cellar, and somebody had taken the boards off the sewer to find out how to drain the water, and he fell in the sewer. He came out a brilliant green. He said, 'I don't think we're going out to dinner tonight.' We never knew what was going to happen; it was fun."

John Rich's father, Nelson, was a mill employee who represented Groveton in the New Hampshire Legislature in 1943: "I think him and the old man Wemyss, they had a run-in then. Because my father went to the legislature, and there was a timber bill that the old man wanted my father to vote for, and he wouldn't vote that way. I don't know what it was all about, but he was pretty ornery too, either one of them." When Jim Sr. expressed his displeasure in strong terms, the legislator quit his job at the mill.

Wages could not keep up with prices, thanks to wartime inflation. Unions had pledged not to strike critical industries during the war, but they persuaded the War Labor Board to support a five-cent-an-hour wage increase. When the Groveton mill and its two locals failed to agree on a wage adjustment in the summer of 1944, the War Labor Board ruled the mill should grant the wage increase to workers retroactive to February 25, 1943. Old Jim agreed to the increase, but he balked at seventeen months of back payments. On July 21, 1944, the Groveton unions voted 427–27 to strike, and two days later, a Sunday when the mill was ordinarily closed, Wemyss shut down the mill. At the end of the month, labor and management agreed to a compromise that gave the strikers the five-cent increase immediately and 55 percent of the retroactive increase. Work resumed at the mill on August 2.[10] As part of the strike settlement, Old Jim forced the unions to move the expiration date for future contracts from June 1 to September 1, a concession the local unions would regret for decades.

The Second World War claimed the lives of eighteen Groveton soldiers. Jim Wemyss Jr. had barely turned nineteen when he saw action in the final months of the war in Europe. He credited a war experience with his decision to live in Groveton: "I was in France with a platoon, and I ran them into a graveyard to get behind tombstones. I figured, 'Pretty safe.' Smart, huh? I was talking to the sergeant, and I was lying on the other side of the tombstone, and a mortar came down like this [*he indicated a near vertical descent*]. It must have hit him on the top of the head. Must have blown the tombstone over on top of me. And I said, 'You know, if I ever get these boys out of this goddamned mess, I'm going back to Groveton, New Hampshire, and I'm never going to leave. So here I am. I got shot up later."

Toward the end of February 1945, as American forces pressed toward Germany, Young Jim was badly wounded: "It's not like in the movies. You're running down the streets, throwing hand grenades in windows at night, and the tanks are firing, and the glass is flying around, and all of a sudden you're lying on the ground. They said, 'Who shot you?' 'I didn't catch his name.' I don't know what happened. All of a sudden I'm bleeding like hell, and hurting like hell, and they put a tourniquet around my leg and rolled me against the building and said, 'We'll try and come back and get you.' They gave me a couple of toothpaste tubes full of morphine [and] said, 'When it gets too bad, don't forget to relieve that thing.'" Wemyss would be on crutches until September. Ever after, he walked with a limp, and he had to have additional surgery on the leg years later. I asked him about the pain after all these years; "It never stops," he answered.

Rosa Gaudette Roberge vividly recalled her childhood during the war years. She was about seven when her father died in 1942: "The night my father was sick, he was having such pains. He sent my sister up to the doctor's office to have him come to the house. Back then they'd go to your house. [The doctor] was drinking; he wouldn't come. So my father walked from behind the high school down to that house where [the doctor] lived. He knocked on the door, and the doctor opened the door, and my father dropped dead right on the doorstep. You always heard that line about, 'You opened the door and fell on the floor.' Well, it happened to my father. He was dead before he hit the floor."

Old Jim Wemyss had closed the company store on October 31, 1942, and shortly thereafter Rosa's mother moved the family to one of the apartments above it. "When my mother went to get [an apartment], the guy came there. He says, 'My goodness, you've got five kids. Isn't that a lot of kids?' She said, 'What am I supposed to do? Shoot 'em?' [laughs]. He didn't want to rent that to her with all those kids. We never destroyed anything. We were taught different."

Her father's World War I pension and Social Security could not support the family. Her mother strung a clothesline from their apartment across to the mill's converting plant, and she took in washing and ironing. "We didn't have any money," Rosa said. "I remember every once in a while we'd take a cart up to the town. Behind the bank there was a barn there. We'd get surplus food. If it wasn't for that — we didn't eat very good."

"Across from the company block, on the mill side, there was great big stacks of coal dust. It was like sand almost," she said. "We'd take an old cardboard box and cut it down and slide down the coal pile, winter and summer [laughs]. It was fun living there. I enjoyed it because we had all kinds of kids to play with, and everybody knew everybody. Everybody got along with everybody."

It is inconceivable today that small children could roam freely around the mill premises. Rosa and the neighborhood kids would sneak into the mill on Sundays, when blue laws required the mill to shut down: "We used to go in and play around the paper machines. We used to hide under them. Just to get in there and see what was in there, trying to get away with something."

"Behind the blacksmith shop there were these big iron [tanks]. There was a hole in the top. I guess they filled it with some kind of chemicals or something. I thought I'd be smart one day, and I got down in the hole," Rosa recollected. "It was empty. And I was short. I couldn't get out [*laughs*]. I was panicking; I'll never forget that. Finally, I don't know if I jumped up to grab way the hell above me. Scared me. Nobody was with me, so nobody knew I was there."

The lumberyard sawdust pile was another dangerous but irresistible place to play. "They had a thing that brought the sawdust up into the boxcars. It was like a conveyor belt, and we used to go over there and jump in the sawdust in the boxcar. Of course there was probably air pockets in there. We could have sunk right into the sawdust and suffocated." And then there was the river: "They used to have the boom logs to keep the pulp from going down the river. We weren't supposed to be on them, but we played on them. Never fell in or nothing."

Rosa witnessed the same prejudice against poor families that Shirley Brown had suffered: "My oldest brother was blamed for robbing a store, Bouchers. Somebody broke into the store, and they stole beer and cigarettes and stuff. First thing, the cop comes to the house and says something about Arthur was supposed to have broke into the store. [Mother] said, 'I don't see how he could have. He was in bed.' Come to find out it was [Boucher's] own relative that broke in the store."

Despite the family's poverty, Rosa remembered the war years with fondness: "We didn't have much, but we made our own fun."

Chapter Seven

CROWN PRINCE

"THE WAR HAD JUST ENDED," Jim Wemyss Jr. recalled. "Gas stamps, rationing and shoes — you were allowed two pairs of shoes a year. [Rationing] went off pretty quickly, but there wasn't the supplies in the pipeline to make any difference. It was a tremendous revolution in this country after the war ended. A lot of women didn't want to leave their good jobs. They were getting paid pretty good, and everybody was worried that some soldiers coming back wouldn't have any jobs because the women wouldn't give them back to them." Old Jim Wemyss's plans to modernize and expand the mill guaranteed abundant jobs for returning soldiers. Many of these hires — "the class of '46" — would remain at the mill for the next three or four decades.

Because of his responsibilities to his family, Ray Jackson was discharged before war's end. He immediately returned to the mill. Soldiers were permitted thirty days off before they had to reclaim their prewar job. Len Fournier, discharged in January 1946, thoroughly enjoyed his free time: "[I was] full of piss and vinegar."

Neal Brown's father, Bud, was hired shortly after the war: "I don't think there was a lot of mobility in those days," Neal said. "You grew up; you were familiar with your surroundings, and you didn't feel the necessity to go some-place else to check out the pastures to make sure they were greener on the other side. A lot of those guys never finished high school. They went into the war. They came out, and they had a lot of skills that they didn't have when they left; they had the leadership skills; they had the work ethic skills; they had everything else that was highly regarded. Of the kids that I grew up with, every one of our fathers had served. They didn't talk a lot about it, but we knew where they had been."

Neal's mother, newlywed Shirley Perkins Brown, recalled the postwar prosperity that allowed the Browns to buy their own house: "When Bud got out of the service and went to work in the converting plant, he was making $39 a week. We paid $2,000 for the house, and we paid $200 down and $13 a month.

Some of those months that $13 came hard. Then the pay started increasing and benefits started coming in like life insurance and health insurance."

The converting plant produced stationery and school supplies such as spiral notebooks, blue test booklets, and graph paper. Its rapid postwar expansion meant jobs for young women, including sixteen-year-old Irene Paradis Bigelow. When she received her first pay envelope, she was on top of the world: "You didn't have to make out an application for work or anything. If they needed somebody to work, they hired you right there. When I went to work in there, oh God, it was fifty-two cents an hour and I thought I had the world by the ass with a downhill pull. I'll never forget, Polly Sawyer had a store, and the first paycheck I got I went in and bought a red trench coat."[1]

James C. Wemyss Sr. became head of the family paper mill business during the war when his father's health began to decline. On April 17, 1946, James Strembeck Wemyss, age sixty-seven, died of a cerebral hemorrhage. His grandson revered him: "I had a very positive relationship with that man. To say he was like my father — he was. He and I, just he and I. He got along with the other grandkids. He was polite to them and nice, but he really, I guess, enjoyed my company as a young boy. He called me the Crown Prince. He wanted me to be head of these companies, and he made no bones about it." "When my father walked down the street, they took their hats off," Young Jim asserted on another occasion. "Not me, but they did for him. And my grandfather, *definitely!*"

After the war, prices had begun to rise steeply, and, all across the country, labor demanded significant wage and benefit increases to compensate for wartime wage freezes, lost work time due to prolonged military service, and inflation. In early 1946, most New England paper mills gave workers raises of at least fifteen cents an hour, even though labor contracts were not due to expire until June.

The average minimum wage then paid to a male mill worker in Maine and Berlin, New Hampshire, exceeded the Groveton mill's rate by twenty cents an hour. In May, Local 41 of the International Brotherhood of Papermakers and Local 61 of the International Brotherhood of Pulp, Sulphite and Paper Mill Workers requested that Groveton also grant raises in advance of the termination of the labor contract. Following lengthy negotiations, Old Jim offered a ten-cent increase to be paid in three installments: five cents on June

1, 1946, three cents on September 1, 1946, and two cents on January 1, 1947. The six hundred Groveton mill workers rejected the proposal and called a strike on September 12, 1946. Jim Wemyss suggested the strike didn't phase his father: "He said, 'Everybody needed a rest after the war anyhow, including me.'"

The unions demanded a twenty-two-cent-an-hour increase; time and a half for Saturdays and double pay for Sunday; a Christmas bonus of forty hours for employees with more than five years' service and twenty hours for all others; and increases in paid holidays.[2] A representative of the International union stated: "The workers at Groveton are not asking any more than has already been granted and is being paid by employers elsewhere."[3]

Old Jim agreed to the Christmas bonus but rejected the wage increase. Mill management suggested that Groveton workers, by working forty-eight-hour weeks, instead of the forty-hour weeks in the other mills, were actually being paid a sum "equivalent" to the weekly pay of workers in other New Hampshire and Maine mills. The union declined the honor of working six days for five days' pay.[4]

The union also demanded that future contracts expire in June to keep Groveton on the same schedule as other mills in the region — and to accelerate wage increases by three months. Wemyss insisted on retaining the September deadline. That later date allowed Groveton Papers' management to see what concessions the other mills had made; and it discouraged long strikes that stretched into November and December. As winter approached, workers on a tight budget became nervous about paying the winter heating bill. Electrician Herb Miles was friends with the Wemyss family: "I never was for strikes. I wasn't a striking man. But when it come fall, Mr. Wemyss said, 'They'll be back when the weather gets cold.'"

While some strikers picketed, others found jobs at the Gilman, Vermont, paper mill twenty miles to the south; a few families picked potatoes in northern Maine. "My husband and I had gotten married in June," Shirley Brown remembered. "The men picked potatoes on their hands and knees with baskets. We spent all our time trying to clean up the hotel because it was awful. It was not a happy time."

During the second week of the strike, a small fire broke out in some bales of waste and scrap paper in the Number 3 paper machine room. Firefighters, including fifteen striking mill workers, quickly extinguished it. Fire chief

Thomas W. Atkinson blamed "spontaneous combustion."[5] Because of the hard feelings during the strike, Dave Miles's father grounded his teenage son: "My father just said, 'Dark, you stay home. You don't go down street.' And I didn't go down street."

Jim Wemyss relished sharing the family version of how his father ended the strike: "Father didn't give a goddamn if they went on strike. He cared, but he wasn't going to take any bull from anybody. He was a very tough guy. I was going to college at the time, and the union couldn't find him for about three weeks, and they came down to the college. 'You've got to find your father.' I said, 'I don't know where he is.' I had dinner with him every night [*laughs*]. They said, 'You've got to find him. We've got to talk.' So I talked to him. 'Oh,' he said, 'Tell them we'll have a meeting at the Parker House [in Boston] next week.' I set it up. They had some real tough guys from New York and Boston. Some of the men from the mill. Father walked in with a big paper bag of walnuts and a hammer. And he sets down and one of the guys starts making a speech, and my father is rustling in the bag, and takes out a walnut and positions it like this and 'bang!' Breaks up. And this guy is speaking, and he breaks another walnut, and finally, [someone] said, 'Jim, are you listening?' 'Oh, yes, I'm listening.' He [the union representative] said, 'We're not getting anyplace, are we?' [Father] said, 'No.' He said, 'Could we all have some walnuts?' [*laughs*]. He opened the bag and said, 'Now, this is the way it's going to be, gentlemen [*he thumps the table several times in cadence to "this," "way," "going," "be"*], or I can disappear again for another six months.' That's the end of it. That's how he negotiated."

The strike ended on November 1. All employees received an immediate twelve-cent-an-hour increase with another five-cent increase to take effect on March 1, 1947. Minimum wages were raised thirteen and fourteen cents per hour. Workers received three holidays with pay and three more, if worked, at time-and-a-half pay. In a victory for management, the contract ran until September, not June, 1947.[6]

Jim Jr. claimed the government paid for the strike: "Taxes were tremendous at that time to pay for the war. And we were making money during that period of time. I actually think the six-week strike, the United States government paid for the whole strike, because you didn't have to pay any taxes that year. The strike didn't financially hurt Father that much. And, he kept saying, 'Don't do it.'"

Postwar construction at the mill. (Courtesy GREAT)

"Wemyss don't want to give nothin'," Puss Gagnon remembered. "Wemyss would go down to the diner and drink with the boys. They'd get drunker'n hell. He wouldn't give. Oh, no. He said you was going to get so much. You could go on strike if you want to. It wouldn't amount to a piss hole in the snow." Zo Cloutier said: "Back then you had to fight for what you wanted. If you didn't, you wouldn't get nothing. They used to go out on a strike for three or four cents. After a Depression, people want a little bit more money. The only way you could get it was to fight for it. The unions, to me, were a great thing. Back then you needed to have people all stick together when you wanted something."

Once the strike was settled, the transformation of the mill commenced. Fred Shannon's father was part of the construction crew that was replacing a leaky cement wall by the filter plant. They had installed rebar for the eighteen-inch-thick, new walls, but they had dropped some short wooden sticks among the rebar, and they needed someone small to retrieve them. "Somebody come over and asked me if I thought I could crawl in there, because I was just a little fellow; I probably didn't weigh only forty pounds," Shannon recalled. "I was able to crawl right down through all that stuff, and pick out all those sticks. I got paid a whole dollar for that."

"Everybody knew everybody," Fred remembered. "Everybody got on good, as far as I can see." Young Fred and his mates thought the mill was a wonderful playground. On occasion, they commandeered a railroad handcar from behind the mill: "We'd push that all the way up on the main tracks, way up, and then get on, and ride all the way down through behind the mill — have a good ride. Hey, back then, no television. There wasn't much to do, except find things to do."

"We did everything we could to make a penny," he said. "All summer long we'd pick berries and sell them, and we'd go to Emerson's and buy a couple of boxes of .22 shorts. Then we'd go up to the dump and spend the rest of the day shooting rats. It kept us out of trouble. After a while they wouldn't let you shoot at the dump anymore. Too close to town. They'd see kids up there throwing a bottle up in the air and then shooting at it with a .22. That could be kind of dangerous, I guess."

The mill's river crew was casual about leaving explosives lying around the riverside woodpiles. Fred and his buddies took notice: "By every pulp pile, there was a little shack where they used to have dynamite. Three or four of us got this little half stick of dynamite and a piece of fuse. We went way up Bag Hill somewhere and set it on a rock and stuck a hole into it and put a fuse into it and lit the fuse, and we run like hell. We waited and waited and waited, and nothing happened. We didn't know you had to have a cap on that fuse. The dynamite was smoldering, but there was nothing to make the dynamite blow. One of them that we was with — I won't mention his name — picked it up, carried it down, and set it on the road. One of us had a .22. So we was pulling up with that .22 trying to hit it. *PEEEEYOUUUU. PEEEEYOUUUU.* About the third time, the whole earth shook. The loudest noise you ever heard. Now there was four young guys going down that Bag Hill Road right in a race. I never was so scared in my life. That .22 bullet set that off."

Jim Wemyss Sr. installed a large new boiler in 1948 and a new General Electric turbine. The old paper machines had been run by steam-driven shafts. During the late 1940s and early 1950s, mill electricians installed electric motors to operate the older paper machines at faster rates. On one occasion, Herb Miles was using uninsulated pliers: "I reached in to get hold of a wire. I had a hold of the conduit. Of course, a conduit is grounded. There I hung. Pulled me right up — pulls your muscles right up. The fellow with me there — I said, *'Pull the switch!'* That's all I could say. *'Pull the switch!'* There's another

Number 4 paper machine's twelve-foot-high Yankee dryer (left and center) and dry end (right) at the time of installation in 1948. Jim Wemyss believed that the man in the straw hat at left was Guy Cushing, a longtime paper machine operator. (Courtesy GREAT)

fellow stood down there looking up at me. If he'd taken me by the pant leg, he could have pulled me off. He thought he was going to get a shock if he got ahold of me. If I'd had a weak heart, I'd have been dead. Finally I kicked the eight-foot ladder out from under me, thinking I might drop. But the [wire] kept me right up there. Finally the wire broke, and down I went *kerploof,* right on the cement floor, weaker than a rag. After that we got insulation for the handles of our pliers."

During the war, Old Jim had ordered new tissue machines from Pusey and Jones for Groveton and the mill in Gouverneur, New York. Pusey and Jones had suspended manufacture of machines in order to construct battleships and aircraft carriers. After the war, the Wemyss family order was at the head of the queue.

The new machine, named Number 4, was installed in 1947–1948. "That was one of the largest tissue machines in the world at that time," Jim Jr. said. Unlike fine-papers machines, this much shorter, 160-inch-wide machine had a single twelve-foot-diameter "Yankee dryer" instead of a series of presses and dryers. As the tissue came over the Yankee dryer under high pressure, it hit the creping blade, called the "doctor blade," that peeled the thin tissue off the dryer and fed it onto a reel. Fred Shannon and his chums thought the installation of Number 4 was quite a spectator sport: "They had that great big old monstrous dryer, and they had taken out the brick wall and brought it in on a railroad and then rolled it into the machine room."

Number 4 paper machine was a twenty-first birthday present for Young Jim, who went to work full time at the mill in 1948: "[Father] said, 'That's yours. Now learn how to run it.' I said, 'OK.' I didn't know anything about it, period, but it was a good learning program." Decades later Joan Breault observed: "Jim Wemyss Jr. was probably the best man on tissue machines probably you could ever find. He could take a piece of beater pulp and chew it in his mouth and tell you if it had enough of any chemical in it." When I mentioned Breault's comment, Wemyss replied: "Paper to me is an observation. It's just a trick of knowing what you're doing."

Jim Wemyss Jr. never attended business school, yet he claimed he earned his MBA at age eighteen: "When you have two very fine businessmen that talk to you ten hours a day from the time you're fourteen years old, at the breakfast table, at the lunch table, the dinner table, about what happened with this, what happened with that. It's a case history, basically, an MBA. My grandfather, how did he come out [of the stock market] before the Depression? Why did he know to get out? These things are all I heard all the time. We never talked about any ring-around-the-rosie stuff. It was always business around me, and I had to learn to run everything in the paper mill. Everything."

"When I first went to work for my father," Jim Jr. remembered, "I said, 'What do you want me to do?' He said, 'Walk around.' I said, 'What's my job?' He said, 'Walking around.' So I walked around one day, and I came back, and I said, 'I walked around.' He said, 'Go walk around some more.' I walked around, and I walked around. All of a sudden I was walking by, and one of the paper machines was shut down, and so I said, 'Why is this paper machine shut down?' I found out why and what they had to do to make it run again.

I learned what was wrong with pumps, or electric drives, or steam engines. I kept walking around. I was in the digester room, and there was a problem. 'Why are we having a problem?' It was the greatest education I ever had. 'Walk around.' I kept walking around, and pretty soon I got quite knowledgeable."

Around this time, the Factory Insurance Agency (FIA) announced it was canceling Groveton Papers' policy. "I walked into [Father's] office. He said, 'Well, son, I think you'd better hear this. This is pretty serious.' The head of FIA for this area was there. [Father] said, 'They're canceling our insurance.' Because the mill was dirty. The war had just ended. It was not being taken care of. It was not what it should have been. I said, 'You know, sir, I just came back from the war, and I got shot up a little bit. I came back to this family business, and I don't want you to do that to me. I went to military school for four years, and I was in the army, and they have ways of doing things to make things clean and neat. I want you to give me a break. I'll take charge of this mill, and I guarantee you, in sixty days you won't know it.' He said, 'Really, soldier? Will you come down to our fire school in Hartford?' 'Yes. I'll be there.' He said, 'I'm going to give you six months.' And he looked at my father, and he said, 'He's in charge?' 'Yes. He's in charge.' And Genghis Khan came to work [laughs]."

After he returned from fire school, Genghis went to work: "We had the women in the finish room shutting off sections and taking the sprinkler heads out. They were all corroded. They were cleaned with wire brushes and washed out, and all the pipes were blown out, and the steam pumps and the high-pressure water pumps in the mill were all taken apart and put back together in perfect shape. Every paper machine once a year had to be cleaned and painted. This place was sparkling. When I got through, the president of FIA said: 'Any mill you have, Mr. Wemyss, we'll insure.' I was fanatic about it. I think the disease caught. Everybody had pride in the mills here and wanted the mill to be clean." Wemyss's longtime assistant, Shirley MacDow, called him "a real neatnik." "Cleanliness in the mill was godly to him," she added.

"It had to be immaculate," Wemyss emphasized. "There was no excuse for it not to be immaculate. And if you did, you were talking to me, and you didn't want to talk to me about that [laughs]." A clean mill was a safer, more profitable mill: "It pays in safety. It pays in maintenance. It pays in everything."

Most of the mill workers of that era approved of the policy, often con-

Jim Wemyss Jr. starting up Number 4 paper machine in 1948. (Courtesy Jim Wemyss)

trasting it with the filth they encountered in other mills. "I've had all kinds of people come up to this mill," John Rich said. "'How the hell do you keep this mill so clean?' And I say, 'When you ain't doing your job, you grab a broom. They've got all kinds of brooms setting around. You use it.' And they did. He was fussy about that, and it was a good thing. You know how it is; dust builds up. You cleaned that finishing room every day, every shift. Three times a day. Blow that out, clean it out."

Dave Miles remembered the chemicals they used to clean the floor once a week: "They would burn you if they got on, but you had a spotless floor when you got done. It smelled kind of bad, but it did the job. I was sent to a couple of other mills. I thought the Berlin Mill was very dirty as compared to our mill." Lawrence Benoit also recalled cleaning the floor: "You'd wash the floor with [Oakite]. That stuff was so strong, if you had rubber soles on your shoes, you'd feel it stick to them. When you got done washing that off with a hose, that cement would look just like brand new. It'd eat the stuff right out of the cement. If you left that too long on the side of the paper machine, it would eat the paint right off on the bottom."

Puss Gagnon was not an admirer of Genghis Khan's campaign: "[Jim Wemyss was a] miserable son of a bitch. I never liked him; he never liked me. When we were over in the new fire room [c. 1948], he come out one day [and said], 'You ought to clean up these feeder motors.' I said, 'You got a cleaner here to do that stuff.' He said, 'It wouldn't hurt you a bit.' 'No,' I said, 'probably not. But it wouldn't be within now or June, it would be just as fuckin' dirty.' 'I'm gonna show you different,' he says. He gets himself a bucket and some cleaning stuff. He starts cleaning the motors. The cleaner happened to come by. I said, 'Go up on the top floor and take the air hose and blow the top floor down. The shit started to come. [Wemyss] throwed the fuckin' bucket. He told [head of the union, Dick] Currier, 'Come back at three, and I'll show you these fuckin' motors are clean.' When [Currier] come back, he says, 'I wonder where Jimmy is.' I said, 'I don't think he'll be back.' He said, 'What did you do to him?' I told him. 'You dirty son of a bitch,' he says."

JAMES C. WEMYSS SR. dominated the Groveton mill throughout the 1940s. "He's a man that worked twenty-four hours a day," his son recalled. "That's an exaggeration. But he was up at five o'clock in the morning. He was there, and he knew everything about everything. Until he got seriously ill, he was purchasing director; he was the sales manager; he was the plant engineer. That's probably why he broke his health. He had to have absolute control over everything. He lived nicely, but he was not a playboy. He was a fellow that really wanted to be there and see things done. He was respected by the men in the mill; they liked him; they knew what he was capable of doing."

Young Jim described his father's early morning routine: "He'd be up at six thirty in the morning, and he'd meet the machine tenders and the back tenders and the pulp mill men walking home and stop and talk to them. By the time he got to his office, he knew what happened all night long. I'd walk in about seven o'clock. 'Did you know this?' 'No, I didn't. I haven't had a chance to look around. How'd you know?' Then he told me. I said, 'Hey, that's pretty good. I like that.'"

Young Jim came in late one morning, and his father said: "'So we've got a banker in the family?' 'Well, gee, I was up the last five nights in a row here.' He said, 'You want to stop that? When they call you in, call everybody else. Call *everybody*. You're in there; you don't want to be alone.' Pretty soon they stopped calling me."

John Rich described Jim Sr. as "a temper-y old boy." Edgar Astle, a machine tender on Number 1 paper machine in the early 1950s, told his son about one of Old Jim's outbursts: "[He] would walk through the mill every now and again, and boy, people would tremble. I guess they'd run over the chests and the stock had come out on the floor, and he threw a fit. He took a handful of change out of his pocket and threw it into the gutter, and he said, 'You guys are throwing my money away.'"

Shirley Brown, whose husband had a celebrated run-in with Old Jim in the mid-1950s, thought: "He wanted to take Willie Munroe's place, because Willie Munroe — his famous saying was, 'I own this town and everybody in it.' When Old Jim, as we used to call him, came, I think he wasn't as fair as Willie Munroe was, because whatever Willie Munroe said, people knew that was a fact. But with Jim, it depended on whether he was sober or not [*laughs*]. I'm sure you've heard some of these stories."

After decades of hard work and hard drinking, Jim Wemyss Sr. nearly killed himself. The *Democrat* reported on August 17, 1949, that he was seriously ill in the Weeks Memorial Hospital in Lancaster. Jim Jr. vividly recalled his father's brush with death: "My father became gravely ill. Had two-thirds of his stomach removed with ulcers. My father was bleeding internally, and he passed out. I drove my father to the hospital, and [Dr. Merriam] put a needle in my arm [to draw blood for a transfusion], and we lay down on the street, right in front of the hospital. He stabilized him. He came out of shock. I sent a message to the mill; we all had dog tags from the war with your blood type on them. Mine was O, so I said, 'Any man with O that wants to come down and help my father out, just walk off your job and get down here as quick as you can.' They liked him; there was fifty people down here in twenty minutes."

Young Jim was not yet twenty-four years old: "When [Father] was back, rational in the hospital, his brother-in-law walked in, Dr. Hyatt. My father looked at him and said, 'I had a serious operation, didn't I?' He said, 'Yes, Jim, a very serious operation.' He said, 'I suppose I won't to be able to eat properly or do anything the rest of my life.' [Dr. Hyatt] said, 'No, no. Within reason, you can do that.' And then he said, 'But there's one thing you can't do. You have to walk away for one year. And never look back. Hire a professional manager to run your companies. Get a manager and go someplace. Or you'll be dead within a year.' Just like that. So [Father] said, 'I've taken care of that matter already. I've hired the man.' I happened to be in the hospital room, and I said, 'Who's the new manager?' 'You.' I was in charge, but nobody knew it. My signature and his, you could not tell the difference, except I would drop off the 'Jr.' Every time somebody came to me and said, 'What do you think about this?' I said, 'My father's not feeling well, and he's up at the company house. I'll go up and ask him.' He wasn't there, but I'd go up and then come back and say, 'Do this.' Who would question me? So that's how I fell into it, so to speak. I owe that to my grandfather and my father. It really wasn't that difficult for me. My father basically left me alone from then on."

Chapter Eight

THE PERFECT
BALANCE

THE 1950S AND 1960S stand out as a kind of golden age for the Groveton Papers mill. This was the period of unprecedented economic prosperity in postwar America, a time when most families had a car or two and a television set. The economic, social, and cultural forces responsible for those good times also contained the seeds for the slow demise of the mill and Groveton's downtown business district. The railroads began their steady decline after the war. The Amusu, Groveton's movie theater, shut down in 1956. The near universal ownership of autos allowed mill workers to move out of town. The clothing stores, food markets, and even Groveton's beer joints began to disappear as families headed to shopping centers an hour or two away and watched TV in the comfort of their living rooms at night. Northumberland's population peaked in 1950 at 2,779; the 1960 census recorded a 7 percent decline.

When Jim Wemyss Sr. had recovered his health and returned to the mill in 1950, the family embarked on a second major project to diversify the mill. Father and son were not happy with Number 3 paper machine. "It had old presses, and it was not a good [bond] machine," Jim Jr. said. The old digesters could not make enough pulp for three fine-papers machines and the new tissue machine. The mill was paying high prices for additional pulp.

There was a nationwide shortage of the fluted, corrugated medium paper that gives cardboard boxes their strength. Friends from the Mead Corporation suggested Number 3 would make an excellent corrugating machine. Old and Young Jim Wemyss "revamped" Number 3, installing two new suction presses and a new suction cooch. Several New England region box manufacturers committed to buy a certain tonnage of the new product. The mill began to manufacture paperboard in the summer of 1951, and soon it was producing 125 tons a day.

For years, the mill had been dumping improperly cooked pulpwood, called "screenings," down by the river above the Weston Dam. Old Jim decided to dig them up and use them as a cheap source of pulp. The mill had also been dumping hard coal screenings from the old Hynie boiler on top of some of the pulpwood screenings. One day Jim Jr. received a phone call from a customer with a problem: "I go out to his corrugated box plant. All the men standing around were black. White circles around [their eyes]. 'What do you suppose that is?' I said, 'I don't know. We did put a little something in to make the fluting stronger' [*laughs*]. That was coal."

The mill soon completed a new hardwood pulp mill to supply the converted paperboard machine. A pile of hardwood pulp logs arose across the river on Brooklyn Street. A conveyor transported the logs directly to the chipper. Legend has it that sometimes six-packs purchased at Cloutier's Store also rode the hardwood conveyor.

Until 1952, most of the tissue finishing operations were performed at the Northumberland mill where four old paper machines together produced less tissue than Groveton's new machine. The Northumberland mill building was in terrible condition by the early 1950s. "To call it rickety was a compliment," Jim Wemyss Jr. once said, "and today OSHA would give you eleven seconds to shut it down." Zo Cloutier was hired to work weekends as a sixteen-year-old in the mid-1940s. "I was making fifty cents an hour," he said. "My father was an oiler down there. [Old Jim] Wemyss said, 'You go down and help your father.' You had to crawl in places underneath the machine. It was filthy. Aw, Jesus, it was awful. I went with a hose and pail and hauled stuff out and washed everything down and cleaned it. They were satisfied, because it wasn't too long they gave me a ten-cent raise."

"The whole mill shook; you could feel it quivering all over," John Rich recalled. "You walked in down in the cellar, and there were so many posts holding it up, somebody put a sign up, 'No Hunting Allowed.' That always struck me funny. I was telling my uncle about that; he said, 'They do quite a lot of hunting up there. They bring in their .22s and they shoot cockroaches on the walls' — .22 pistols. Right out through the walls, old boards, shiplap. Quite a few times they got it — fifteen feet away."

At age sixteen, Joan Gilcris Breault, whose father, Duke Gilcris, was a supervisor in the Northumberland finishing room, was hired for the summer in the print room on the three-to-eleven shift. "You know what I made for money when I started in '47, the year before my senior year — that summer?"

she asked me. "Fifteen cents an hour. They paid it in cash in an envelope. You got cash money, and you didn't get pennies because they kept all the pennies from everybody as part of a flower fund for anybody that had died. Might not sound like much, but nobody lost over four cents a week, and it added up."

Working in the mill was an education: "It is a whole new way of life," Breault said. "Some people will carry on and do things that they wouldn't do outside. We had one napkin machine operator that watched his machine from a stool where he could look at the girls taking off napkins and see through their dresses. He was a dirty old man. Just sit there and have his evil laugh going a lot of the time."

After Joan graduated from high school in 1948, she went to work full time on the napkin machine, unloading and wrapping packages of napkins. She took maternity leave in 1951 and was still on leave in June 1952. That spring, Old Jim and Young Jim demanded that the union extend the old contract for two to four months owing to uncertain business conditions. The United Mine Workers Union Local 50 overwhelmingly refused on May 8, 1952. The union demanded increases in wages and paid holidays and a group insurance plan that would be paid in full by the mill. The Wemyss family insisted on significant wage and holiday cuts. On May 10, millwrights moved some of the Northumberland mill's perforators to Groveton,[1] and negotiations grew increasingly bitter. Even the pro-management *Democrat* wondered "whether any machines so moved would be . . . returned to Northumberland."[2]

Virginia Ward, a member of the union negotiating committee, wrote to the *Democrat* that mill workers in Groveton were paid more for the same jobs. She asked "why a man is worth from eight to fifteen cents more per hour for common labor in Groveton than in Northumberland?" The Northumberland mill's 270 workers struck on June 1. By then, most of the finishing room equipment and machinery had been removed.[3]

On June 23, the Northumberland strikers picketed the Groveton Papers mill to protest the transfer to Groveton of five perforators, one roller towel machine, two core machines, and four napkin machines. The 721 members of the two locals in Groveton honored the picket lines, even though their leaders took pains to explain that they had no grievance with Groveton's management. The Groveton mill was shut down for four shifts. The non-union wood yard and the converting plant, operating in a building beyond the mill, continued working.

Jim Wemyss Sr. returned to Groveton that afternoon, and at noon on June 24 he announced the closing of the Northumberland mill.[4] The defeated pickets left town, and the Groveton mill resumed operations that afternoon. In late June, Local 50 voted to end the strike so its members could file for unemployment benefits and improve their chances of finding another job.

Jim Wemyss Jr. later explained the rationale for shutting down Northumberland: "Around that time, I had a choice to either fix Groveton up or fix that up, and that was not a mill to fix up. It had very old machines. OSHA today would tremble if they had seen it. Open belt drives would not be tolerated today in any sense of the word." Some Northumberland employees were able to find jobs at the Groveton mill, but a great many people lost their jobs following the strike. Sixty years later, Wemyss remained sensitive to the charge that he and his father had cost people their jobs: "Never did I shut a department down in the mill to eliminate anybody. When I shut the Northumberland mill down, I had three hundred people working down there. It was absolutely archaic. You've got to make sound decisions as to what's the best thing for this community. That's what I did all my life. What's good for here?"

Number 4 finishing room in Groveton was located just beyond Number 3 and Number 4 paper machines. Duke Gilcris was transferred to Groveton to direct the new operation. "Dad had come home one noon hour," Joan remembered, "and he said to me, 'Would you like to work for a couple of weeks?' I said, 'Doing what?' He said, 'Teaching new girls in Groveton how to pick napkins [off the napkin machine].' So I said sure. I went up the fourth of June. I taught them all how to pick napkins. The second week I was there, [Dad] was shorthanded on the Teal folder, which was facial tissue, and he said, 'I'm going to take you off the napkin machines today, Joan, and put you down there.' I said OK. So I learned that job, and then he was shorthanded on the perforators, and I had done some of that in Northumberland, so I went to work on the perforators part time. I worked all around. My two weeks turned into forty-three years."

"People don't realize how hard we worked," Breault maintained. "We worked full tilt." Her friend, Pauline Labrecque, who was hired June 5, 1952, concurred: "I had to bend down, pick 'em up, put 'em in my case. Five rolls of toilet paper — and maybe more. The fellow who was putting the boxes down, he liked it to get a certain amount in each eight hours. You don't sleep on that job, and you don't sit. You're busy. You had to watch your fingers. I told

James Campbell Wemyss Sr.,
known as "Old Jim." From a
1955 Vanity Fair sales catalog.
(Courtesy GREAT)

them, I lost this [pointed to her left eye patch], and I'm not about to lose [my fingers]." Every eight-hour shift, Pauline and her coworkers were expected to pack 120 cases of toilet paper. A case contained ninety-six rolls, each of which had to be wrapped before placed in the carton. To meet the quota, Joan and Pauline had to wrap and pack twenty-four rolls a minute, or one every two and a half seconds.

Two decades later, Bill Astle, a student at the University of New Hampshire, worked in the mill during summer vacations. One of his jobs was to spell the women in the finishing rooms on their periodic breaks. "It was always women who took the napkins off the machine and put them in the conveyor," he recalled. "And these women would be talking about their grandkids and what they watched on TV the night before, and they were dealing these things into the conveyor like they're cards. And I'm there struggling for all I'm worth. All I could think of was the old *I Love Lucy* sitcom where she's in the chocolate factory trying to keep up with them."

Pauline continued to work late into her pregnancy: "I had no choice. I was brought up poor. One of seventeen in the family. I probably could have got done earlier, but I was trying to get ahead to try to have a little nest egg because my life was hard before I met up with him [husband Gerard]. I didn't miss out on any work unnecessarily. I never called in like a lot of them did: 'I've got a headache,' 'I'm sick,' 'I've got to go home,' for an excuse. I worked. Because for what I didn't have in years past, I wanted to be able to make my life a little bit easier. Follow me? So I worked right up until something here [*pointed to her abdomen*] told me, 'You've got to stop.' And when the boy was born, he had a cord around his neck."

The women of that era felt it was unfair that they were paid less than the men at the mill. Joan Breault said: "That's aggravating. Probably the women were doing a more thorough job of everything than the men were. As a rule, most women are more conscientious, maybe because we've had to work harder to get where we are." Pauline's starting pay was ninety-five cents an hour, whereas her husband, Gerard, hired shortly before her, started at ninety-eight cents an hour. "They always paid the men more anyway," Pauline noted with some bitterness, adding: "I think because the men were mainly the head of the family. I don't think it's right." Gerard agreed: "If you're going to do the same work, you should get the same pay."

Gerard and Pauline rarely worked on the same shift, so that one could always be home to take care of the children. When both were working, Pauline's niece would babysit. "A lot of times he [Gerard] ended up doing the washing, take care of the kids," she recalled with a laugh. "It wasn't no worse for him than it was for me. I'm a hard egg, ain't I. But I want to tell you what. Made fifty-four years last July [2009], and I'm still with the same rooster."

The "hard egg" took no guff from coworkers or bosses: "I went into work from three to eleven, and the boss for that shift, he was at the punch clock waiting for me. He said, 'Paulie, don't bother to punch in. Go home. You were supposed to have been in here this morning, not now.' I said, 'Nobody ever told me about it.' It was not going to end there. They had a special meeting with one of the union fellows in with the bigger boss that was in the office. I said, 'Nobody told me to come in days. There was no list put up to let me know when I was supposed to be working. I came in for the shift that I was told to come in. I'm not about to lose a day's pay through his fault.' And I fought it. I had enough mouth on me. I got my day's pay. *Then* they started putting the list up on a bulletin board. So and so works this shift, that shift. That straightened that out, didn't it?"

Joan enjoyed her young female coworkers. "I can remember back, way back, we had a quota in the tissue finishing room," she said. "Once you got to that quota, you could shut down for the night. You probably wouldn't have been able to if the bosses had been around — but they weren't. Probably I shouldn't say this on tape — we'd go sit in the girls' room and play cards. Play cribbage. Probably three-quarters of an hour, an hour. Or just visit. In fact, I didn't have to worry about a hairdo. I had two girls I worked with all the time that were better than most hairdressers. And they liked to. We'd all work on each other's hair. I had nice hairdos from those girls."

By the mid-1950s Groveton was having difficulty competing with stationery firms located nearer to Boston because of high shipping costs for converted products. Late in 1955, father and son decided to relocate the converting plant to a building in Canton, Massachusetts, that was five times larger than Groveton's converting space. Young Jim was delighted: "It was a transition. [Father] had a nice home in Stoughton, Mass. He didn't bother me, and I didn't know what he was doing. It was something to keep him busy." Old Jim would remain owner and president until 1968, but he generally left the management of the Groveton mill to his son.

The move meant that about one hundred employees of the converting plant in Groveton had to choose between leaving their community or risk losing their job. Belvah King recalled: "There were quite a few single girls; a lot of them moved down. And some other men did. There was more that didn't go than did go. It was a troublesome time. You didn't know what was going to happen. I finally got into Number 1 finishing room. Seems as though I was out of work maybe a year."

Bud Brown, the young supervisor of converting, was charged with setting up the new plant. His widow, Shirley, recalled: "My husband walked into an empty warehouse, and when he left it was a converting plant. He set up the whole thing. He was very, very proud of it. When Old Jim came down, Bud said to Old Jim, 'What do you think of this?' And Old Jim said, 'You've played around enough. Now it's time to get to work.' My husband told him what he could do with that mill." Neal Brown elaborated: "My father turned to him and said, 'You can take this mill and shove it up your ass' [laughs]. [Old] Jimmy fired him on the spot, which I guess he was prone to do. He was pretty short-tempered."

Coleen Mills and Coleen Ledger removing napkins from the napkin machine in Groveton's Number 4 finishing room, from a 1955 Vanity Fair sales catalog. (Courtesy GREAT)

"[Old Jim] had him blackballed all throughout New England," Shirley Brown said. "He couldn't get a job. Bud would have an interview with a paper company, and then we'd get this notice that the employment fee had been paid by Jim Wemyss. Old Jim would buy up the contract so he couldn't work." Bud Brown's blunder, his widow bluntly stated, was that "he stood up to him." Brown was forced to find work in midwestern mills.

Shirley MacDow, who served as Old Jim's secretary for a while in the mid-1950s, tactfully referred to him as an "unusual individual. Very austere, but at other times he could be down to earth." Herb Miles called him a generous man: "If he saw me somewhere to a restaurant, [he'd] buy you a drink or a meal, or say, 'Send over a drink to so-and-so.'"

Sylvia Stone was a young woman in the accounting department in the 1950s: "The thing that I hated the most was that Mr. Wemyss Senior came in. He'd call us down, and he'd go through the cost sheets item by item. If there was anything that was a red flag for you, you'd be called down on the carpet. We'd have to look up the invoices, and I would get pretty nervous then. We had to prove everything that we set down." Stone witnessed one of Jim Sr.'s angry outbursts in the old Red Office: "God his face would get as red as a beet. He'd come into the main office. Oh, he'd storm around; it was unreal. Boy, you knew when he was on the rampage. He came out to his secretary, kind of shouting around. I said I was glad I wasn't his secretary." Arguments between Jim Jr. and Jim Sr. at the mill were common, Bill Baird remembered: "I heard Jimmy and his father arguing, and I thought he was right outside the door, and he was maybe fifty feet down the aisle towards the paper machines. The two of them, you could hear a hundred yards, I think."

Old Jim's relations with the town were equally stormy. In 1950 the town debated building a $150,000 high school gymnasium. He issued a statement threatening to close the mill. The *Democrat* reported: "The company might need to seek tax abatement if its mills were to continue to operate in Groveton, where, he said, the tax rate is already too high. Offers of tax abatement have been made to the company as an inducement for them to move to the South." The town voted not to build the gym.[5]

A decade later, Mickey King recalled, when the town considered a warrant article authorizing the construction of a community swimming pool, "Old Jim got up, and he was drunk. [*In an exaggerated, high voice:*] 'If you think for one minute that I'm going to pay taxes for this swimming pool then you — ' Well, of course, the people voted it in, thanks to that speech. It was wonderful [*laughs*]. I'll never forget that. He walked — la da-da-da — like Jack Benny." Belvah King added: "Best thing that ever happened to this town, that pool." In the 1970s and 1980s, Young Jim routinely dispatched mill workers to the town pool to repair its plumbing and concrete work.

In 1953 Jim Wemyss Jr., who had steadily assumed greater responsibilities from his father, took over the job of negotiating new one-year contracts with the two unions. That year, for the first time, union and management reached an agreement without any fireworks. Young Jim recognized that America was changing, and labor unions everywhere were winning higher wages, increases in paid vacations, payments for pensions and health insurance, and other benefits and perks.

For the three decades Jim Wemyss Jr. dominated the mill there were only two strikes and a short work stoppage. Young Jim was no pushover during negotiations. However, his war experience, the zeitgeist, and his carousing with many of the younger mill workers in the postwar years ensured that contract negotiations never degenerated into the sorts of battles his grandfather and father fought with the unions.

I asked Wemyss once if his war service had affected his management philosophy at the mill. "Yes, it had a great influence," he replied. "I went into an infantry outfit, which was coal miners, steelworkers, big families, three or four kids sleeping in a bed. Peanut butter and Marshmallow Fluff for breakfast. I went to some of their homes because they wanted me to see them before we went overseas. I had never been exposed possibly to the real America that was fighting this war, and seeing how people were poor, as poor as they were, because I lived in a pretty nice neighborhood in Connecticut when I grew up. I started to understand that there was another world, and it affected me greatly. I was very concerned about people who worked for me in later years and their families. Of course, having men die in your arms. . . .

"I had a lot of men in my outfit who couldn't read or write because they grew up in the Depression era. One fellow got his nerve up and came over and said, 'Could you read a letter for me?' 'Sure.' It was a letter from his wife or somebody. He said, 'Could you write her a letter back for me?' 'Yes. What would you like me to say?' Then the word got around that I would write letters. I was amazed at how many men came to me. I've known a lot of guys who had to work during the Depression, didn't get a chance to finish school. That was quite a thing. That's what the service does to people. Everybody is the same. We're all together."

AS THE MILL FLOURISHED, jobs were abundant. Many of the mill workers I interviewed were hired in the postwar decade. Nearly all described the mill hiring process as a mere formality. Gerard Labrecque was hired in 1951: "My God, they put me to work right off [on the drum barker], and I wasn't dressed up to work." Two decades later, Bruce Blodgett recalled, "You could almost quit today and go back tomorrow."

Greg Cloutier, a childhood friend of Jim Wemyss III, admired Jim Jr.'s commitment to the community. "He made them feel special. He also made an effort to bring in professional people, and have them stay in the community. He made an effort that you try to buy local, you try to do local. The school system, I thought, was quite good, considering that it was just a mill town.

He encouraged professional people to come there and put their kids in the school, be a part of the school board."

Mill workers who entered the workforce before World War II often had little education. When Lolly LaPointe bid into the stock prep department in the mid-1960s, he worked with an older man near retirement age who kept asking him the time: "He would come up to me, and he would say, 'What time is it?' I'd tell him what time. I was telling the guys: 'Jeez, his eyes must be terrible.' We had a huge clock in there. They said, 'No, he can't tell time. He's completely, totally illiterate.' A guy said, 'I'll prove it to you.' They used to have to make a report. They'd write down what they used. Another guy said, 'I'll put like he made two pulpers of apples.' That old guy would come in and relieve him, and — just beautiful handwriting — he copied what the other guy had. That's the first person I believe I saw that was illiterate. I was dumbfounded by that."

Sometime in late 1950s, Wemyss decided the mill would only hire workers who had earned a high school diploma: "Kids used to say, 'Aw, the hell with it; I'll go down to the mill, and I'll get a job.' I said, 'You can't do that anymore.' So, they didn't." Older men and women who had dropped out of school during the Depression and war years to support their families were not penalized by this policy.

Wemyss realized a small New Hampshire paper mill could thrive only if it modernized in an efficient and thrifty manner: "I never stopped," he boasted. "We had forty-two men in our construction crew, or more. I kept them busy all the time." In 1960 the construction crew began the largest single addition in the mill's history, a thousand-foot-long building adjacent to the two buildings that housed the paper machines. Wemyss named it in honor of Bill Verrill, his longtime plant engineer. The new offices were at the end of the Verrill Building, nearest the town and adjacent to a spacious fine-papers finishing room. The remainder of the building housed a cavernous shipping complex that included a warehouse and railroad tracks with a capacity for sixteen railroad boxcars and six docks for tractor-trailers. Shipping department crews were especially grateful for the indoor railroad-track loading facilities when it was thirty below zero outside.

The steel for the Verrill Building came from the Grumman Aircraft building in Bethpage, Long Island, that built World War II dive bombers. Wemyss crowed: "They practically gave it to me for four cents a pound, delivered to Groteton, match marked. My father said, 'You've lost your mind. Do you realize how much that building's going to cost?' It was one thousand feet long and 150 feet wide: $580,000. That's the price of a house today in a lot of places. Can you imagine that? There's no buildings in New Hampshire or any place that are built as rugged as those buildings are."

Once I asked Wemyss how he dealt with major screwups during the construction process. "We couldn't afford them," he snapped. "It's a family business. You didn't make a decision and then forget it. No. You were there too. If something came up, and a decision had to be made, you could make that decision or correct it. Everybody worked together. That's Groton. We wouldn't bring in outside people to do it. We did it ourselves." Wemyss's policy sustained scores of local jobs, saved huge sums of money, and built up a construction crew with intimate knowledge of the entire mill.

Fred Shannon and the construction crew loved working for Jim Wemyss: "He always treated us like kings. He could have had the president of the United States in his office, but if we showed up to see him about something, he'd kick that guy right out; he didn't care. We were important to him. That's what made you feel good. He'd always come right up and talk to us." When Boston-based steelworkers picketed the mill to protest Wemyss's use of his local construction crew, he told John Gonyer, the crew supervisor: "It looks dirty around here; get that fire hose and wash that street up a little." The soggy pickets eventually departed.

Wemyss loved his wild construction crew: "They were a tough bunch. I used to have to get 'em out of jail sometimes on Monday morning. The jail used to be right there by the railroad track." He took pride in the crew's ability to do anything on short notice: "John Gonyer and people like that were the steel riggers. The best. 'John, put up a building from here to there, will you?' That's all you had to say to John. That's the type of people who were in Groton."

"A lot of times, Jim would ask me if I could handle a job," Gonyer recalled. "I'd say, 'Piece of cake.' Make it sound good. That's my boss I'm talking to. A lot of times he'd say, 'You know what I want, order the steel.'" Gonyer's best friend and coworker, Fred Shannon, said Wemyss "had his blueprints right in his head."

When the construction crew built the bleach plant in the early 1960s, it had to devise a way to install heavy machines thirty feet in the air. "We fabricated all that steel from the ground up," Gonyer said. "It was quite a project, because it had no crane. We'd always find a way. I think we had cables strung from one building to another and would hang up chain falls from that to get a [sixty-foot-long] column up in the air. Now we've got to put in these I-beams for the roof part of it. You've got to have room above the column for your chain falls and everything to hang on. I made up a bracket that went on a column with kind of a gooseneck on it, and it clamped onto the column, and it probably went we'll say four to six feet above the existing column, and I put my falls on that and pulleyed the beam into place. It was slow work, but we got it done.

"We had heavy equipment in there too. Some of it had to be jacked from the ground floor, I'm guessing thirty feet in the air. Eight-by-eight cribbing as we went up. It was pretty shaky work. We would stabilize the cribbing to the existing building as we went up. You'd go up a ways, and then you'd tie off to keep the cribbing from tipping. We bulled. We worked hard. I guess we put enough thought into safety, but back then you kind of stretched it a little at times." I asked about OSHA, and Gonyer retorted: "Never heard of them."

Despite the hair-raising nature of the work, the construction crew suffered only one fatality. On April 25, 1960, four men, including thirty-seven-year-old James Ledger, were forty feet up on a catwalk removing a high-pressure steam valve that weighed about three-quarters of a ton. The men put a chain around the pipe so that it could be lowered after it was cut loose. Inexperience led to a tragic mistake. "The falls were all rigged up ready to take this valve down," Gonyer remembered. "And the bolts were all cut; they had to be drove out. The valve was upright, and he made a hitch on the valve, but he hooked on the bottom part of it. So when he picked it [cut it loose], the valve flipped, and it hit [Ledger], and there was an inch-and-a-half angle-iron rail in there, and it put him right through it and he went down on his head."

Until the early 1960s, blue laws required the mill to shut down on Sundays. Dave Miles, a conscientious paper machine operator, described how the weekly work stoppage tormented him: "We'd shut down on Sunday [morning], clean the machine up, get it all ready, and then go home. I may be in bed an hour and I'd think, 'My goodness, did I shut this valve off?' I'd get up and go down to the mill. I couldn't help it. I don't think I ever failed to do something important, but it just didn't stop me."

Wemyss considered the blue laws a wintertime curse because boiler operators had to start up cold boilers at 4 a.m. on Monday in "goddamn twenty-five below zero." He explained: "Every time you start a motor up that's been down, you blew one. Starting up and shutting down is the worst thing you can do in a paper mill. You've got a turbine as big as this room, and you let it cool off, then you've got to get it balanced up and heated up and bring it up to temperature."

Shortly after the Verrill Building was completed, Wemyss attempted to run the mill seven days a week. This provoked a brief strike on September 23, 1962. Two days later, Wemyss withdrew a controversial clause in the proposed contract that mandated work on Sundays when the mill was operating.[6] The following evening, both locals voted to end the strike.

The era of blue laws ended when the mill negotiated a new labor contract in 1964. The new contract instituted the "southern" swing shift for paper machine operators and stock prep workers. The swing shift rotates four crews on three shifts. Each crew works seven consecutive days and then takes two, two, and three days off. At the end of twenty-eight days, each crew will have worked twenty-one days and had seven days off. To compensate for the roughly three hundred work hours lost annually under the new system, workers received a sixteen-cent-an-hour raise when the swing shift system was implemented. This meant that an average worker who worked no overtime and took no holidays or vacations would earn about $130 a year less under the new system but enjoy forty more days off from work every year. Few workers suffered that $130 loss, because they could quickly recoup it through overtime opportunities that also increased as the mill ran full time. Additionally, the mill hired more workers to fill out the fourth shift. Maintenance and construction crews continued to work day shifts (with ample overtime opportunities), and the finishing rooms and shipping departments remained under the old blue law schedule of closing on Sundays.

It had become necessary to abolish the blue laws, Wemyss explained, because "what happened is everybody wanted paid holidays, Christmas, New Year's, Fourth of July. Then all of a sudden everybody wanted health care. Then everybody wanted two weeks, three weeks — we ended up with five or six weeks vacation. Either run full, or you can't support it. The whole industry went seven days a week." Gary Paquette, a longtime paperboard machine tender, wryly suggested: "Jimmy wanted to make more money."

Wemyss acknowledged that working a swing shift was "very debilitating." Research into the health risks of shift work suggests that disrupting natural rhythms often leads to diminished exercise and an increased consumption of junk food that can contribute to obesity and diabetes. The risk of cardiovascular disease in shift workers may increase. Many shift workers suffer serious gastrointestinal problems, including higher risk of peptic ulcers, nausea, diarrhea, and constipation. There is also evidence of problems with pregnancy among shift workers, and a significantly higher risk of breast cancer for women with more than twenty years on a swing shift schedule.[7] Shift workers may be at greater risk of depression and mood disorders.

Swing shifts wreak havoc with family life and social activities. "Summertime, you might be mowing your lawn," Dave Miles said, "and I'm trying to sleep. Kids might be out playing on a hot day; you're trying to sleep. For some reason or other, you just can't sleep." Ted Caouette said most workers hated the three-to-eleven shift, "because it's like the best part of the day; it's the end of the day. The kids are coming home; things are starting to happen; you can enjoy supper together. You couldn't; that was gone." Workers on the night shift also usually missed out on evenings with the family because they had to sleep until about 10 p.m. "Most of the time when you woke up," Caouette recollected, "you were grouchy because you knew you had to go to work."

Bill Astle observed: "Studies have shown that the older you get, the more difficult it is to reset your internal clock. I can remember my dad's comment, 'As the years go by, I mind shift work more and more.'" That may be one reason a very high percentage of mill workers opted to retire at age sixty-two, even though their Social Security and pensions would have been 18 percent greater if they had worked until sixty-five. Astle's father, Edgar, died of a heart attack shortly before he could retire.

Some loved the night shift. "Most people think I'm absolutely nuts," Sandy White laughed. "I loved the night shift because I'm a night person. As hard as you worked, you could have some fun as long as you got your work done; nobody ever gave you any problem. All the foremen were good. It was quieter, nobody bombing around bugging you. You just went in there, you did your job, and that was the end of it. Day shift, there was so many people [from management] wandering around."

When he was hired, Lolly LaPointe said, "It used to be fun to go to work.

On the night shift we used to have big fish fries and corn on the cob. We used to use steam lines to cook it. And we used to have big breakfasts sometimes. We'd designate a cook. Somebody had to cover his job when he was cooking. [The supervisors] knew exactly what was going on. Most of them would have breakfast with you. It didn't hurt nobody; everything was getting done."

Wives tended to have their own parties while their husbands worked evenings or nights. I asked Francis Roby if the men had their own parties. He snorted: "The men never hung together. We had enough of each other down there." Late in his career at the mill, Dave Miles had to transfer off the paper machines because of the wear and tear on his knees from four decades of working on cement floors. He took a day job and marveled at the luxury of "having the night to yourself. I never had weekends off [on shift work]. If you wanted to invite us to supper tonight, we could say, 'Yeah, we'll be there.' Whereas before, it was 'I'm sorry, Dave's working three to eleven,' or 'I'm sorry, Dave's got to go to bed.' When I was working eleven to seven, I'd go bed as soon as I'd get home, usually sleep till ten, eleven o'clock, go back to bed usually at six [p.m.] so I wouldn't be too tired at night, get up at ten, have something to eat, and then go to work. It was just brutal."

THE PAPERBOARD OPERATION had been a huge success since its inception in 1951. The two highest-paying union jobs in the mill throughout the 1950s and 1960s had been "boss machine tender" and "machine tender" on the paperboard machine. By 1965, however, the venerable Number 3 paper machine could no longer compete with more modern, faster, and wider machines. Jim Wemyss approached Groveton's customers and suggested they join him in forming a new company, Groveton Paper Board, to buy a new, specially designed, corrugated medium paper machine. The Wemyss family would own 50 percent of the new company. With Mead Corporation, St. Joe Paper Company, and Diamond International as partners, Wemyss was able to design and buy a new paper machine from Black Clausen. He borrowed an additional $7 million to construct a new building along the north wall of the Verrill Building.

During the construction of the Paper Board building, John Gonyer had a Tarzanesque confrontation with Wemyss. "Things were going good; the steel was flying," Gonyer recalled. "They wanted us to get one bay a day. A lot of steel. You've got to put steel in for the ground floor. You're putting steel in for your siding and their brace work, and it's a lot of work. A bay is probably twenty feet between columns. I had been after my boss, Earl Livingstone, to get a raise. He said, 'When I can get the young fella [Wemyss] in a good mood.' This went on for a month, and so one day Wemyss come a walking down through, and I was up on top of the steel there. I timed it just right, so that when he went by this steel column I come sliding down the column, and I landed right by his feet. I said, 'I want to speak to you.' 'Yes, John, what can I do for you?' I said, 'I want more money.' He stopped and thought a minute. 'Yup, I can give you more money, John, but when this job is done, I can kiss you good-bye, too.' I had on a pair of welding gloves, and I threw the welding gloves down by his feet, and I said, 'Plant one right here, I'm on my way.' I struck off, and he said, 'Get your ass back here!' So I went back, and we negotiated. Jim and I got along good." Tarzan got his raise, and, thanks to Gonyer, so did all the lead men from the other departments.

The crew moved the massive new paper machine parts into the new building with a forty-ton crane, and Black Clausen specialists assembled it. Wemyss named the new machine "Love in the Afternoon": "I said, 'I'm tired of having it called "Miss Rock Mountain" and "Mr. Granite," and "Mr. God." That's what they name paper machines. We printed up labels, 'Made with "Love in the Afternoon,"' and we put it in every load that went out. The guys in the converting plants we were selling to [said], 'Go out and get me a roll of "Love."' It got to be a joke with everybody." Whenever I asked Wemyss why he chose that name, he evaded the question. One time I told him I'd read in a news story that while the construction crew was working around the clock on the Paper Board job, Wemyss would give crew members a couple of hours off in the afternoon; he smiled and said, "That could be."[8]

Number 5 paper machine was dedicated to Old Jim Wemyss on July 28, 1967. When it came time for a trial run of Love in the Afternoon, the crew shut down Number 3, switched a valve, and began pumping stock over to the new machine. Gary Paquette was a back tender on the first run: "They had some high-pressure hoses that had just clamps on them. The pressure was so great, it blew the clamps right off the hoses, so we shut down. Went back over on the other side on Number 3 and started that up again. That was only a couple of days. Then we come back, and after that, we did get started up on it. We started up at around seven hundred feet a minute, seven fifty, right around there. Overall, it started fairly well. We was making paper quite well after two or three weeks."

The new machine had fifty-four dryers, each sixty inches in diameter, whereas Number 3's forty-eight dryers were forty-eight inches. The old machine was operated by hand. Paquette thought the new one, which was controlled by instruments, was easier to operate, but changing a felt was more difficult because felts were heavier. Many crew members wanted to remain on the slower Number 3 when it returned to action. This allowed younger, ambitious men like Paquette to bump up from third hand to back tender. It meant more money, and, Paquette said, "I wanted to make as much money as I could."

Paquette worked on Love in the Afternoon until he retired in 1996. Many people hated Number 5 because of the heat, smell, and noise. Paquette learned to cope: "At that time I was young enough that I could take the heat. I'd hate to try to think of it now." His wife, Beverly, recalled, "When he came home half baked, just leave him alone." "The first thing I'd do," Paquette said, "is sit in the chair and go to sleep because it was brutal in that heat sometimes. We had a thermometer setting there against the wall. One hot summer day, 128 degrees. You run over to the water cooler, and you run the water on your wrist; it helped a little bit to cool. That's the hottest. Most of the time in summer, it was 112, 113, 114. But some of them days, the air just don't want to go anywhere. That was the toughest shift in the summertime, working three to eleven, because it would be that hot when you'd go in, and it would be ten o'clock before it starts to cool off. The night shift, even in the summertime, wasn't too bad as far as the heat goes, unless you had some trouble where you had to get right up next to the dryer." The machine heated the building even in winter, and crews worked in T-shirts year-round.

Number 5 made "a really loud whistling sound, very shriek," Paquette remembered. "I had to wear earmuffs." Paquette's hearing, unlike that of a great many former mill workers, remained "pretty good." After his retirement, he and his wife went west in a camper: "We got into South Dakota, and they have those underground caves. I went into one [two hundred feet down], and the park ranger said, 'I'm going to put the light out, and everybody be really quiet, and you'll see how quiet it is down here.' When everybody stopped talking,

I heard this, 'rrreeeooo, reeeoo, reeeoo, reeeoo.' I was still hearing the cooch roll from the mill two years afterwards. It was really strange."

Paquette thought making corrugated paper was easier than fine papers: "When you make the corrugated material, it just goes in the digesters. There's no looking to see if there's dirt in the paper because everything goes in the corrugated. But when you're working on fine paper, you've got to make sure it's good and white. It was a lot touchier job. It was a lot easier with the corrugated. It didn't matter because they chewed up the bark and everything." Paperboard stock was smellier because fine paper stock had been thoroughly washed and bleached.

As soon as Love in the Afternoon was running smoothly, Number 3 was rebuilt to make fine papers again. Dryers manufactured by Sandy Hill Company replaced the old dryers that had gotten out of round during the Depression. The rebuild included a new head box, an expensive new size press, and a new calender stack. When it resumed operations, Number 3 produced one hundred tons of fine paper a day, double the output of Numbers 1 and 2. The ancient pulp mill could not satisfy three fine-papers machines and a tissue machine, and the mill had to purchase bales of pulp from other mills.

The Paper Board expansion, the installation of Number 5 paper machine, and the rebuild of Number 3 were completed by the beginning of 1968. Jim Wemyss believed the small Groveton mill was "the perfect balance" in the 1960s. It produced an impressive array of tissues, fine papers, and stationery products, as well as paperboard. The world the mill had operated in, however, was in flux. Although it would be a decade and a half before people realized it, the era of local ownership was about to end.

Chapter Nine

THE DARK SIDE

WHEN SEVERAL HUNDRED people converge morning, afternoon, and night to labor under exhausting and harsh conditions, there are bound to be social problems. The smell, noise, heat, chemicals, swing shift, stress of meeting production expectations, breakdowns in machinery, labor-management conflicts, dangerous work environment, and human frailty test one's endurance.

Some conflicts were inevitable under old-school management practices. A member of a paper machine crew bid onto another job to escape his supervisor: "He treated everybody like a dog. Hollers. Bellow at you. After I got out of there, oh, I don't know — quite a while — I wouldn't even speak to the man. How many times would I see him in the store, 'Hi.' I turned my head and walked right away; I had nothing to do with him. I was ready to quit any day of the week. Otherwise than that, it weren't too bad."

Union representatives handled grievances of their members — mostly small matters involving a few hours of overtime or issues of seniority. The union and management usually worked out a compromise on more serious issues such as chronic absenteeism, personality conflicts, drinking, and stealing. Joan Breault sadly recalled an occasion when the union could not protect a worker who was being bullied by coworkers: "We had a squabble once from some finishing room people. A couple of guys were harassing a fellow that wasn't too bright. It ended up he threatened to kill a whole bunch of them. The company had to get rid of him because he could not work around those guys. Even though they were told to leave him alone, they wouldn't leave him alone, and nobody could prove when they were harassing this man. We tried our darnedest to get the company to find some way to keep him. We knew what was going on. We couldn't get proof of it. Not all things are fair."

A few mill workers teased a colleague by alleging that Web Barnett, head of the local union, was cutting a deal with management to hurt this fellow. The victim of the prank was so angered he took a gun to Barnett's house to shoot him. Fortunately, the Barnetts were out of town, and the following day the union president was able to convince the man of his innocence.

Mill managers tolerated the inevitable pranks and stunts pulled on fellow workers because they helped release pressure and stress. When a convert to the Jehovah's Witnesses stood atop some bales and began preaching to his coworkers, a couple of them "got the high-pressure hose and turned the hose on," the widow of one of the pranksters laughed. "Then they put the hose back, and they ran so he wouldn't know who did it. They never saw him get up to preach to the boys again."

Mill workers were allowed to take home a couple of rolls of toilet paper, and supervisors tended to turn a blind eye when employees also took flashlights, gloves, and other low-cost supplies. I asked one longtime worker about pilfering. He replied: "Nobody ever stole nothing. Nobody ever stole nothing." "Borrowed?" I suggested. "Yes. Nobody would say anything if you went up and took a couple of rolls, four rolls [of toilet paper], put 'em in a bag and took 'em home. But always somebody, 'I'll take a case.' After a while it gets out of hand."

One 1960s-era college student was having car engine troubles. His wife described how it was repaired: "His older coworkers, longtime mill employees, [said] 'Why don't we see what we can do.' This man took it upon himself, and through the mill ordered the part that [he] needed, and one in reserve. [My husband] said, 'I can't take that.' 'Yes you can' [laughs]. [My husband] felt he didn't have a choice because it was the standard mores. If he had refused it, it would have been an insult, so you kind of have to go along with it. But [he] was very nervous that he had pilfered this part, that it might someday come back to haunt him. He was under the impression that it was done all the time."

Alcohol consumption in the mill posed a more serious problem. "The Wemysses didn't care as long as you done your job and behaved yourself," Herb Miles thought. "You could bring beer in. Up on the paper machines, on Number 4 and 3, they had a sink with a spigot of water running cold all the time, floating with beer. The guys would go along and have a beer, think nothing of it."

The pipe shop was one of countless celebrated hiding places, Thurman Blodgett said: "You could put your hand in any piece of pipe or elbow or something and pull it out with a jug. A lot of times you went in there sober and came out drunk." Lenny Fournier said electricians encountered hidden bottles in every nook and cranny of the mill: "We used to get around a lot, changing lightbulbs. It was all screw bulbs — big black ones. We'd go behind some of those tanks, and God, there'd probably be a case of beer cans and beer bottles. Bottles then more than cans. They'd be in someplace where there wouldn't be any light."

The old warehouse was another celebrated spot for hiding the evidence. Bill Astle became superintendent of shipping in the 1980s: "I recall Leo Rich, whose position I took over when he retired, telling about adding on to the warehouse [around 1960]. There was a section that had an old wooden floor. When they came in to tear the floor out, he said, 'My God, you've never seen such a stash of beer bottles and whiskey bottles.' It was everywhere. Everyone threw it when they were done consuming it."

Thurman Blodgett's earliest job was as a pool laborer on the construction crew. One day he was running a jackhammer; the next day he was moving cement. Often there was temptation: "Down in construction — 'Hey, come on over here behind this wall and have a drink.' Sometimes if you're working with a wheelbarrow, it gets pretty crooked down there."

Older mill workers often sent the younger men on booze runs. "When I was working at the mill driving the bark truck, a lot of times when the boys were doing a lot of drinking on weekends, they'd send me to get them a couple of cases of beer," Hadley Platt recalled. "Boucher's Grocery Store was right across the street. I drove up there with the bark truck and picked up two cases of beer and put them in the truck, and who walked out of the Eagle Hotel [across the street] and saw me doing it was Jimmy [Wemyss]. I took it back to the boys on the drum barker. He never said a word, and I never said nothing either."

As a fifth hand on the paper machines in the early 1950s, Lawrence Benoit often was sent on errands: "They used to send me to the liquor store all the time. Castile's and, I think, Fleischmann's. Pints mostly. Most of the time they'd go on the back side of the paper machine because all the bearings were water cooled. You had water going in and water coming out. They'd take that pint and lay it right in the gutter. Nice cold water. When I first went in there, just about everybody drank on the job."

Gary Paquette spent over four decades on the paperboard machine: "I wasn't much of a boozer. Once in a while a guy would bring in a bottle or two. But you don't want to be fooling around with booze on the paper machine." Puss Gagnon advanced the counterintuitive theory that the mill was a more dangerous place when one was sober: "I never heard of anybody getting hurt drinking. They'd get hurt quicker sober."

Christmas was the one occasion when drinking in the mill was sanctioned. "At Christmas it was the supervisors, the big superintendent of the paper machine, all the tour bosses would chip in," Lolly LaPointe, who was hired in 1966, remembered. "After you got the machines shut down, and everything was washed up, they'd open up the laboratory down there, and they'd had a shelf completely full of liquor that they'd buy for the crew. Some of them guys would get totally, absolutely shitfaced. It ended up some guy fell down, got hurt, or something. He was still on the clock. I don't think Wemyss ever came in there; I never saw him in there, but I'll guarantee he knew what was going on."

Wemyss had his reasons for not attending the workers' Christmas parties: "I couldn't get involved with them because anytime people that aren't used to drinking have two drinks, all of a sudden they'd decide to become argumentative or start to tell me everything that was wrong with me. A lot of genius comes out of a drink. To avoid their later embarrassment, [it was best not to] be there. But I did hear they were dingers."

Cat-and-mouse drinking at the mill frequently masked more serious drinking-related problems at home where alcoholic husbands verbally or physically abused wives and children. Neal Brown recalled: "I think perhaps behind closed doors, things weren't always as pleasant as they could have been, either due to the mill [or] the stresses of not having a lot of money. A lot of men who came back from the war, and had significant life-changing experiences in the war, perhaps had found alcohol as a way to get past it. There were some kids that you knew that were beaten pretty regularly, but you didn't talk about [it]: 'We know that what's his name drinks and beats his wife and kids.' But it wasn't something that you would openly confront. In retrospect, you would recognize if one of your friends came down to play and had a black eye. You knew they had been batted around a little bit."

Mickey King and Bill Astle were sons of lifelong mill workers. In the 1970s both served as social workers at Alpha House, a home for troubled and abused boys that operated from 1971 to 1977 in Lancaster. "I remember [working with] a number of kids whose fathers worked at the mill," King told me. "Alcoholism was the problem. There were those people that died young, too, because of alcoholism. It complicated things like diabetes. Just so wrapped up in the alcohol that they couldn't deal with the illness of the diabetes. I saw a number of cases like that."

"There's a certain amount of negativity that took place [at the mill]," King said. "Just dealing with the lack of safety in the early days; there were a number of deaths and amputations and all kinds of things. Working with the pollution, and there was a very high rate of alcoholism. I think the anger sometimes from the monotony of the work ended up coming home with a lot of men. There was a fair amount of abuse of families, children, and wives. People needed work, but it tended to be monotonous. It was not always cheery." Although abuse occasionally was physical, usually it was verbal, he thought, adding: "It's unbelievable how much resilience children have."

"There were hair-curling stories of people that didn't live that far from where I grew up," Astle recalled. "I can remember a family that I was friends with. The kids basically were fending for themselves. They were as close as a little town like Groveton would have to street kids. They did have a house, and there was an older sister who held things together. But the father was no longer in the picture, and I'm thinking the mother died, or she was very sickly. She wasn't functioning as a parent. Not to say that Groveton was a bad place to grow up. It was more of an enlightenment for me; what seemed like such a quaint little town, that everybody meets at the church social, and gets along, and belongs to the same fraternal organization. There was a lot more to it than that, and there still is."

In the 1950s and 1960s, Astle remembered, heavy drinking was considered socially acceptable at the mill: "You worked hard, got the loads out; once the work was done it was OK to send somebody over to town to pick up some beer, and they'd kind of finish up their shift that way. The drunk was considered an amusement. 'Gee, did you see so and so at the Christmas party. My God they had to carry him out.' And everybody would chuckle. If that was to happen today, it would be, 'My God, can you believe the scene that this guy made. He needs help.' It was kind of a culture of drinking was glamorous."

"An awful lot of people who worked at the mill were very passive folks,"

Mickey King observed. "They were raised here; they stayed here; they lived through the Depression, although the Depression didn't hurt people here anywhere near as much as it did in urban settings. People had gardens here; they survived. No one was jealous of anyone else because everyone was in the same boat, and you put up with it. Then you were taught all kinds of values at home. 'If you want to eat, you've got to work.' It sort of transferred to the mill. 'I've got money; I'm making money.' The reason that the town was bubbling and moving was that it needed just hands. It didn't need anything more complicated than that. You had bull teams; you had forty, fifty men — well, they weren't building pyramids, but it was similar. You had to have strong back and good hands."

His mother, Belvah, interjected that workers did not have to use their minds. "Nothing up here," she said as she pointed to her head. "They were jobs that maybe people shouldn't have been doing anyway," Mickey continued. "It was like — dehumanizing. It's like, 'You're a cog in a wheel.' And I'm sure that really affected people's minds and attitudes. You'd come home, and you weren't really satisfied with things. 'All day long I've been doing this.' I'm sure people were soaking their feet. And the dust — I'm sure it caused a lot of medical problems. I remember, even as a kid, that there was a lot of hand shoveling done of chemicals. Talc and stuff. And a lot of guys — on their way home — they'd look like ghosts. They were just covered."

I remarked that I had expected to hear many more negative stories about the mill than I had been told. King responded: "Perhaps somewhat more from my generation you'll hear it. There's not a lot of reflection on the part of people; they were just happy to have work. A lot of the negative stuff, they would push it out of their mind. There was a lot of drinking on the job. And there were a lot of people who came in on their shift who were not able to work, and their peers would protect them. 'Go lay down in the corner, and I'll watch your machine.' The company knew it. They wanted you to have your job, and you probably did your job pretty good. But they didn't realize what they were allowing to happen. It wasn't until I think really the Wemysses left that that was not tolerated anymore. You really needed to get help for these people. They really needed to deal with their issues because they were not going to be valuable employees, and they were risking their own health. Then actually the company would be put at risk."

Television, radio, and automobile travel in the postwar years expanded the worldview of Groveton's children. Perhaps there were options in life that did not involve working in the mill. As children of the town's doctors and mill bosses aimed for college, many daughters and sons of mill workers also began to dream of pursuing higher education.

Greg Cloutier's parents made it clear they wanted "a better life" for him. "I wasn't going to learn any French," he recollected. "I was going to learn how to speak English correctly, and I was going to get an education, and I was going to leave Groveton. I found them to be disappointed when I returned. Not unhappy to see me. Their view was that success was somewhere beyond, that it was going to be a better success somewhere else. I think it was that post–World War II group that fought the war, worked very hard to recover from the war, catch up, and didn't want their child to work as hard as they did. Which, in some respects, probably is not good."

Enrolling in college or pursuing a career in the military service gave many Groveton boys and girls opportunities denied their parents. There was, however, a poignant cost to this liberty — the classic "brain drain." "We developed certain skill sets that we did not bring back to Groveton because all that was here was the mill," Neal Brown reflected. "A lot of people from my group, particularly the class of '64, went away. They never came back."

In September 2010, nine months into the mill oral history project, I shared some of the liveliest stories I had gathered at a public presentation on the mill's history. During the subsequent discussion, Kathy Mills Frizzell, who never worked at the mill, urged me to investigate the impact of the mill's presence on the lives of children. I immediately contacted her to ask just those questions, and I continued to ask every subsequent interviewee about her or his childhood memories of the mill.

"I was from a poor family," Kathy began. "My father did not graduate from high school. He was very intelligent, as were both my parents. My mother aspired to be a nurse. That didn't happen. They were married at quite a young age. And my father just had a series of temporary, seasonal jobs. He loved being outdoors. He loved kind of being his own boss, but he moved from construction jobs, to logging, to driving the oil truck. Related businesses to the mill, but not an employee of the mill. . . .

"I am a social worker; I was a born social worker. Everything I'm going to tell you is going to seem strange coming from a kid's perspective, but it was how I felt and how I thought at the time. I was the middle of three children, and I was aware of how poor we were, how little we had. And I always thought life would be so much better if my father could have worked in the mill."

Kathy said the oral history project had altered her understanding of why her father had never worked at the mill. She had always been told it was because the mill only hired people who had earned high school diplomas. At the conclusion of my presentation, she spoke with Jim Wemyss, who remembered cavorting with her father when they were young. Wemyss recollected that Kathy's father had never worked in the mill. "I didn't want Jimmy to feel bad, so I said, 'That's because he wasn't a high school graduate, and you had that rule that you couldn't work there unless you were a high school graduate, and that is a good thing — it kept people in school.' Jimmy interrupted me, and he said, 'That wouldn't have applied to your father. We could have gotten rid of that rule in an instant. That applied to people from 1950 on. Anybody who grew up in the hardscrabble times of the '30s and '40s could have gotten a job here anytime.'"

Kathy continued, "I grew up with the belief that my father could not work in the mill, wished he could have worked in the mill because things would have been better in terms of a stable income. This was a life-story script changer. I think my father was prideful enough that he would not have asked his friend, Jim, for a favor. The other thing is my father was an outdoors person and liked working on his own terms and kind of being his own boss. He never really was his own boss. He drove somebody else's trucks and things, but he worked on his own. And I cannot see him punching a time clock and going to work inside. I cannot see him conforming. So I have since thought, 'Well, maybe my mother knew all that, and to save face for my father, or offer something like a more reasonable explanation, we were just told, 'No, he couldn't work in the mill.' But it shook up my story, my sense of my childhood and what could have been. I don't think there was a misunderstanding; I think it was by choice that my father didn't ask for that favor."

I suggested that she seemed to have "adult-like concerns in a child's body." She responded: "That was true of me. Maybe in my family because there was such a concern about the bills and enough money and paying for things. That was not kept secret. Maybe we did not know all the details, but we knew when there were money issues. Tapping into that, there's still a sadness in me that in elementary school, maybe around third grade, we had an opportunity to say if we wanted to learn to play an instrument. I badly wanted to learn to play the clarinet. As a kid, you would censor your own self: 'Should I ask for this?' Or, 'I know they can't do it, so should I even ask?' And if it was something that you really, really wanted to do, then you would ask, but there was not enough money for me to get an instrument. Same with Girl Scouts. There wasn't enough money that I could afford a uniform or the materials or the supplies.

"Now my brother says — and I agree with this — to some degree [we] have an advantage because we knew whatever we were going to get out of this life we have had to work for. Nothing was going to be given to us. I got a special permit to work in the drugstore with Bob Styles, when I was young, fourteen or fifteen, whatever the rules were — it was before I was sixteen. And from that point on, I bought my own clothes, I started going to the dentist because I could pay to go to the dentist. I wasn't taken care of in a lot of ways children might expect that they would because there wasn't that much money in my family. It went to alcohol and cigarettes; I mean there was always that in my family. And as a kid, I really resented that, but I just kind of understood my place. I think we were raised as my parents were raised, that you didn't necessarily get anything from your parents. You did it for yourself. My brother thinks we're better off for it. . . .

"I don't even think that we as kids knew why we were moving so much until we got in high school. Then it was a little embarrassing. But it did not make a difference in town what you had, or how much money your family had. We kind of all had this notion nobody had very much, and some of us knew that we had less than a lot of others. But nobody threw that in your face or anything like that. . . .

"My mother got married at a young age, family right away, and when my father was unemployed, she would work in the drugstore. [In] the early '60s' Manpower Development and Training Act, she got to go to school, and she was thrilled. She did some sort of secretarial, clerical course. Then she finally got a skill that would make her employable at the mill. It was the beginning of my high school years where my mother was employed in the mill, and from that point on, there was a steady income. . . .

"We never had health insurance, but she must have gotten it when she went to the mill. She worked in the mill office in production. My mother was proud of herself, and that was very nice to see. I don't think she would have said that about herself prior to that, because I think she felt as though she wasted a lot of potential or lost the opportunity for a different kind of life. But she, I think, had a wonderful time working in the mill. She worked with Tom Atkinson in production, and would love to tell us the stories of what happened that day in the mill. She was very good in her job, and the steady income made a difference in our family. And for her."

Kathy could not wait to escape from her family's poverty: "Throughout my years, I was raised with the belief: Try to get out; don't settle for life in Groveton. Don't stay here. This was parents — I think because they wished they had gotten out. It was teachers; it was family, friends. It was, 'Don't stay here, there's nothing for you.' It kind of came to represent a little fear, the way coal miners' families talk about the coal mines, like, 'I'm willing to do it for my family, but I hope for better for my kids.' So it really was an expectation and a belief that you had to leave, that it would be better for you to leave. I definitely got the message that if I stayed, people would consider me a failure.

"I had a freshman year at UNH, but I felt like I was thrown in there unprepared. I felt like I didn't know how to take advantage of it, and I ended up getting married to my current husband, also a Groveton guy, after my freshman year. Everybody who saw me said, 'Kathy, you're making a mistake. You'll never go back to college. You shouldn't be getting married.' That kind of steeled my will even more. But I definitely had the feeling I was letting them down. You could sense the pride of the townspeople if someone did get away. I don't really mean in any way to put down people who stayed. It's a choice. It's a difference. And in many ways, I think quality of life might have been better here."

She was pained by the low self-esteem of many of her classmates: "I think my age mates would have expressed it as, 'What are you going to do after high school?' 'I'm *just* going to go to work in the mill.' They would say it without pride, without gumption." She added: "It wasn't I was ashamed coming from Groveton. I'm very proud to have come from there. We had wonderful teachers, wonderful school. Not that I appreciated it then as I appreciate it now. Some of my teachers were my parents' teachers. They knew my family. They would always ask me if I could sing because my mother was such a good singer. Achievement was of value in town, and of value in my family."

Kathy and her husband, Leon Frizzell, raised a family in Illinois, but they always felt that Groveton was home. They built a vacation and retirement home on Maidstone Lake in Vermont, about twenty minutes from Groveton: "Many of us find a way to come back because you realize what's up here geographically, and quality of life, and how it's unique, and you can't get the quiet and solitude and the clean lake anywhere else. And it feels like home. I kind of chuckle to myself as I'm driving down the roads, 'Whoever would have thought I would be here and happy to be here?' We've arranged burial spots in the Northumberland Cemetery, and I've found a quote that we're going to have engraved on the gravestone, and that's, 'Bound to the place we have come from.' And that's what it feels like."

Chapter Ten

A FATEFUL

DECISION

JIM WEMYSS UNDERSTOOD paper mills would soon have to spend millions of dollars on expensive technology to address mill-generated pollution. Groveton would have to build a much larger and cleaner pulp mill to satisfy the demands of its paper machines for pulp and to comply with recent air- and water-quality laws. Wemyss also worried that if Old Jim, still fighting him over how to run the business, should die, estate taxes could force the sale of family assets, including the mill.

During the 1950s, 1960s, and 1970s large, multinational paper corporations were buying up local, often family-owned, paper mills. In neighboring Maine, Scott, Georgia-Pacific, and Diamond International acquired paper mills and hundreds of thousands of acres of timberlands. The giant conglomerate Gulf and Western swallowed the Berlin and Gorham mills in 1968.

By 1968, Groveton was purchasing large amounts of dry pulp from Diamond International's struggling mill in Old Town, Maine. This growing relationship gave Wemyss an idea: "One day, I said, 'You know, Dad, you're getting older, and I'm getting older. We should do something that's constructive for us and for Groveton.'" The solution, Wemyss decided, was to merge with Diamond International: "When you get with a big company, you can raise the capital any way you want." Young Jim and Richard Walters, son of the chairman of Diamond, were friends. Jim Jr. told the younger Walters, "'You've got a stinking mill [in Old Town], and you should straighten it out.' He said, 'Why don't *you* straighten it out?' I said, 'Maybe we should merge.' He said, 'We sure like the identity of Vanity Fair. It will help our company expand.' So we made what I considered was a reasonable arrangement." It was a fateful decision.

The planned merger was announced early in February 1968. Shortly before the formal signing in May, there was a glitch. "My father had his way of doing things, and Mr. William Walters had his way of doing things," Jim Jr. said.

"They were both similar in age, and they were about as flexible as blue cobalt steel. When you're merging a company such as ours into a large company like that, you have to identify what's merging, down to some details that seem ridiculous. Who owns the computer? Who owns the typewriter? It gets childish to some extent, but they have to identify as many things as they can."

Old Jim had a Persian rug, a wedding present: "Father had an affection for it. For some reason, I didn't think about the rug, so I never mentioned it. After we were 98 percent done, my father said to me, 'Where's my rug? Make sure I get it. I don't want you fellows to have it.' I said OK.

"Not thinking too clearly about a rug that was fifty years old that hadn't been taken care of, I said to Mr. Walters Sr., 'I just remembered, my father had a Persian rug in his office down in Canton, and I wanted you to know we are going to take it out.' That was the dumbest thing I ever did. He said, 'Jim, is it in the agreement?' I said, 'No, sir. It's something I overlooked.' 'Then,' he said, 'it's my rug.' I said, 'Mr. Walters, it isn't really anything you'd want to put in your house, sir.' 'No, Jim, the discussion's over. It's my rug. It belongs to Diamond. If you didn't put it in there, that's the way it is.' So I said to my father, 'Dad, I'm sorry about that rug. It seems to be a big issue. I'll buy you a new rug.' 'Ohhh no, you're not going to buy me a new rug. That's my rug.'"

The morning of the formal signing of the merger contract in New York City, Young Jim made one last pitch to the elder Walters: "I was standing out in front of the [Diamond] office, reading the newspaper, and he came down the street. 'Well, this is the day, Mr. Wemyss.' I said, 'Yes sir, I'm looking forward to it. Just one question, sir. There seems to be some mild discussion about some stupid rug in Canton, and I'm sorry I didn't think about putting it in the agreement, but my father feels very strongly that he wants it in the agreement.' 'Jim, if it's not in the agreement, it's my rug.' Oh, Jesus. I go back over to the Plaza. 'Dad, Mr. Walters said that [rug] belongs to them.' 'Goddamn you, I'm going to insist on having it.'"

Father and son arrived at the meeting with Diamond. "There's five lawyers here, and five lawyers there. Mr. Walters was here, and my father was here, and I looked at them and said, 'I'm very happy that we're going to do this. I think it's going to be good for both of us. And, now gentlemen, I don't want to have any more discussion about a rug. Dad, will you just waive on that rug and forget about it?' [*Very loudly*,] 'NO!' 'Mr. Walters, will you forget about the damn rug? I assure you, sir, it isn't worth three hundred dollars, and I'll give you a check right now for it.' 'Jim, it's not in the agreement; it's mine.' There was a holder with pencils, and I reached in and grabbed [a few] and I held them up and I went 'whap,' broke them in my hand and threw them on the table. I said, 'The arrow's broken, and the hell with you all.' I turned around and walked out."

Walters and his staff stormed out, and Old Jim headed back to the Plaza Hotel to celebrate. Young Jim continued: "Father and I and my brother sat down and had a bottle of champagne for lunch. Father was so happy: 'I'm so proud of you, son.' Over a Persian rug. Jesus Christ. I said, 'Dad, they printed up in their annual meeting—Vanity Fair and how wonderful this was for Diamond. It was the right thing to do. I'm trying to straighten out a family business to make us have high liquidity in case something happens to one of us.' He said, 'I don't care. We're going to live a hundred years more.' I said 'OK.'"

A few days later, Young Jim flew down to Greenbrier, North Carolina, for a gathering of the presidents of many of the large paper companies. He was discussing a possible merger with the Mead Corporation when Richard Walters appeared: "Richard said, 'What the hell happened?' I said, 'It's too childish to talk about.' He said, 'Jim, you and I are making the deal. I'll tell my father to go off in the woods someplace, and we can put this goddamned thing back on track.' 'What can we do with that rug?' 'Jimmy, stick it up you know where. I don't want to hear that word again. Wrap up your father in a roll like Cleopatra.' We made the deal, and that's why a month later it all went back together."

On June 6, 1968, the *Wall Street Journal* reported: "Diamond International Revives Plan to Buy Groveton Papers Co." The Wemyss family received nearly four hundred thousand shares of Diamond International stock, worth $18.2 million based on Diamond's June 5 closing price of $15.50 a share.[1] Forbes ranked Diamond the 219th largest corporation in the United States.

What happened to the rug? "The rug was not mentioned, sir. It was never in the deal to start with. The rug disappeared. Maybe the rats ate it. It was very comical. Nothing had changed [in the contract] except the stupid rug. Not one dot, period, comma, nothing."

Following the Diamond merger, employees at the mill naturally worried their jobs might disappear. Wemyss acted promptly to allay fears, telling his management team: "'Folks, we're going to be part of Diamond International. Not one of you are going to get fired. Not one of you are going to lose your job. I'm still the president of Groveton, and everything is going to be fine.' I kept my word absolutely one hundred and fifty percent." Few former mill workers recalled significant changes in Groveton following the merger because, as Fred Shannon explained, "Wemyss was still in control."

In the accounting department, Sylvia Stone remembered, there were significant changes: "We had to adopt [Diamond's] system. They changed a lot of the account numbers in the ledger. It was horrible, but we finally got it straightened around, and it worked out OK. It might have been five months."

Soon after the merger, CEO William Walters tapped Jim Wemyss Jr. to run Diamond's paper division. "He became my greatest ally," Wemyss proudly remarked. "He would let me get away with things in Diamond that he would have had [other Diamond executives] guillotined." The merger also liberated Young Jim from further clashes with his increasingly irascible father. Old Jim was one of Diamond's largest stockholders, but William Walters made it clear from the outset that he was not going to play an active role in the company.

For two decades, Jim Jr. had prowled Groveton's mill day and night, intimately familiar with its workings and forging strong bonds with the mill's workforce. After the merger, Wemyss succeeded his father as president of the mill, and he remained in charge of overall operations, but his new corporate responsibilities limited his time in the Groveton mill. He delegated the day-to-day running of the mill to his management team, led by Charles Brand Livingstone, who assumed the position of executive vice president of Groveton in July 1968.

A year into the merger, wild nature and human error nearly put the Groveton paper mill out of business. Seventy-five years earlier, Weston Lumber Company had built a dam that created a shallow, two-mile-long pond in the swampy headwaters of the Nash Stream. The Nash Stream and Phillips Brook watershed due east of Nash Stream were sportsmen's paradise. "John Veazey and Owen Astle went to the Nash Stream Tuesday for a few days outing," the Locals correspondent for the *Groveton Advertiser* informed readers on August 1, 1919. The mill owners welcomed hunters, fishermen, and even firewood cutters, provided they had secured permission and did not interfere with the procurement of pulpwood for the mill.

By the 1960s, there were over one hundred private camps on lands leased from the mill in the Nash Stream watershed. Most of the camps were built after International Paper reserved access to its Phillips Brook lands for its executives. Groveton mill workers who were displaced approached Old Jim. Jim Wemyss Jr. remembered: "So the people in Groveton who worked in the mill said, 'What are we going to do?' And my father said, 'Come on over to Odell [the township where the Nash Stream Bog is situated].' That's all. Just like that. 'You'd be welcome.' That's how it happened."

In February 1969 there was a record snowfall, and snow lingered in the woods until May. On Saturday, May 17, temperatures reached eighty-five degrees, and the Connecticut and Androscoggin Rivers flooded, causing an estimated $400,000 in damage in Colebrook, Berlin, and Gorham. The previous day, the New Hampshire Fish and Game Department had stocked the 250-acre Nash Bog Pond with a thousand eastern brook trout. The fishing was good, Herb Miles remembered: "I was up there the week before with the boss, Ralph Rowden. Friday night, Saturday, Sunday. Took a day off. We stayed at the Company Camp. It had been raining a lot. The water got up within a foot and a half of the dam at the top. We cranked the gates up to let it down." By Tuesday, May 20, the gates were again closed.

That morning, Armand Gaudette, foreman of the river crew, and four others were ordered to open the gates. When they arrived, the bog had already begun to overflow and had cut a channel around the western side of the wooden dam. The dam held, but the breach prevented Gaudette's crew from reaching the dam's gates on the eastern side. There was no telephone communication with the mill. Forty years later, Jim Wemyss was still exasperated: "There was three feet of snow in the woods; it was seventy degrees and raining. Instead of opening the gates, they didn't want to let the trout get out, so they let the water keep building up. I came back into town. I had to fly my airplane in, and I went over to Nash Stream to see what was going on. I called the superintendent in charge of that and said, 'You get up to that dam as quick as you can and open all the gates, and the *hell with your fish!*' He didn't get there in time. He spent the night in a tree."

Superintendent Ralph Rowden headed up Nash Stream a short time after Gaudette's crew had been dispatched. The earthworks adjacent to the dam washed out at 11 a.m., and a mass of water, trees, boulders, and other debris started to rumble down the Nash Stream toward Groveton thirteen miles to the south. Rowden was a couple of miles downstream of the dam when he realized he was caught in the flood. He scurried up a yellow birch, later dubbed "Rowden's Roost," and hung on for dear life for four hours as uprooted trees and pickup-truck-size boulders tumbled down the stream.

Construction and maintenance workers rushed out to open the gates at the Brooklyn Street Dam adjacent to the mill as the floodwaters approached. "Those old things, you had two men on a crank trying to get them up," Hoot McMann recalled. "That was hard work. Looked up the river, and here come this thing. Looked about twenty feet high, just moving toward us. No big rush or anything, but coming right towards us. It was just a mess of trees and stumps. You really couldn't see the water. There was so much stuff ahead of the water itself. It looked like a dam coming at you — a beaver dam."

The flood hammered the mill's two pulpwood piles, and hundreds of cords of pulpwood washed downstream. Miraculously the old covered bridge survived the battering. The Route 3 steel highway bridge also held up, but the abutment at the southern end washed out, and the floodwaters carved a deep ravine at the bridge entrance. The mill basement was flooded to a depth of about four to five feet.

In an ordinary year, the mill would shut down during the week of July 4 for "maintenance week," to address annual maintenance requirements while disposing of a significant number of employee vacations with the least disruption to mill operations. Wemyss announced that May 21–27 would be maintenance week, and he ordered non-maintenance workers to take a week's vacation.

Fred Shannon spent that first week removing roughly two hundred wet, silted motors from the basement: "All the electric motors had to come out. They had to be sent away and get dried out, checked out, to see if they were shorted. That's what we done, remove motors, remove motors. It was just nasty."

After May 27, the mill started calling workers back to help with the cleanup and to repair the Brooklyn Dam. The basement was a foul mess. "It was devastating when I went back in there the first time, down in that cellar," Dave Miles shuddered. "Everything was piled up on this end. The barrels, some of them, the labels were off of them, and you didn't know what was in them. Haul that stuff out of there." In the wood room, Francis Roby found "mud and

The covered bridge took a pounding by the flood but survived. Photo taken from the highway bridge just downstream from the covered bridge. The highway bridge abutment (off the picture to the right) washed out. Though the highway bridge survived the flood, it was closed for twelve hours while highway crews repaired the washed-out approach. The mill's wood piles, acid tower, pulp mill, and smokestack are in the background. (Courtesy Warren Bartlett)

dirt and stuff. Oh, Jesus. Fish and everything else was in there." *Who cleaned it out?* "We did," he laughed. "With a wheelbarrow. That was a nice smell."

By late June, the mill was again making paper.

The flood was another nightmare for Sylvia Stone in the accounting department: "I remember a lot of hard work because they brought all that inventory up to me from down in the stock room — the motors and all that stuff. I had to go through my depreciation schedule and write it all off. It was a mess. It took me longer than [a month]."

She added: "[Jim Wemyss] said that if Diamond had not purchased the mill when they did, the mill would have gone under. We had that much loss. Jimmy Wemyss said that himself." Forty years later, at a public interview I conducted with Wemyss, he quipped: "If we hadn't been with Diamond International, it might have been very serious. Instead of a catastrophe, we had a good bath. Diamond paid for it" [*laughter from audience*].

Three months after labor and management pulled together to clean up the mill, the two-year union contract expired. Jim Wemyss was proud that his mill managers and union members generally enjoyed a positive relationship. Web Barnett, president of the Groton union from 1973 to 1977 and 1983 to 1993, agreed: "We were especially lucky with the type of negotiations we had here, because everybody got along pretty good. And they got decent contracts. Once in a while you'd get a bad one. Mr. Wemyss, I had no problem with the man at all. If we'd get into real tough things, we'd get together, and we'd have an agreement. Sometimes he was tough; sometimes we were tough. But it wasn't a war. There was arguments and disagreements; but it's all right to get together if you're going to disagree, but not be disagreeable."

One former shop steward suggested some union officers were too cozy with management: "I thought that the higher ones up at the union and the ones negotiating were kind of working together, you know. Maybe the one in the middle would get a few favors, or something."

Whereas grandfather Wemyss had fought to keep the Northumberland mill from unionizing in the late 1930s, his grandson refused to run a nonunion mill. "You don't want to talk to three hundred people or two hundred," Jim Jr. explained. "You want to talk to one person. Now, if they become so obnoxious and so difficult you can't work with them, then you have a strike, and then you teach them how you are, so they understand when they have a strike with you, you're not a pleasant person to be around. A strike was not a pleasant thing for the town, and I didn't want it to happen. I said, 'You're not hurting me; you're hurting yourself. That's what bothers me the most.'"

Negotiations foundered in August 1969, and mill workers voted to strike on September 12. The unions insisted future contracts expire July 1, not September 1, but Jim Jr. refused to yield: "There was no reason for a strike ever to be in Groton. All the big mills in Maine and coming across to Berlin — May, June, July, August — is when they negotiated their contract. We were in September. If they get an extra paid holiday, I knew we were going to get an extra paid holiday. If they got another week's paid vacation, I knew we were going to have to give a week's vacation. If they got two cents or five cents more, I knew we'd have to do the same thing." When the union made a demand not conceded already by Maine's mills, Wemyss would say, "That's not negotiable."

Shirley MacDow offered another reason management was adamant about the September deadline: "We always tried to have our negotiations in the fall because we knew all the employees were thinking about, 'Oh, I've got to buy my winter fuel.' It might have some bearing on how long they'd be out on strike." *Sounds like a cat-and-mouse game?* "It was," she chuckled. "I'm not sure who won."

In the weeks before the strike, Joan Breault noted the change in atmosphere around town when she went shopping: "It almost seemed like every time a contract come up, prices come up in the stores. Like they're already planning on us getting more money, so they'd get more money. Maybe it's just my imagination, but we all thought the same thing. It cost more to live. So I guess it's a catch-22 situation, isn't it?"

The strike divided union members. Francis Roby refused to picket during the strike because "I didn't want the damn strike. You didn't gain a thing by striking. They lost." Thurman Blodgett, who served a year as a union shop steward, had mixed feelings: "Nobody gains in the strike; nobody. But you've got to try to get the best you can."

The timing of the strike was terrible for Joe Berube: "I had bought this house in mid-August of '69, and two weeks later we were on strike down at the mill. That was not very cost-effective for me. I had a mortgage I had to pay off. I'd just come out of the military, and I was thinking of getting married, so everything was kind of snowballing on me. I was tickled pink when they went back because it meant I could start drawing a regular paycheck again."

The union paid strikers to join the picket line. Some, like Belvah King, opted out: "[I] just came home and waited. I didn't like the strike because there was no money coming in, but I kind of liked the time off." Pauline Labrecque picketed on a raw night: "Brought me a little bit of money. You ought to seen the rain suit I made myself. It was rubberized on the outside, like a little cloth, and then pants. I said I ain't going to freeze my tush off. But it was cold."

Ted Caouette, a young paper machine crew member, remembered: "Nobody had any money. You couldn't pay your bills. You didn't make any money anyway, so you lived week to week. Even when the mill was running. When you're raising your family — I had four children — it took all the money you had and then some. My wife was working at the bank; she worked at the grocery store. Even then it was hard to get by. But we did; we managed to."

Many strikers found construction jobs during the strike. Armand Dube, a machine tender on Number 4 paper machine, worked at the Waterville Valley ski area an hour and a half to the south: "They loved us down there. I guess they never had help like we was. Oh, they loved us. Then we told them we was coming back here; they didn't think too much of that. They said, 'You guys know how to work.' Because them stupid clowns they had down there, they wouldn't do nothing." Fred Shannon drove a big truck on a crew building Interstate 93. He supported the union, but with six children to feed, he needed a steady income: "We worked every hour we possibly could."

Shirley MacDow, by then Wemyss's administrative assistant, noted that despite his new responsibilities with Diamond, he "had his pulse on everything." "He always had his own ear to the ground, especially with the union guys," she said. "If the boys were in Dinty's having a beer, he might be in Dinty's having a beer with them. He'd pick up a lot of things there. I think, in truth, the union probably was in awe of him. He wasn't about to be bamboozled by any of their antics."

John Rich, a piper, recalled having a little fun with the boss during negotiations: "[Wemyss] wasn't there too much, but when he was, we'd give it to him. He'd get pissed off. That was part of the deal anyways — piss them off a little because they was trying to piss you off. Jim and I was always good friends."

Jim Wemyss claimed he settled the strike with the following stunt: "I took my Cadillac convertible. It was a sunny day in September, and I drove it right by the bank, in the middle of the street. Parked it. It has a long hood on it, and I went out and lay in the sun. The picket line was standing by the railroad track, and they all came over. 'Mr. Wemyss, are you OK?' I said, 'No, I'm not.' 'What's wrong?' I said, 'It's hot here. Let's have a beer and talk this over.' We all went [into Everett's Diner], and the strike was over. And the International representative was mad as hell. He said, 'You can't talk to people like that. You have no right to.' Yes, we did some crazy things. Not crazy; they were good."

The new, three-year contract gave workers a seventy-two-cent raise over the period, including a 7 percent immediate raise. It also included increases in sickness and accident benefits, life insurance, and five weeks of vacation for employees with more than twenty-five years of service at the mill. However, union contracts continued to expire September 1.

Joan Breault said Diamond gave the union its first big pay raises: "The

Wemysses never gave that much of an adjustment. A nickel was a big thing to them. After Diamond took over, the raises were in terms of dollars and stuff as well as benefits and things."

Jim Wemyss's position as a major shareholder of Diamond and his rapport with William and Richard Walters paid dividends for the Groveton mill at this critical juncture. "I'd say in the 1970s we spent more money on environmental problems than we did on anything in the mill," Wemyss speculated. *Was this due to recent federal laws such as the Clean Water Act or because it was the wise thing to do?* "I live here," Wemyss shot back. "I didn't want everybody living like that. No. We have an obligation to do it. We did it. Everybody was doing it, or they were going to go out of business. It's as simple as that."

Throughout its history, the mill had dumped "white water," primarily from the paper machines' dewatering process, directly into the Upper Ammonoosuc River. In response to the 1965 Water Quality Act, the mill embarked on a two-phase pollution abatement program. Phase I, costing nearly $15 million, separated clean water from polluted water so that the mill could recirculate the unpolluted water instead of paying to clean it unnecessarily. By September 1970, the mill had reduced its daily water use by three million gallons a day.[2] From 1972 to 1974 the mill spent about $600,000 on the construction of two clarifiers — 110-foot-diameter cement tubs — downstream from the mill.

The workplace environment for the mill's roughly one thousand employees was also transformed during these years. Following the establishment of the Occupational Safety and Health Administration in 1971, the practice of shoveling toxic chemicals into wheelbarrows and shuttling them around the mill gradually ended. OSHA mandated that mill lighting be adequate and that workers wear eye and ear protection. Lolly LaPointe was one of the older workers who found the transition difficult: "There's all kinds of noise in a paper mill. That's why there aren't too many of us guys, me included, that can hear anything anymore. My girlfriend, 'Turn that [TV] down.' I say, 'Jeez, I can't hear it.' There again, when OSHA came in, they really recommended that everybody wear ear protection. Some did, and some didn't. I hated it, but I got to the point where I couldn't hear anything anyway, so I guess it didn't sound too loud to me. I hated wearing the plugs. Especially when it was hot. There's a lot of heat in a paper mill. They were hot and sweaty."

Routine maintenance tasks henceforth had to be performed according to

OSHA standards. LaPointe described how OSHA regulations transformed the process of cleaning the stock prep chests: "When I first went there, we wouldn't even turn the agitators off. It was stupid, but we done it, and nobody ever got hurt. Then, of course, when OSHA steps in, you've got to get an electrician, and it takes you longer to flag out the chest and get ready to go in and wash the chest out. In these later years, you had to have a guy with an air gauge monitoring to see if there was any chemicals. And it was a good thing. But it was funny. Union people were actually the ones that instigated OSHA. A lot of the older supervisors, they hated it because they knew that five, ten, fifteen years before, you'd get into the chest and wash it out and get the hell out of there, and you were ready to go again. Most of it was good; some of it was ridiculous. But then you'd get these younger guys that didn't want — my comment was, 'You were the guys that wanted OSHA, not me. So get your suit on.'"

Until 1972, Groveton mill workers employed on paper machines, in the stock prep department, the finishing rooms, and the shipping department had been represented by Local 41 of the United Papermakers and Paperworkers; workers in the maintenance department and the sulfite mill had belonged to Local 61 of the International Brotherhood of Pulp, Sulphite and Paper Mill Workers. In 1972 the two unions merged to form the United Papermakers International Union. Henceforth, the mill negotiated only one union contract, with Local 61 of the UPIU, which covered all unionized mill workers.

Following the passage of the Equal Employment Opportunity Act in March 1972, some women with considerable seniority began to bid on jobs that had always been filled by men. Jim Wemyss recalled, with exasperation, an early, unsuccessful attempt at gender integration on the paper machines: "When all of a sudden the emancipation of women came in, and they started wanting to work on paper machines, I said, 'Oh, Jesus, well start them on Number 4.' The girls couldn't do it. When you've gotta climb up twice as high as this room and lift up a ten-ton roll and slide a felt on, they didn't want to. If you hadn't done it, you'd have been sued and put in jail."

Joan Breault encountered resistance when she took a job on the wrapper machine in the finishing room: "One guy that I worked with on the toilet paper line was kind of lazy. He'd leave me doing his job as well as mine, and he'd go sit in the break area and laugh about it: 'What can you do about it?

I'm the one that gets the money.' I finally decided maybe I could do something about it, so I signed the next bid that came up for running a wrapper machine. I got a lot of flack from some of the guys. The lead man there was against me going on that job.

"One day I went in, they had shut down the wrapper because it needed a change of film — a roll of plastic [that] weighed about a 120 pounds or so. You had to lift it into slots. I couldn't lift it from that angle. I didn't have enough leverage to get it up, and I couldn't change it. They told me I might as well go home; I couldn't do the job. I went to the boss, and I said, 'I guess you've got me because I can't lift that.' He said, 'No, I didn't figure you could. It's a man's job.' So I sat in the break area, and pretty quick my union president came up, and he went in to see the boss."

Web Barnett continued the story: "I went down, and the boss came over and said, 'Goddamn them. These women, they want this, and they want that.' The men were sticking together, except this one guy that said, 'They're lying. Those girls are working like hell. They are lifting the rolls, and too bad because they can't do it. It's too much. The guys don't do it. The guys always helped each other, but they won't help the women.'"

"The thing that came out of it," Breault concluded, "was that nobody — man or woman — was ever to lift those [rolls] alone. They were to have two people lifting. You had to get through these things. They're natural in any environment, I think." Breault emphasized that most of her male coworkers who had worked at the mill a long time treated her fairly. The ones who gave her trouble usually were recent hirees.

In 1971 Wemyss decided to scrap old Number 2 paper machine, installed in 1896, and to replace it with a new two-hundred-foot-long fine-papers machine — Number 6 — built by Manchester Machine, a Diamond subsidiary. Wemyss dubbed it "Queen of Diamonds" in honor of the corporation that paid for it.

Machine crews on Number 2 were assigned to the thirty-man crew dismantling the old machine and installing Number 6. Wemyss noted proudly: "When we got ready to start the machine, those men knew more about the machine than the engineers did. I said, 'Give them a job' — why lay them off and hire outside people to come in and do it? They're your mechanics. Plus our mill mechanics. That's why we had a very good start-up with the machine."

The Queen, capable of making 150 tons of paper a day, started up on June 27, 1972. Dave Miles, a back tender on the Queen, thought the start-up was "an awful job." For the first two or three months, while working out the bugs, two five-man crews worked side by side on twelve-hour shifts. Miles described the nightmare: "The first day we started Number 6 up; we tried running it until about eight o'clock. We just couldn't keep it running. So [Wemyss] said, 'That's it. Shut it down; we'll come back tomorrow and start again.' We made a tremendous amount of broke. It would break everywhere. I don't think it ran more than fifteen or twenty minutes steady, and it would break somewhere else. We'd try again. Once in a while a bolt might come loose, or something like that, and they'd have to tighten it up, or a rope would come off and we'd have to put it back on. It was a disaster trying to start it, to be truthful. That first day, I don't think we made half a reel of paper. Then we got better at knowing what to expect, and we'd catch it ahead of time. It was definitely a learning process to get it running. Lots of times I've gone in there in the morning and set your lunch box down here, and it would be there when you come home."

Ted Caouette was working on Number 1, and during those early weeks he would put in time helping out on the Queen. A decade later, he became a supervisor of the fine-papers operation. "It never ran well," he said. "Number 6 machine was another headache in the mill. You were always trying to do something. If it didn't break on the machine, it would break on the winder. It would be the same thing day after day. You never really caught up to what exactly was wrong with that machine."

The foul-smelling, ancient, inefficient sulfite mill in Groveton was one of Wemyss's greatest headaches. According to several former mill workers, Dr. Robert Hinkley, a much-beloved figure in Groveton, regularly complained to Wemyss about the correlation between the horrible sulfur smell emitted by the sulfite mill's digesters and the high incidence of asthma and other respiratory ailments of townspeople. "I think Dr. Hinkley did more to clean that up than anybody," John Rich asserted. "Because one night, I guess, [Hinkley] got a charge, and he went down: 'Shut down the sulfur burners. If you can't run them better than that, they don't run.' One guy used to get in there and fire [the sulfur burners] right up. He did it for a joke. Some people had real bad trouble with breathing, lived right here in town, lived all around. Hinkley said, 'You kill one of them, and you're going to pay dear.'" Jim Wemyss denied that Hinkley ever challenged him over sulfite emissions.

A single blow pit, where the digesters emptied cooked chips and their acid bath, drained about ten thousand gallons of water with a pH of about 3 into the river. "I think it would have killed fish on the Amazon," Wemyss observed. On one occasion, he had his outboard motorboat in the Connecticut River, downriver from its junction with the Upper Ammonoosuc: "I pulled the motor out to check something, and the propeller was glistening. I said, '*Whooo*. Something's cleaning that propeller.'"

When Diamond International's Old Town pulp mill faced a monthlong shutdown because it could not sell enough bleached pulp, Wemyss shut down the Groveton sulfite pulp mill on April 29, 1972, and increased the mill's pulp purchases from Old Town: "Here I am, the president of the company, what the hell would you do? I said, 'Wait a minute. SHUT GROVETON DOWN, NOW! Not tonight, now. All pulp for all of our mills must come out of Old Town starting yesterday, now.' All of a sudden [Old Town] had a 150- or [1]60-ton-a-day customer here, bang, just like that. We shut the [Groveton] sulfite mill down, cleaned it up, and stopped polluting the river practically overnight."

Most of the fifty-six workers in the pulp mill's digester building, its bleach plant, and the acid tower found other mill jobs. Gerard Labrecque began driving a Towmotor forklift that ferried five-hundred-pound bales of Old Town pulp, called "hogs," from railroad cars to the pulpers in the stock preparation department. The four wires around the bales had to be cut and removed before dumping the bales into the pulper. "The one who drive the Towmotor had to get off his Towmotor, go cut the wire," Labrecque explained. "The [operator of] the pulper had to hang on to the wire. And the one in the Towmotor used to push a bale in the pulper. Lots of time [wires] did go in the pulper. It would get caught on the pump underneath, down in the cellar. You had to go down there, open the pump, get them outta there and clean up the pump. [The wires] used to get in a big ball."

Forty years later, Jim Wemyss was still sensitive about accusations that the shutdown of the pulp mill had caused job loss in Groveton: "We were going to have to spend millions of dollars in this pulp mill over here, which was antiquated and old. They had a pulp mill over there that didn't have any customers. It's sound business. I didn't do it to hurt people in this town. Are you crazy? I did it to make the town a better town. Why would I want to hurt the town? I lived here. That's just a logic of business decisions you have to make."

Campbell Stationery, a subsidiary of Groveton Papers, played an important role in the mill because it used paper that failed to meet fine-papers standards. Wemyss enjoyed telling of the time in the mid-1960s when he was giving the president of Mead Paper a tour of the mill. His visitor remarked: "I don't see any reject rolls here." Wemyss replied: "'We don't make reject rolls.' He said, 'Jim, stop the baloney. Everybody makes reject rolls.' I said, 'We don't, sir. Anytime we see the paper isn't quite up to spec, we put it in the rewinder and cut it up to 34.5 inches wide.' He said, 'Yeah, what do you with those?' I said, 'Come with me.' I took him up to Campbell. 'That's where you put it on the back of the ruling machines. You rule it.' And he said, 'Oh, my God. Every time we make bad paper, we give it to people in New York for nothing.' I said, 'You're a generous man.'" A month later, Mead acquired Westab, a venerable stationery company.

Campbell had moved from the old Northumberland finishing facilities to a large new building in Groveton in 1969. At that time Campbell shifted from school-oriented products to a broader, more commercial, product line. Its business grew so rapidly that within three years it had outgrown its new building.[3] The mill purchased the shuttered plywood mill in North Stratford early in 1973 and, after renovating it, moved one hundred employees of Campbell Stationery into it later that fall. The 190,000-square-foot building provided ample space for Campbell to expand; it had direct access to the Grand Trunk Railway line for shipping, and it saved the mill the need to erect a planned new Campbell warehouse at Groveton.[4]

The Equal Employment Opportunity Act probably played a role in the Campbell move. Relocating to Stratford allowed Diamond to pay Campbell finishing room workers at lower rates than workers doing similar jobs in the Groveton finishing rooms. The move angered union officials, and decades later, Wemyss defended his action: "I didn't do it with malice towards the people in town. When you have a paper machine man running a big paper machine making five hundred tons a day, you pay him umpteen dollars an hour. And if you have a little girl working on a ruling machine in the tablet division, she says, 'I should get the same pay. I work here too.' If you gave her the same pay, you would not be in that business very long because your competitors weren't giving that type of money to their people who were running the ruling machines all over the country. That's a sound, simple, clean decision to make. Not with malice and hate." A more apt comparison would have been with wages paid to finishing room workers in Groveton, not high-paid paper machine tenders.

Old Town's new tissue paper machine, also manufactured by Diamond's Manchester Machine, ran so poorly that Old Town's finishing plant was operating far below capacity. Wemyss recalled: "My brother calls me up and said, 'You're shipping finished facial tissue over to Old Town so we can make up a car properly, and it's costing us a fortune. What are you going to do?' I said, 'It will be taken care of tomorrow.' I went into the mill here and said, 'We're shutting the facial tissue line down." On June 8, 1973, mill vice president Walter MacDonald announced that the tissue converting plant would close in twenty days, and that those operations would be transferred to Old Town. Number 4 paper machine would continue to run in Groveton.

Most of the finishing room employees found work elsewhere in the mill, although not always with the happiest results. Pauline Labrecque used her seniority to bump into Number 1 finishing room, where she wrapped reams of fine papers. A coworker made her life miserable: "The fellow that was behind me didn't like it because I bumped down there. He was dirty to me because I was new. I was learning. And he was pushing that to the hilt. The paper was piling up on me. Just made me more nervous."

There were no jobs for college students in the summer of 1973 because of the transfer of facial tissue finishing to Maine. Bill Astle recalled: "A lot of union employees were laid off, and they weren't about to let summer kids come in and take jobs that could have gone to a union employee. So I didn't get to work that summer."

When the mill announced it was closing Number 4 finishing room, union president Web Barnett, fearing the loss of a hundred jobs, urged town officials to go down to the mill and learn what was going on. Several town leaders toured the mill, and one expressed concern that there was "not a good working relationship" between Wemyss and Groveton's municipal government.[5]

Barnett blamed town manager Dana Kingston and the selectmen for job losses at the mill: "I say you are against the working man in this town. . . . It will be the blackest day this town will ever see if Mr. Wemyss gets out."

Selectman Jay Gould, who had recently lost a high-paying salvage job with the mill, said, "We're willing to talk it over; we'll break the ice, but the ice is pretty thick."[6] Two weeks later, Barnett and Gould again exchanged insults. Shep Mahurin, a local political leader, attempted to calm Barnett: "The people of this town would do anything in their power to make sure that this mill stays. But they have to know what to do."[7]

Jim Wemyss claimed the selectmen wrote to Diamond's president, Richard Walters, urging him to fire Wemyss. According to Wemyss, Walters said: 'Jim, tell them to go to hell, shut the mill down, and come on over to Old Town. You've got that big mill over there.' I said, 'I don't walk away from problems. I'll take care of them. Leave me alone.' That's when I ran for selectman and fired every one of them."

Wemyss was elected selectman in March 1974, and for the next dozen years he dominated the town government. I asked Wemyss if he ever felt there was a conflict of interest between mill and town interests: "No. Absolutely no. There were no problems. There were no problems. I'm telling you there were no problems." *Did anybody challenge you with a conflict of interest over mill taxes?* "Who'd do that?" he smiled. "It was good for both sides." He once was criticized at a Diamond board meeting: "They were talking to me about taxes. I said, 'You don't understand. I'm the tax assessor, and our taxes are right.'"

THE DEMOCRAT'S HEADLINE on October 25, 1973, read: "Fuel Reserves Dwindle at Groton; Mill Shutdown Narrowly Averted." The mill used sixty thousand to eighty thousand gallons of fuel oil a day, and the oil tanker carrying the mill's resupply had been delayed at sea. When the tanker reached Portland, Maine, the oil was speedily delivered mere hours before the mill would have run out.[8] This was the first hint of the oil crisis that fall and winter. Middle Eastern oil-producing nations had set up an embargo against countries that had supported Israel during the October 1973 Yom Kippur War. The price of crude oil increased by 70 percent as OPEC nations moved to secure a much greater share of the revenues from their massive oil reserves. By January 1974, oil prices had quadrupled. The era of cheap energy, one of the cornerstones of postwar American economic growth and prosperity, had expired. Skyrocketing and unpredictable energy prices would torment the energy-intensive Groton mill for the remainder of its existence.

On December 3, 1973, the mill learned that its fuel supplier, Texaco, would reduce Groveton's allotment for the month by 75 percent because of OPEC cuts in supply. "It was serious, really serious," Jim Wemyss reflected. "I wasn't sure we were going to survive. Paragon [a subsidiary of Texaco], who was selling us all our oil, told us, 'We haven't got any.' I said, 'You can't do that to me. We've been with you for so many years.' I went to military school with a fellow who was a vice president of Texaco in later years. I went down to the Chrysler Building and said, 'I want to see him.' 'You have to have an appointment.' 'Just give him my name, and tell him I want to see him.' I did see him, and I got my oil [laughs]."

Spurred by the 1973–1974 oil crisis, Wemyss decided to convert one of the mill's recovery boilers to an incinerator that would generate some energy for the mill by burning mill waste and town garbage. A ton of garbage burned in an incinerator yielded the equivalent of sixty-three gallons of oil and saved the town fifteen dollars in sanitary landfill fees.[9] The $250,000 incinerator began operations in October 1975.

Two or three times a day truckloads of mill trash, skids, and bad rolls of paper were delivered to the incinerator; on Wednesday and Thursday afternoons, town trash was delivered. "When they put it in, they said you could burn everything, don't even have to separate the glass," Thurman Blodgett, one of the incinerator crew members, said. "But every Monday morning, we had to go in with a jackhammer. It melted up front, but when it got to where it dropped down on the chain, it cooled. It solidified right there and kept building back. We'd spend all Monday, four of us, digging it out. It was shut down over the weekend. It was still hotter 'n a devil." The incinerator experiment ended in the early 1980s. By then, environmentalists were warning that incinerating plastic and other manufactured products released PCBs, dioxin, and furans.

Fuel costs would play a major role in the demise of the mill. In its final decades, the mill would convert from oil to wood chips, back to oil, and then to natural gas in a vain attempt to secure a stable, low-cost supply of energy to keep itself running.

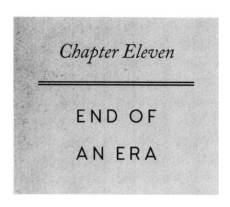

Chapter Eleven

END OF
AN ERA

THE OVERTHROW of the shah of Iran in January 1979 triggered another sharp rise in oil prices, the hostage taking of fifty United States Embassy officials in Iran in November 1979, and a war between the new Iranian government and Saddam Hussein's Iraqi regime in 1980. Uncertain oil supplies were an even more serious threat to the mill than price rises. Wemyss and his managers were losing control over the mill's destiny.

Saddled with a $25 million a year energy bill, Wemyss decided to convert Number 1 boiler to burn hardwood chips. In August 1981, mill general manager Jack Hiltz optimistically wrote: "The conversion of No. 1 boiler to wood chip burning seems to be coming along quite well, and we expect to be starting the converted boiler in October. We certainly will need it before the snow flies."[1]

The wood-fired boiler missed the intended November 1, 1981, start-up date by two months. It used oil for several weeks while the system was "debugged." Early in 1982, during a bitterly cold stretch, the mill started burning wood chips, and quickly discovered all sorts of problems. The belts alternately froze or slipped. The hopper over the boiler plugged up with chips. Although the boiler worked well when fed wood chips, design flaws with the tubing prevented running the boiler at more than half capacity.[2]

Unknown to the Groveton mill community, Diamond was fighting for its life, and Wemyss was under tremendous pressure from the Diamond board. Greg Cloutier, son of two mill workers and nephew to a dozen or so others, was an engineer who had recently directed the installation of the first large industrial wood-fired boiler at Georgia Pacific's Gilman, Vermont, mill. One day Jim Wemyss Jr. paid him a visit. Cloutier remembered: "[Wemyss] basically says, 'Hey, we're trying to build a wood-fired boiler in Groveton, and it's killing us. It's not running.'"

Not long thereafter, Wemyss flew Cloutier down to a Diamond board meeting: "Mr. Wemyss says, 'This guy doesn't work for us. He's got no skin in the game. I want you to hear him out. He's making it work.' At the time I was doing a lot of ice climbing. I just got done with a predicting avalanche class, certifying to do some guiding. Jimmy's kind of rubbing [the Diamond engineer's] nose in it a little bit. I come in, and the crescendo of the meeting is this guy says, 'Tell me this, if you're so smart, how do ice crystals plug up those feed conveyors and it doesn't flow? Why shouldn't it just slip?' I said, 'Clearly, you don't know or understand the metamorphosis of a snowflake.' The guy was completely taken aback. I could list at that point the four dynamic phases of ice crystal formation changing to a grain. And I then said, 'That's why you don't have wood falling into the boiler.' The guy was completely dumbfounded, and Mr. Wemyss said, 'See, he knows what he's talking about.' Then I left the room. [Soon Wemyss] came out, and he said, 'Oh! That was so good! That story you made up on the metamorphosis of a snowflake was terrific! We've got the money to make the modification.' I don't know if it was then or on the way back home, he made me an offer to come work for Groveton for substantially more money than I was making at Gilman. I think the fact that I volunteered to do something for Groveton without pay was important to him. He was always convinced that [my] family was all bullshitters. This confirmed a theory he already had."

After Cloutier had had an opportunity to study the Groveton boiler conversion project, he told Wemyss it would be necessary to make substantial changes in the design of the fuel delivery system and the method of removing the wood ash. Three million dollars later, the wood-fired boiler started up in November 1982, a year behind schedule. The boiler produced two hundred thousand pounds of steam an hour and was expected to supplant 85 to 90 percent of the mill's fuel oil requirements. The mill saved money and was buffered from OPEC oil price swings and embargoes. The boiler consumed about fifty tons of chips — roughly two and a half tractor-trailer loads — an hour.[3] A huge pile of chips appeared in the wood yard where the pulpwood piles had been prior to the closing of the pulp mill in 1972.

"A wood-fired boiler was tough for the men who ran it," Cloutier acknowledged. "It really meant that they had to work. Making good paper on the paper machine was an art; firing wood was, in my mind, the same thing. You get a feeling about the system you are running. If [the crews] weren't paying attention, it was tough."

Cecil Tisdale, a boiler room supervisor, thought it was the "worst thing they ever did." "We had more trouble with that, more maintenance," he grumbled. "Wood causes problems. As far as I'm concerned, the equipment they put in just didn't work good. They never could get the steam pressure they wanted because the boiler would smoke all the time. Call-ins in the middle of the night. Conveyor's gone. Motor's burned up. They used to have a conveyor to take all the ash out. That blew up twice. Once I was headed in there to find out what the trouble was. I opened the ash house door, and it blew right then. Whoa, I got back outside pretty fast." Eventually the ash house burned down.

While the mill was grappling with the fallout from the oil crisis, Anglo-French financier Sir James Goldsmith had embarked on a campaign to take over and dismantle Diamond International. Late in April 1980 Goldsmith offered to buy shares of Diamond International for a "premium." When Diamond's stock jumped $3.25 on April 28, the *Wall Street Journal* took note. Rumors of an impending sale swirled. On April 30, the *Coös County Democrat* headline asked: "Diamond's stock sold?" The brief page-one article noted that Diamond's corporate headquarters had no comment, and Jim Wemyss was out of town.[4]

Few in Groveton realized that Diamond was fighting a losing battle for survival, but they could feel the gloom descending upon the mill. To boost morale, mill managers launched an in-house newsletter, the *Papermaker*. Jack Hiltz, production manager, wrote in the December 1980 inaugural issue: "One of the reasons for having a newspaper is to keep people informed about events that affect their lives and the society in which they live."[5] An unspoken additional reason was to allay fears stoked by the local rumor mill.

The *Papermaker* published four to six times a year until 1992. It reported on promotions, retirements, safety issues, new mill projects, the mill's bottom line, and birthdays. It also included cheerful prattle and quirky photos of employees in Halloween costumes as it tried to put the best face on an increasingly hostile economic environment. Vice president and general manager L. J. Alyward wrote in that first issue: "Our company has been very fortunate in obtaining enough business to operate fully (with one exception) during the past year."

To improve its competitiveness, in 1980 the mill began to experiment with making alkaline paper. The traditional acid paper was made by adding common alum to the pulp. Alum allowed papermakers to add rosin to the mix; rosin improved paper's ability to absorb ink without blotting. Papermakers also added white clay to the stock to fill pores and make fine papers smoother. Since clay is cheaper than wood pulp, the more clay fill used, the lower the production costs.

When chemists developed a substitute for rosin, it became possible to replace the acidic alum with an alkaline system that used calcium carbonate, or lime, instead of clay as filler. Alkaline paper is stronger than acid paper; it lasts far longer, and it does not turn yellow and brittle. It is cheaper to produce because a higher percentage of lime filler and a correspondingly lesser amount of pulp can be used in the process.

Early in 1981, the mill made a trial run of the alkaline process on Number 1 paper machine, using high-quality, finely ground calcium carbonate from Vermont's marble quarries. A writer in the *Papermaker* hailed the trial run as an "outstanding success." A subsequent alkaline trial was a disaster. "We had a young man here who wanted to change to alkaline paper, which is more or less the standard of the industry today," Jim Wemyss explained. "I said, 'That's a good idea. Let's see how it works. Take the smallest paper machine and make a small run, package, and distribute it, and let's find out what the reaction is.' What did he do? He put the whole mill on alkaline. We ended up with a million dollars worth of paper that we had to burn or bury, and almost lost one of our biggest customers [Gestetner] because of his arrogance in doing such a thing. He left the mill, and I happened to come back into the mill. The people said to me, 'What are we going to do? This is god-awful. We can't run the paper machines.' The whole place was chaos. We were hauling it to the dump. All the [fine-papers] machines were terrible. I said, 'There's only one thing to do. Dump all the chests, and we're going to put it back on acid in the next — [*raises voice*] immediately! [*Pounds desk*] Right now!'" Wemyss fired the manager. "If he'd been there, I would have been upset with him, but I would not probably have been as severe in my judgment. But when he put the whole mill on [alkaline], and then left and was a thousand miles away, playing golf, and his troops were in chaos — that's not excusable to me. I said, 'You no longer work for us.'" Rule number one for Jim Wemyss: An officer never abandons his troops when they are under fire.

"Gestetner could not use that paper. Every office all over the United States that had their machine — all of a sudden, it wouldn't work," Wemyss continued. "Normally, that's an unforgivable sin, and the people throw you out. Because of my friendship with the chairman and president of the company, we were able to pull it out of the fire."

It would be nearly a decade before the mill successfully converted to alkaline paper using a synthetic calcium carbonate. The ground calcium carbonate used in the early trials was so abrasive that it destroyed pumps and wires on papermakers. A $15,000 wire that should last a month or two was destroyed in a few days.

Susan Breault concluded an upbeat report in *Papermaker* on two trial alkaline runs in early 1982 with this jarring exhortation: "Success in the [alkaline conversion] process can only be accomplished if everyone works as a team. This is a strong healthy town and with everyone's help we can make it grow in wealth, health, and bring back the spirit and moral[e] which once lived here in these walls."[6]

Mill morale had taken a huge hit in the fall of 1981. Negotiations for a new union contract broke down. On September 12, 1981, Local 61 struck the mill over wages, the pension plan, and proposed changes in seniority rules. Years later, Jim Wemyss still angrily referred to the union president as an "idiot."

The *Democrat* editorialized: "The strike comes at a bad time. The paper workers can not stand getting along on $45 a week for very long, and if reports of the mill's financial status are accurate, neither can the mill stand to lose those daily shipment revenues for very long."[7] "I can remember not eating that well," back tender Dave Miles said, "or paying the bills."

The strike grew ugly. The mill reported it had found ten sticks of dynamite in the boiler room. When an injunction prevented the union from picketing the Campbell plant in North Stratford, someone slashed truck tires, and the radiators of three Mack trucks in a locked garage were smashed in by crowbars. Two men in North Stratford were arrested for trespass and criminal mischief. A salaried employee's wife reportedly received a threat over the phone that her house would be torched.[8]

Shirley MacDow, a vice president of Diamond, had a nightmarish time: "They came down and ruined our garden. Threw tomatoes all over my house. Our little girl was only a few years old then. So, Mr. Wemyss instructed, probably Joe Lacroix and a couple of others, to keep an eye on me. Maybe they'd set the house on fire. We didn't know. The mind-set changed from, 'Hi, how are you, Shirley?' to 'You're our worst enemy.'"

Roger Caron reluctantly joined the picket line: "I remember part of getting your strike benefit was walking a picket line. I really didn't like that. People would drive by and look at you. Even Wemyss came along, and I'd known him all my life. He lived right behind my folks' house. It just felt like an adversarial position to be in."

Pam Styles, a nonunion office worker, had to cross the picket line. "I didn't have a problem with the people maybe because I was friendly with a lot of them," she remembered. "One of my friends had a guy spit on her. It's a small community, and people know everybody, and it's just I'd never do that. I know I'm upset if somebody is doing my job, [but] we need the work too."

Styles was assigned to work in the fine-papers finishing room to run off reels of paper that had been produced prior to the shutdown. "I worked on the Wills machine," she recalled with amusement. "That was the machine that cut the paper to eight-and-a-half by eleven, or eight-and-a-half by fourteen. It was fun because for a while we didn't know what we were doing. It was something different, out of the ordinary. I'd get right up on the machine when we got a jam and pull the paper out. It kinda gave us firsthand knowledge of what they were doing."

During the monthlong strike, rumors swirled: Boise Cascade was going to buy the mill; a paper machine was going to be moved to Old Town. When the strike ended on October 11, the new agreement gave the seven hundred union workers a 9 percent pay increase in the first year and an 8.5 percent increase in year two.[9] No paper machine was shipped to Old Town, but old Number 1 paper machine never restarted, and a couple of weeks after the strike ended, it was scrapped. Murray Rogers said: "It was kind of a retaliation move because of the strike." As many as eighty jobs disappeared with Number 1.

A month after the strike ended, the *Democrat* ran a short page-one article headlined: "Diamond Intl. Could Be Sold."[10] Readers of the paper learned that over the previous three and a half years, Sir James Goldsmith had bought up 40 percent of Diamond's stock.

Goldsmith and his merchant banker collaborator, Ronald Franklin, had made a stunning discovery: timberland-owning corporations, such as Diamond, listed the value of their forest holdings at a fraction of their potential market value. If the hostile takeover bid succeeded, Goldsmith could sell off Diamond's pieces, including the Groveton and Old Town mills, Diamond's playing-card business, Manchester Machine, and other non-timberland assets to pay off the huge, high-interest debt, while retaining the timberlands, valued by Goldsmith at $723 million, as profit. Franklin later explained the rationale: "Diamond interested us because of our philosophy which pervaded everything we did in America: that the sum of the parts of most conglomerates was worth a great deal more than the whole."[11] Diamond's undervalued timberlands made the corporation irresistible to a corporate raider.

"[Diamond] was a fantastic company until Jimmy Goldsmith came along," Jim Wemyss told me. "You know what was wrong with Diamond? We were too rich. We had no debt. We had four million acres of land on our books for twenty-five dollars an acre. We were a very, very successful company. Any company like that was a target for these people. You couldn't stop them." Diamond owned eight hundred thousand acres in northern Maine, ninety thousand acres across northern New Hampshire and northeastern Vermont, and another ninety-six thousand acres in the Adirondacks. I asked Wemyss why Diamond had valued its timberland at one-fifth or one-tenth its market value. "The trees are growing every day, and so their value is increasing every day," he explained. "You don't have to report it as income on your company and pay taxes on it." Wemyss acknowledged that the low valuation translated into a lower capital gains tax rate paid by the seller if and when the land was sold.

Jim Wemyss led the fight against Goldsmith on the Diamond Board of Directors. "I kind of remember sitting in his office and listening to him vent — frustrated vent," Greg Cloutier said. "Mr. Wemyss really saw this [takeover] as potentially the end to Groveton and the way Groveton worked and the way all of the different entities worked together to make the Groveton facilities profitable."

In the fall of 1981, two major Diamond shareholders, Conley Brooks and Old Jim Wemyss, sold their shares to Goldsmith for forty-two dollars a share, thirteen dollars above the price fetched on Wall Street. Jim Wemyss Jr. did not agree with his father's decision, but he did not blame him either: "My father wasn't happy with Diamond about that time. In any mergers like this, when your stock is selling for twenty-eight and somebody offers you forty dollars for it, and you've got many thousands of shares, it's a lot of money. Father, in his inner thinking, said, 'That damn son of mine, I know him, he's going to screw this deal up. I'm getting up there, and I want to get my estate in order. This might be a good window for me to do this.' Goldsmith called him up, and [Father] said, 'I've got so many thousand shares; I want you to nail it for me right now: forty dollars, forty-two dollars.' Maybe he asked a little bit more. Goldsmith saw the chance to grab that big hunk of shares, and they made a deal. The next thing I knew, [Diamond president Bill] Koslo said, 'Your father just sunk us.' I said, 'I had nothing to do with it, Bill.'" Early in November 1981, as Koslo agreed to discuss terms of the takeover with Goldsmith, the New York Stock Exchange suspended trading in Diamond shares.

Over the next year, as the final stages of this boardroom drama played out far from Groveton, most mill workers heard rumors but were in no position to take any action. "The guys on the machine knew there was something going on, and you'd hear rumors here and there, but no, we did our job, and waited to see what was going to happen, just do your job and that was it," Ted Caouette recalled. Finally, on November 1, 1982, Bill Koslo recommended that Diamond shareholders accept Goldsmith's offer, and 89.6 percent of Diamond's shares voted in favor of the sale.

To pay down his $660 million debt, Goldsmith moved quickly to sell off all Diamond's assets except the timberlands. James River Corporation of Richmond, Virginia, had bought the Brown Company paper mills in Berlin and Gorham, New Hampshire, late in 1980. In May 1983, James River (JR) agreed to pay Goldsmith $171 million for Diamond's paper division, which included the Groveton Papers mill, Campbell Stationery in North Stratford, and Old Town's pulp and paper mills. JR paid $75 million in cash, common stock in JR worth $19.8 million, and preferred stock with a value of $76 million.[12] Goldsmith paid Jim Wemyss $150,000 a year to remain on his Diamond board. However, when Sir James asked Wemyss to help dismantle Crown Zellerbach, following another successful hostile takeover of a paper company in 1985–1986, Wemyss refused.

Jim Wemyss tried to persuade his fellow board members to consider the rights of other stakeholders, but to no avail: "I couldn't get rid of Jimmy Goldsmith. I tried, but nobody would support me. I knew what he was trying to do. The board's position was: Let the stockholders vote. If you don't allow that to happen, you're depriving the stockholders. They just, 'I'll take the money,' and the people that are working there — 'The hell with them. They lose their job, but I've got my money.' And I don't like that." Thirty years later, Wemyss was still enraged by mention of Goldsmith's name. "Goldsmith didn't even know where Groveton was. Never did know to the day he died."

The arrival of James River in Groveton in July 1983 ended forty-three years of Wemyss family ownership and management of the Groveton Papers mill. Jim Wemyss Jr. would remain a presence in the mill complex for another fifteen years as president and chairman of the board of Groveton Paper Board. Diamond had assumed the Wemyss family's 50 percent ownership of Paper Board in 1968; James River declined to buy Diamond's share, and for the next two decades, two independent corporations shared the Groveton mill complex. Almost immediately, the relationship between Young Jim and James River turned hostile.

The bad blood between Wemyss and JR was common knowledge throughout the mill. While Wemyss railed at his successors, Bill Astle suspected James River "took it more with amusement than feeling that they were really getting beat upon, or that they needed to teach him a lesson." Louise Caouette had known Wemyss when she was growing up. She thought JR might have "exposed him as being a human being." "Groveton had really put Wemyss on a pedestal," she explained. "I think James River was pretty free at making sure people knew that Mr. Wemyss was no longer calling the shots; that they were dealing with a corporation, and it wasn't Mr. Wemyss. I would think that that would have been hurtful to him."

Wemyss had modernized the mill. He knew its remotest corners intimately. He cared passionately about the mill, the workers, the community, and his legacy. And he had no experience taking orders, or watching other people give orders he could not countermand. "They didn't like me," Wemyss said of the James River managers. "I tried to be good to them because I wanted to keep the people working." *What did JR do that was wrong?* "They didn't listen to me; it's as simple as that. We knew the business; they had a new theory of running the business. They'd have paper machines down in Groveton, and Conway Process meetings up at the Legion with all the millwrights. I said, 'The paper machines are down.' 'We're having meetings. That's more important.'"

Greg Cloutier observed: "The James River group really spent a lot of time polishing teamwork and problem solving, communication. That was perhaps a [strength] Mr. Wemyss didn't have. He was the single focus for everything. Everybody worked together almost because they hated him, or because they feared him. But they worked together. You could take extremely capable men who had terrible people skills, but had extremely good skills at making paper, and they would work under Mr. Wemyss because in many ways, he could control that sort of guy. He could take a high-energy individual that was a pain in the butt to work with and make that guy work well for him. He had that strong leadership, commanding leadership — I mean, he was the alpha dog. There was no question about it."

Cloutier offered an example of the contrasting management philosophies: "When Mr. Wemyss was there, if you were a key department head and the power blinked so the lights go out, you saw men run from wherever they were. The meeting stopped that second. You ran to your department to get it back on line. [Under] James River, your men were supposed to solve that problem. If you'd done your job right, they had the ability and the skill to make those decisions. They didn't need you, and you stayed in the meeting. I don't think that set quite the example."

Jim Wemyss's management philosophy was *Keep the mill running*. He expected bosses to be there when there was trouble and to remain until the problem was fixed. "Don't tell me you can't fix it; fix it!" he would holler. When the machines were down, Cloutier explained, "[Mr. Wemyss would] walk through; he didn't keep on walking. He took his coat off. He stayed. Maybe he was mad to stay, but he stayed. 'What can I do?' 'Rethink what you're doing here.'"

Chan Tilton, a retired paper machine tour boss, admired Wemyss's commitment: "If that tissue machine was in trouble, he'd be there. He was a papermaker. He'd come and talk to you. You couldn't buffalo him. He was an intelligent guy, a little autocratic, but fair. If you needed to replace equipment, you'd get it. [While he ran the mill] there was nobody out of work in the town."

The key to success for a small, family-owned mill, Wemyss believed, was to offer a diverse product line; don't rely on one large customer; always upgrade to remain competitive; encourage innovation; waste nothing; operate a clean, safe mill; and maintain a huge inventory of spare parts so that the mill never shuts down for want of a pump or a bearing or a bolt. When orders were down, he directed the crews to run the paper machines at a slower pace, rather

Jim Wemyss with "Jazzo" Kingston, one of Greg Cloutier's many
uncles, at Maidstone Lake around 1966. (Courtesy Greg Cloutier)

than shut them down and lay off scores of workers. Employees kept drawing a
paycheck, and the mill was spared the headache of restarting a paper machine.

"I don't think Jimmy missed much," Iris Baird suggested. "I think he con-
veniently didn't notice on occasion. But if you had tried to take advantage,
he would have known." Wemyss agreed with her assessment: "I was involved
in everything. Little went on that I didn't have some knowledge of it before-
hand." He was proud that he and his father were hands-on owners: "My
father would be working on a paper machine when things were bad, maybe
pulling broke off the top press, and I did the same. We were not the managers
that lived in New York City and came up once a year and walked through in
our tuxedos to see how the paper mill was running. The president was here
at two o'clock in the morning or four o'clock in the morning. That's the way
we were." "We had a very strong work ethic in our family," he explained on
another occasion. "We didn't talk about what time we went to work or how
many hours we worked. If it wasn't [running well] you were not supposed to
be anyplace but where it was."

He was a local owner, who viewed the mill workforce as a large family: "It was a family atmosphere. I always left my door open. Anybody could walk in. 'Hi, what's going on? What can I do for you?' [Groveton] was my home. Always has been my home." There was no doubt, however, that Jim Wemyss Jr. was the patriarch of that family. "He could be a dictator," Greg Cloutier said. Others used terms such as "autocrat," "old school," and "son of a bitch."

Dave Atkinson's grandfather, "Bucko," a stock prep supervisor under Wemyss, had a reputation for screaming and hollering. "You didn't want to screw up for Bucko," his grandson said. "I think he went to the school where it was 'My way or the highway.' Call it the Jimmy Wemyss School of Management. You just scream and holler. I don't want to say disrespect people, but that was the style back then, and [Bucko] certainly fit the style, which is probably why he was promoted to a boss."

Wemyss was legendary for his outbursts when a paper machine wasn't making good paper. He invariably directed his fury at management because the managers were in charge, and Wemyss, the ex-soldier, believed in the chain of command. "I had seen him when he trimmed up some of the bosses," Bruce Blodgett said. "Kicked that sport jacket of his right up and down the floor and scream at those guys and rip 'em apart. He was not bashful at all."

Lolly LaPointe, superintendent of the stock prep department, witnessed a few Wemyss eruptions: "I'd come in there eleven to seven. If [the tissue machine] had been haying all night, he'd take off his jacket and throw it on the floor and jump and rave and rant and raise all kinds of hell, and then he'd walk out of the place. Maybe he was hot. But he'd come in there like on a night shift, and would he ever go into a tantrum, mister."

As always, Wemyss had an explanation: "If you walked into a machine room when you've got a big coat from outside, and it's ninety degrees in the machine room, and it was forty below outside, [and] you're going to be there for two or three hours, what do you do? Get the goddamn coat off and go to work. It worked. I didn't go home until it was running. If it was two days later, I was still there. There's no excuse. It's got to go. It has to run. And I want it running at 95 percent efficiency if it can get up there."

For all the screaming, Wemyss rarely fired people. "You didn't fire people to fire people," he explained. "You knew their families and their kids. You can't do that." Herb Miles maintained that Wemyss rehired most of the hourly workers he fired: "He'd fire more bosses. Jim Wemyss told me himself: 'I can get those fellows a dime a dozen.'" Bill Baird said: "He had a temper. If you crossed [him], he was just as apt to fire you, as not. But he expected you in the next morning to go to work at seven." Iris Baird added: "The first time he fired you, somebody said, 'Don't pay any attention. He'll have forgotten by morning.'"

John Rich recalled a man who was fired for oversleeping: "He was on call. They'd call him. 'Yup, be right in. Be right in.' He never show up. Jimmy got sick of it. He had him canned, and a year later he hired him back, and he give him a garbage can and one of them big old alarm clocks with the bells on top. 'You put that goddamned clock in that garbage can, and you set it. That ought to wake your ass up and get you out of bed in the morning.' I think Jimmy was fair."

Union contracts forbid the mill from firing an hourly worker without going through the union grievance process. Office workers did not enjoy those union protections. "I didn't really know him well," said Pam Styles, who was hired in 1970. "When he was there, I was really, really young. Shirley MacDow was the office manager, so we had dealings with her. Everyone kind of tiptoed around him. I know she bent over backwards to do what [she] could to help him."

"I don't think I walked on eggshells, but I kind of understood where he was coming from," MacDow told me. "I wouldn't challenge him in any way. People would feel like they were walking on eggshells because if he made a decision, or if he walked through the mill and saw something he didn't like, the shit would hit the fan." Characteristically, Wemyss embraced the eggshells image: "If they had something they weren't doing right, they had good reason to walk on eggshells."

In the 1980s and 1990s, Greg Cloutier and Jim Wemyss were notorious for their shouting matches. But Cloutier remained because he admired the older man's commitment to the mill: "You'll find a lot of business people are very strong and powerful people, and the underlings won't stand up and protect them from themselves. Mr. Wemyss would say [something like], 'I expect you to protect me from myself. You've got to do what I ask you, but if it's wrong, don't do it. Tell me what's wrong with it.' He always wanted respect and loyalty. If you did that, you were 80 percent there." Cloutier pointed out that Wemyss liked foremen who argued with him, adding that they remained union members who were protected by union grievance rules, whereas once they were promoted to supervisor, they became management and no longer enjoyed those protections.

Mickey King's father was promoted to tour boss, but despite the welcome pay raise, he soon quit because he refused to scream and holler at his former crewmates. He told his son: "I will not blame my help for things that they did not do. I can't do this." Mickey described Wemyss as a kind of tragic figure: "Jim is a strange fellow. Just a difficult, difficult person. He surrounded himself with lackeys. He always had people who, 'What can I do? What can I do? Do you want a drink? Do you want a drink?' He loved it, and he would belittle them. They were people who were bosses in the mill. People who contracted with him for certain things. He couldn't help himself; he loved belittling people. You'd see a moment of kindness once in a while from him, and you'd say, 'Wow, that's different.' Then he'd go right back to his —. It's always been sad, but that was Jim. If you really stood up to him, he would kind of respect that. If you didn't, he'd insult you right in front of your face. His father was the same."

Bill Astle described a complicated man who often succumbed to the temptations of power: "He was always considered very authoritarian and perhaps more involved in some people's lives than they deserved to have him. My perception is he always looked out for what he believed was the best interest of the town. There were times when Jimmy could be a cruel man. He could belittle people. There were people that were hired and fired five times as a boss because he'd fire them and chew them out and humiliate them publicly in front of all of the people that were working for them, and then Jimmy seemed to get a little bit of levity about that, and then he'd come back the next day and say he hadn't meant that. I think a lot of that was to demonstrate the dynamic of power that he had. One of his expressions was, 'Employees are just like a can of coke. Go over to the machine, you put your money in, you press a button, and another one comes out.' I think he was a fairly complex man. He absolutely wasn't all bad, but ownership meant he could do anything he wanted when he was in his heyday. There really was no check. I suspect he learned many of those attributes from his father."

Because of his dominant role in the town over the course of half a century, even his admirers vented from time to time. "We used to bitch about him, but he kept us working," electrician Len Fournier observed. Francis Roby declared in his characteristically terse way: "Jimmy, he was just the boss. I worked for him. He made the paycheck out. That's all."

Wemyss promoted locals to management positions whenever he could: "Half our management came out of the union. I can't think of all the names of all the men that came in here as young boys out of high school and [became] head of the electrical department or head of the labs or running the paper machines and the pulp mills. When they got up in the thirties and forties, and they had a heckuva lot of knowledge, I'd say, 'Want to try it?' 'Mr. Wemyss, I don't have a college education.' 'You've got a college education; you've got one here.' It's always better to bring them up through the ranks. The quickest way to destroy the morale is to say, 'Gee, I've been here twenty years, and I always wanted to be the head of this department, and look at that, he brought somebody in.' You give him a chance first. You say, 'You want to try it? You think you can do it?' 'Yes.' 'Go. You got it.' It has a great morale boost to the people."

This policy contributed to a much more flexible relationship between union and management. Wemyss recalled a visit to the mill by Leonard Pierce, president of Berlin's paper mill, who wished to observe Groveton's high-speed toilet paper winder. Wemyss introduced him to Jim Doolin, superintendent of the finishing room. While they were talking, as Wemyss recounted, "All of a sudden, Mr. Doolin said, 'Excuse me, sir, I'll be right with you.' He turned away, yanked the adjustable wrench out of his pocket, loosened one of the folding plates on the seventeen-inch napkin machine, and moved the plate a little bit, which you do every so often. Leonard said to me, 'What did he just do?' 'I think he adjusted that folding plate on that napkin machine.' 'What did you say his job was here?' 'He's superintendent.' 'We can't do that in Berlin. [The union would] shut the whole place down.' I said, 'They won't shut it down here. I would adjust it if I felt like it.'"

During a public interview, Wemyss suggested another reason for promoting locals: "The best possible thing you could do was get a good man out of the union and put him in charge of the department. And shortly thereafter he says, [*in an exaggerated voice*] 'Those goddamned union bastards . . .'" The audience of former mill workers roared with laughter, but it was a great insight. Lolly LaPointe was promoted to day supervisor in stock preparation after nearly twenty years as a union member: "In my heart, I was a union man, I guess. Personnel problems really got to me. Towards the end of it, all these young kids they were hiring, I don't think that any of them had ever worked a day in their lives. They were great kids until they got in the union. You'd ask them to do something: 'That ain't my job.' I guess I was from a different generation. You was lucky to have a job."

Despite the bullying and tantrums, Wemyss really cared about his adopted community. Shortly after his election to selectman, he learned the town swimming pool was too run-down to use: "One day I saw a little kid walking out toward my home. He had a tube over his shoulder, and I said, 'Where are you going?' 'I'm going to go swimming in the river.' I said, 'No, you're not. You're too little to do that. Why don't you go in the swimming pool?' 'The swimming pool's broke.' I went down to the mill and said, 'Nobody goes to bed until the swimming pool in Groveton is fixed. Put new toilets in, put new stainless steel valves, pumps, fill it up with water, chlorinate it. Nobody goes to bed. These are your kids that swim there, and I don't want one to drown. Do it!' And they did. I think we spent between $25,000 and $30,000 before we got through, getting that thing right. It never should have gotten down like that."

As a boy, Dave Atkinson witnessed Jim Wemyss's tough love: "My dad worked for Paper Board in the office. I think he was very good at what he did. But he had, at times, a pretty serious drinking problem. It got to the point where it was affecting his work. I can remember Jimmy coming to our house and saying, 'Anne, we're going to get this guy some help. Thomas, you're going to Founders' Hall over in St. Johnsbury.' I was twelve; it would be mid-to-late '70s. 'Tom, I don't give a shit what you have to say. You're drunk right now.' And I think my father was. I think it was during the noon hour, probably in the summer. That's why I was home. 'You're going now, and that's it. If you don't, then don't bother coming back to work. You've got a family here; you've got a wife that loves you; you've got kids that are crying.' It was quite a scene, as I remember. Off he went. I think it was thirty days. It helped my dad; he relapsed and had all those type things. But it was certainly something that I remember about Jimmy. He ruled with an iron fist, but he had a heart for those he wanted to have a heart for. For whatever reason, he had a heart for my dad."

At a time when there were few if any female executives in the paper industry, self-proclaimed male chauvinist Jim Wemyss promoted Shirley MacDow to vice president of Diamond International. MacDow had graduated from high school at age seventeen in 1951. She immediately went to work at the mill as a clerk, earning seventy-two cents an hour, at a time when the minimum wage for women in the union was eighty-five cents. She never attended college or earned an MBA, although she took some correspondence courses over the years.

Wemyss recalled giving her more and more responsibility in the early years. "Shirley was schooled something like me. I said, 'Do it.' Well, how do I?' [Raises voice] 'Do it!' Then I'd kind of watch her. If you give people confidence, they do well. The day I made her a vice president, she walked into my office and started asking me some questions. I said, 'What the hell are you asking me for? Do it!' She said, 'I might make a mistake.' I said, 'Join the club. I've made a lot of them' [laughs]. That's the only way you learn." MacDow said her gruff boss never second-guessed her: "I can never remember him saying, 'Why did you do that?' Or, 'How come you made that decision?'"

"I guess something within me was determined that I was going to be not just an invoice clerk," MacDow reflected. "I wanted to do more than that. If there was an opportunity within the office, I did it; I took whatever job there was next. I wanted to be involved in everything. So I kept pushing away." What made him decide to promote you? "I guess it was because I was doing those things and actually without any recognition until somebody said, 'Who's in charge of the office here?' and all of a sudden, I'm the office manager; I'm the sales manager and whatever else you want to call me. Just sort of materialized. It wasn't easy, but I have to say, bottom line, that I did enjoy it, or I wouldn't have put up with a lot of the tough times when the men didn't want any part of me, didn't want to listen to anything I had to say, even if it was a good idea. I had to work through it. It was tough."

Several male managers resisted taking orders from a woman. "I had to work probably twice as hard to establish the fact that if I made a decision, it was the right one," MacDow said. "I didn't just willy-nilly say, 'This is the way it's going to be.' I had to really work at, 'What should we do here, and how should we make this work?' Because I was the female that was being watched, targeted. Over the years it got better, but it never got totally better even until after I retired. Boy, those first twenty years or so, wow!"

MacDow described herself as "a very detail person." To defend against the hostility of some male subordinates, she said, "I always kept notes of everything on the decision that I made. I wrote who I checked it with. It saved my neck a lot of times because they always were accusing me of doing something that didn't make any sense, just to get back at me because I was a female."

On one occasion a male manager stormed into Wemyss's office to demand he fire MacDow: "He lit into Mr. Wemyss. I'm standing there because I knew you don't light into Mr. Wemyss, and I thought he was going to throw him bodily out the door. Well, he didn't last much longer after that [*laughs*]. No one ever said to Mr. Wemyss, 'You will do this or do that.' He was the boss."

One of MacDow's most important jobs was "gatekeeper" for Jim Wemyss. "I made sure that people calling in, if it was somebody that I thought he should talk to, they could. [Otherwise], I just took care of it, or sloughed it off. I think any good right-hand person would do what I did as far as handling the life of the CEO." Her job was to assure that his time was used efficiently: "Don't bother us with piddling things." For her efforts, she earned some nicknames. "You were known as the Dragon Lady," Jim Wemyss teased. "Other words, too," she replied. "Not quite so nice."

She recalled her maternity leave in 1969: "I worked up until I had to go to [the medical center in] Hanover because I had some problems. Then I was back home in about five or six days. They brought my typewriter to the house. I had probably only another week at home, and then I went back to work. When I walked in the door, Mr. Wemyss was standing there with a bunch of papers in his hands. I thought he was there to say, 'Welcome back.' Instead, he said, 'These need to be typed up today.' Maternity leave — what's that? [*laughs*]."

Did Jim Wemyss ever say "good job" to Shirley MacDow? "As far as 'good job,' forget it. No kudos. No, no, no, no. no. Not ever, never, to this day. Well, maybe the last two or three years [*laughs*]." *Was his way of saying "Good job" to give you greater responsibilities?* "Yeah. Now that's probably the bottom line right there. He would just heap on more, not that I didn't absorb it, because I never backed away from anything."

AT THE CONCLUSION of our public interview in 2011, Wemyss, then eighty-five, said: "All you people, I always considered you — whether you believe it or not — were part of my family. The greatest joy I had was driving around here on a school day and seeing the playground full of kids screaming and running, and going around Sunday and seeing you people fighting to get into your churches, and saying, 'That's a good thing. That's a good thing.'"

Chapter Twelve

THE WORST YEARS

"SINCE THE ANNOUNCEMENT there has been a lot of concern about what exactly will take place. Please try not to get upset over this change. James River has a good record in their previous takeovers and they are capable of recognizing a well-run operation. We have nothing to be concerned over," mill manager Jack Hiltz wrote in the *Papermaker* shortly after the May 10, 1983, announcement that James River Corporation of Richmond, Virginia, intended to buy the Groveton mill.[1] Goldsmith would retain Diamond's timberlands, and for the first time since the early 1890s, the Groveton mill owned no timberland.

Founded in 1969, James River had grown spectacularly throughout the 1970s. JR acquired scores of struggling paper mills via "friendly takeovers." Its rapid growth and unconventional strategy for operating without large timberland holdings inspired *Bradstreet's Business Month* to rate it one of the five best-managed companies in the United States in December 1983.[2] James River touted employee involvement in running the mill and boasted of good relations with unions. However, after each takeover, JR usually fired many of the executives of the swallowed corporations and pressured unions for concessions.[3] In August 1983, James River and Local 61 reached a two-year contract with a 6 percent raise the first year and a 5.5 percent raise the second year. A three-year contract in 1985 gave annual raises of 3, 4, and 4 percent.[4]

Vice President Terry Brubaker from James River's Richmond headquarters informed *Democrat* reporter Peter Riviere that JR's local managers enjoyed considerable autonomy. As part of the new owner's corporate strategy to integrate operations between its many mills, Groveton began to acquire hardwood pulp from the Berlin pulp mill. Groveton also continued to purchase more expensive Old Town pulp that was only 30 percent hardwood.

Groveton Paper Board signed an operating agreement with James River whereby it paid JR a monthly fee to cover the wages and salaries of the JR employees working on Paper Board jobs. This monthly payment also covered mill overhead, energy costs, and other shared expenses, as well as James River's management fee. Jim Wemyss claimed that two Paper Board directors went behind his back to sign the management agreement: "I think someone from James River said, 'We're going to fire Wemyss, and you'd better talk to us because we've got control of all the management here.' They didn't have control of anything."

James River acquired the Campbell stationery and envelope operations when it bought Diamond's Paper Division. "It started going downhill a year or so [later]," Sandy White remembered. "We were told that that wasn't going to happen. They can tell you anything they want. They never come right out and tell you anything. They just let you find out a little at a time. People started getting laid off. Machines started going down. People started bouncing around. You get the message. I hung in until I actually got laid off. I knew then it was for good. It had been touchy for a good year before that."

James River viewed Campbell as a nonstrategic asset, and in April 1985 it transferred Campbell's Customer Service Department to North Stratford.[5] Two months later JR sold Campbell to Ampad, a large stationery company headquartered in Holyoke, Massachusetts.[6] Ampad claimed it planned to maintain current operations, but soon it laid off fifty to sixty workers in an attempt to "adjust our inventories downward."[7] Late in December 1985, Ampad moved Campbell Pads to Holyoke, reducing employment by fifteen to twenty jobs. In six months Ampad had cut Campbell employment in half.[8] Mead Corporation bought Ampad in 1987 and sold it three years later to Bain Capital, headed by future presidential nominee Mitt Romney. On January 10, 1992, Campbell Envelope, reduced to thirty employees, was shut down by Bain. A belated employee buyout attempt fizzled.[9]

"James River ruined Campbell Stationery," Jim Wemyss fumed. "That was a blue-eyed gem. That little plant we had up in North Stratford had the most modern machinery for that type of work in the world. You had a workforce up there which were good, dedicated people. It was very disgusting what happened there." With the sale of Campbell's and divorce of James River and Groveton Paper Board, the mill no longer offered as diverse a product line as it had under the Wemyss family.

Former mill workers' attitudes toward the new owner varied. "I think if they hadn't a come in we'da been done," Dave Miles said. "I thought that things weren't going quite that well. And when they took over I just thought, 'Well, we've got a new life.'"

Ted Caouette was always focused on production, and he felt that the arrival of James River made the mill a better and safer place to work: "The management would talk to you. The other way around was pretty autocratic. You just did your job and didn't say too much. When James River came, now you had to work safely. [JR] put guards everywhere that a person may get hit by a piece of machinery. A paper machine is a million turning parts, so there's always a chance of bumping into something if you're just daydreaming. So they would put guards to keep fingers, hands, arms away from the turning parts. That was a major difference for us."

Many workers welcomed the end of old-school management. "The guy who took her over used to come up and tell you what was wrong right off the bat. He didn't give you hell or nothing," Armand Dube, a machine tender on Number 4, pointed out. "Jimmy was a hard guy to work with because he used to give you hell all the time. Then, of course, he'd get you nervous. When you get nervous, you don't give a shit."

John Rich was grateful that James River significantly improved the pension plan at the mill. Lolly LaPointe thought JR treated its employees well, but wastefully: "They run seminars and schools all over hell. All you had to do was apply. They might have one six months from now coming to Berlin, but the next one happened to be in Seattle, Washington. You went to Seattle. They didn't wait. They were just free with their money. I don't wonder they went down."

James River was notorious for requiring its workers attend meetings on teamwork and cooperation. Sandy White was one of scores of workers who loathed the endless rounds of meetings: "What they basically were trying to teach you is what everybody knows after they've gotten out of the eighth grade — work well together. Standard common sense. The biggest waste of money I ever heard of. If it was on shift, they'd hire somebody to come in and pay them overtime so you could go to these seminars or meetings. There were different times I damn near fell asleep at these meetings."

Not long after James River arrived, Bill Astle was promoted to supervisor of shipping. He thought JR often focused on hackneyed, feel-good incentives instead of efficient production: "A lot of it was just the flavor of the month:

What's management doing these days? It was 'risk taking.' 'If you're not taking a risk, you're not doing your job well.' Somehow that even got contorted to where you got an 'attaboy' if you screwed something up because that meant you were taking a risk. It really seemed a little perverse, to my thinking. Gee, I don't think that's the way risk taking was intended."

"James River had its problems, but when it came to how it treated women, I think they did a really, really good job," said Louise Caouette, who was hired by JR in 1988. "If you could do the job, you could do the job. If you couldn't, you couldn't, and it didn't make any difference whether you were a man or a woman."

The 1972 Equal Employment Opportunity Act had opened the door to women bidding onto paper machine crews. Tough times and the increasing threat of layoffs in the mid-1980s forced a few women to tackle the quintessential "man's job" in the mill. In 1984 Sandy White left Campbell Stationery because of layoffs and low seniority. She was not allowed to count her time worked at Campbell's for seniority and bumping rights in Groveton. Consigned to the mill's labor pool and always facing the threat of layoffs, she was desperate: "I was just trying to stay working. If I'm not working, I'm pretty unhappy and pretty worried. You take what comes along. I begged. I've got to do something; I've got to work. The supervisor out there was a friend of mine, Bill Paradis. A real nice guy. I said, 'Put me out there, put me out there.' He said, 'Andy you don't want to be on those machines; trust me.' 'I gotta work. I gotta work.' He said, 'I'll try it, but that's no place for you girls.' So, he let me go."

She promised her crew she would remain only until she could bid onto another job: "I told them, 'I'm here because I don't have any choice if I want to work. If I don't do something right, tell me. Let me know; don't baby me. I promise you I'll get the hell out of here the first chance I get.' And that's exactly what happened."

Her first day on Number 4? "Oh, my God. You can't describe it. Terror [*laughs*]. 'What is wrong with my head? Why don't I just take a couple of days off and say "forget it" and hope something comes along?' I got to thinking, 'You're on your own; you've got a family to support. Get off your ass. It can't be worse than some of [the jobs] you've been through.' I found out it could be. It was hard work. As long as the machines are running good, everything is really nice. You know what to do, when to do it. But if something goes wrong on those things, oh, my God, it's unbelievable the trouble you can get into, and the danger. I didn't sleep a few nights when I first went out there. And dragging my butt when I came home. But the guys went through it too. There were days on that machine when it would just about kill you, even a good strong, rugged guy. I've always felt that's no place for a woman. I really have. I've always been a super-strong woman. But there are jobs that women just are not made for. There's a difference; don't let anybody tell you any different [*laughs*]."

Ted Caouette, a tour boss, supported the women who worked on paper machines even though he felt it was unfair to ask them to do such difficult work: "I have nothing against women. Nothing. I didn't think it was a job for a woman because it's too darn hard. It's a very physical job. You have to put a wet felt or a dryer felt on a paper machine, it's a difficult task, but these women did it."

A few years later, Sandy Mason bid onto Number 3 paper machine. She described her reception: "There was one crew that was very male testosterone crew, and that was B crew. If you walked out to train on their crew, you knew you were in trouble because they laid it right out for you. I had one guy in specific — he's not alive now, he died of cancer. He told me, 'You're not welcome out here. Women are only good for one thing and one thing only.' I said, 'You want to pay my bills, I'll leave.' He said, 'I'm not gonna do that.' I said, 'Well, then I guess I'll stay.' That's the way we left it. When I got done the first time, that crew wished I hadn't left. They all loved me except for him. Ted Caouette at the time was the head of the paper machines, and I went to him, and I said, 'I don't want to make waves out here.' He said, 'Don't sign off the bid because we really like what you're doing.' I said, 'Try not to put me on that crew.' They would try not to, but if somebody would call in sick, they would call me up, and I'd go right in. Towards the end he [the hostile B-crew member] got so he'd just tolerate me. I grow on you [*laughs*]. I always left him to himself. I would never sit in the break room with them. They always had another table outside, and that's where I would sit. When you go into a man's profession and a man's job, you don't try to win them over overnight because it's not going to work. You just take your time, do your job the best you can, and show them that you can do it too. They're pretty adaptable."

B crew's chief, Joe Berube, supported Mason. "I know who that guy was because she told me about it," Berube later said. "I said, 'Anytime these guys give you any problem, you come see me.' I had a rough crew. Those guys didn't get along with much of anybody. I knew that they were going to give her a hard time. It weren't just that guy; my whole crew gave her a hard time." Web Barnett, president of the union, recalled it took six months to a year to stop chauvinism on the paper machines: "Even the paper machines, when [women would] go on there, they [the men] were stinkers. It usually was a certain few that would bring it on. The girls did well. They'd do the job. Their hands would be bleeding and everything else. We stopped that shit after a while."

Sandy White and Sandy Mason earned the respect of the men they worked with because they combined a strong work ethic with sensitivity for the feelings of their fellow crew members. "My father always taught all his kids good work ethics. Do the best job you can with what you're doing," White said. "I found if you don't go on a job thinking you know it all after five minutes time, you ask questions. Everybody I've ever worked with has been great. I never met anybody down there that I couldn't find something that I liked about them."

White described the different approaches men and women take to difficult and dangerous jobs: "Women have a way of figuring out things to make it easier. A guy will just go ahead and do a job. 'That's what you've got to do, go do it.' I'll think to myself, 'How the hell can I do that a little bit easier?' That's the difference. Sometimes there is no easy way; you just have to do it." *There weren't instances where you could use your feminine wiles to —* She interrupted me, laughing: "I wouldn't even think of trying it. No way. No, you don't do that, if you're smart."

Based on her time working with both men and women, White observed: "You watch your back with a bunch of women. Women have a tendency to cut each other up. The bigger the group, the bigger the cut. When you work with a bunch of guys, if you do your job right, you don't have any trouble; you don't get the backbiting. Men are right up front. If you're doing something they don't like, they're damn well going to tell you. Sometimes it's a nice way, sometimes it isn't. But you're going to know where you stand. Women will go around this side; they'll go around that side; they'll go over; they'll go under; they'll take forever to get a message across. Sometimes it's nice; sometimes it isn't. There's a lot more competition, I think, when women are working together."

Sandy Mason was sensitive to the changes men were being forced to make when women joined their crews: "Back in the '70s and '80s, they felt that they were making a home for their family, and you were coming in and taking your job away from them because you've got the seniority. They get kind of nose out of joint. You have to work harder to prove yourself. When I first started for James River, there were some guys [that] did not want to see a woman out there. I had some guys that once I proved myself, they would ask for me for their crew because I'm a worker. I don't stop going. But you just have to prove yourself."

As time passed, the women blended into the crew. "When you work on the same crew, you get to know each person's way of doing things so you can pick up where they left off," Sandy Mason explained. "I worked with Larry Breault, Larry Davenport, Steve Colby for a long, long time. We knew when one person needed what they needed. If somebody come in not feeling good one day, you knew you'd have to pick up this load, and they'd help you the next day. It was just like clockwork, a nice oiled machine. We worked really good together."

Eventually, the pranks began. Crew members put holes in her soda can so it drooled on her when she drank from it, and she was occasionally sprayed accidentally on purpose by someone washing the machine. "When they did that to me, too, I felt I was part of the crew," she laughed.

In May 1986, JR had again doubled in size when it took over the paper division of Crown Zellerbach, another hostile takeover victim of Sir James Goldsmith. Doubling a large corporation overnight, however, incurred massive debt. Between 1984 and 1988, James River shareholders' earnings fell from 26 percent to 10.7 percent as soaring costs for pulp also ate into JR's profits.

Northern New England's paper industry had by then entered a period of decline. The Fortune 500 corporations began to redirect major investment to newer, larger, faster paper mills, especially in the Southeast. Employment at New England's older, smaller mills had grown steadily until the late 1960s. After two decades of no growth, mill employment began to decline after 1985. Advances in mechanization and automation replaced many of the labor-intensive jobs formerly performed by bull gangs.

Because of its growing debt, James River did not have the capital necessary to invest in modernizing its many, old, noncompetitive mills. Bill Astle, head of the shipping department, explained: "It struck me that Halsey and Williams [heads of James River] were the masters of the art of the deal. They went in and bought up paper mills at pennies on the dollar valuation, and then their stock just went crazy, and so they'd go buy another one, and they were very successful until they'd done that too many times to double the size of the company again. Finally they got big enough that the growth strategy wasn't going to work anymore, so then they decided, 'Now we have to find those [synergies], to bring mills together in groups,' and all of a sudden, rather than a sales force just for the mill in Groveton, it's a sales force for James River printing and writing, and it's out in Oakland, California.

"They didn't seem to have enormous abilities to run the business. The buying and schmoozing with Wall Street — they understood how to make that work. We went from that fear [of Wemyss] to you didn't have to worry about anything. There seemed to be this lack of accountability. There wasn't the sense of urgency around everything. It was the start of the dog-and-pony-show era where every month all the departments would come, and they would show charts and graphs and the folks with the company seemed more impressed with 'Oh, you've got colored graphs, great.' As opposed to 'Gee, what happened to production?' That didn't seem to be where their concern was. They were more interested in the process than results."

By 1987 the position of general manager of the Groveton mill became a revolving door. Managers lasted only a year or so before moving on. Greg Cloutier asserted: "There isn't a single mill that's successful unless the mill manager has a passion for the facility." "Who was sitting in the corner office in Groveton? [Managers would] come, and it was just part of building a résumé to move on to someplace," Bill Astle lamented. "Their concern really wasn't about Groveton."

He added that the strong bond between labor and management deteriorated under James River. During the Wemyss regime, managers and supervisors were expected to reside in Groveton. "That got lost when James River came in," Astle said. "It had reached the point where the only people that were still in Groveton seemed to be the hourly folks that had always lived there. I would say the majority of upper management didn't live in town anymore. And, consequently, the relationship between the mill and the town was not really relevant to them."

"Mr. Wemyss's view of the mill at that time was that it had become [James

River's] turkey farm," Pete Cardin recalled. "Every big corporation has a turkey farm someplace. That's where they send all their turkeys. That's what this had become."

The Dow Jones Industrial Average lost 508 points on October 19, 1987, and thereafter James River would operate in the red. Resident mill manager Bill Sleeper reported early in 1988 that Groveton was "far from meeting the corporate financial objectives of a 25 percent ROA [return on assets]." Sleeper expected fiscal year 1989 to be another year of "very careful cost control," with the goal of reducing operating and material costs, particularly energy expenditures, which then were $14.8 million a year. A few months later, Sleeper emphasized the need to move away from commodity xerographic paper grades.[10]

Between 1988 and 1992 the United States paper industry largely converted from acid-based paper to the production of alkaline paper, using precipitated calcium carbonate — crystals grown under controlled conditions that did not possess the abrasive qualities of ground calcium carbonate.[11] Early in 1989 JR decided to follow suit in hopes of saving $2 million annually. Local boy Dave Atkinson had been hired in May 1986 following graduation from the University of New Hampshire. In January 1989 he was placed in charge of the alkaline conversion.

To convert to a calcium carbonate slurry, the mill had to install more powerful pumps, and the gauges on the machine that scanned the sheet had to be able to read calcium carbonate instead of clay. The sizing system had to be converted from alum and rosin to acetone ketone dimer, a base. Once the engineering and chemistry changes were completed, paper machine crews had to gain a feel for the new process. Ted Caouette remembered: "It was still a learning process how to refine it, how to adjust the water on the table — the drawers between the wire and the first press, how much stretch you'd want there, how tight you'd want to put it. It seemed to be a more tender sheet; the acid was more forgiving. Just things like that, you had to learn."

The first trials were conducted on Number 6 paper machine in May 1989. For the next year there were frustrating setbacks, including problems with Number 3's colors and Number 6's wet end draw, reel building, and ridges. The finishing room encountered problems in slitting and edge register. By May 1990 the conversion had succeeded.[12]

Paper demand declined dramatically early in 1989, and the mill had to sell some products at below cost. By November, the mill had lost $1.9 million in the first ten months of the year; again management called for greater cost savings. New resident mill manager Jim Bailey arrived early in 1990. He conceded he had been warned that morale in the mill was low.[13] That spring JR announced it had suffered a 13.1 percent decline in income in the past year, and investment was down 16 percent.

As the Groveton mill struggled to compete against newer, larger, and faster paper machines in the low-priced commodity market, James River accounting practices made Groveton's mill appear to be even less profitable. Bill Astle explained: "Who do you want to look good? Who do you want to look bad? Groveton had no pulp mill then, so it was all purchased pulp from other JR mills. James River could price that pulp at whatever they wanted to, and that's what [Groveton] paid. If you went out on the market, maybe you could buy it cheaper than that and improve your numbers." Astle suggested Jim Wemyss had probably played similar tricks in the Diamond years, but to the advantage of Groveton's bottom line: "I'm fairly confident that Groveton always looked the best of that whole [Diamond] group because it was Jimmy's mill."

Pete Cardin blamed "corporate burden." "So much of your profit has to go to corporate headquarters to cover their costs," he said. "It was huge, $10 [million], $12 million a year, and we couldn't call it profit. It went right to Richmond as corporate burden. It was an expense right off the top. They were taking money and not putting money back in the mill. Any business person that had a head on their shoulders could see that."

Ted Caouette added: "They stopped spending capital. Once you stop making your equipment better, and you stay status quo, your quality is not getting any better. If you had a problem, you had to put in some new equipment because people expected better paper. The machine tender and the tour boss and all those, you can't perform a miracle."

On August 16, 1990, James River announced a major corporate restructuring plan that included the sale or closing of thirty of its less profitable, or "nonstrategic," paper mills. Groveton and the former Brown Company mills in Berlin and Gorham were for sale. Rumors swirled that the Groveton mill would be shut down any day. Even in the best of times, most people lived paycheck to paycheck. Morale in the community and in the mill plunged to new depths.

James River executive James Matheson acknowledged that the August 16 announcement "marks the beginning of a challenging new period for all of us. Being for sale but not sold, uncertain of the intentions of a new owner, concerned over the reaction of our customers, and apprehensive about our personal futures, we ask ourselves, 'what can we do now?'" The answer, he suggested, was clear: "focus on the job at hand, and develop an unprecedented commitment to show just how good we can be."[14] Pete Cardin glumly observed, "It was a dynamic, evolving mill up until James River, and then it was a dying mill."

The week James River hung a "for sale" sign on the mill, a wildly hopeful rumor swept through the community: Jimmy Wemyss would come riding to the rescue and buy back the mill. Wemyss, nearing age sixty-five, cryptically responded that this notion was "food for thought." He vowed that Groveton Paper Board would remain in business.[15]

That fall, officials from Domtar, ITT-Rayoneer, and a mysterious group of unnamed private investors toured the Groveton and Berlin-Gorham mills. The local press provided upbeat reports of each visit and later dolefully noted that none of the potential buyers had followed up on its visit. JR headquarters admitted shutdown was a possibility. Mill manager Jim Bailey insisted the mill would remain open but conceded "the shadow that still remains over the mill is the status of future ownership."[16]

Jim Wemyss had no inclination to buy back the mill, but as prospects for Groveton's survival grew increasingly bleak, he began to search for a buyer to keep the mill running. He contacted his friend Arnie Nemirow, CEO of Wausau Paper Mills Company, a small fine and specialty papers corporation headquartered in Wausau, Wisconsin: "I flew out to Chicago and met Arnie Nemirow and told him he ought to come in there. I said, 'We never really wanted you in the East Coast, but I can introduce you to all the customers you can have. You make similar grades to what we do.' He said, 'I'll think about it.'"

Wausau executives toured the Groveton mill on January 23, 1991. That day the *Coös County Democrat*'s page-one headline read: "One Week Layoff at JR Hits 125." Blaming "seasonal slowdowns, the shifting economy, and full warehouses," James River announced a weeklong "curtailment" of its two fine-papers machines, along with associated finishing, shipping, and maintenance operations. Additional cutbacks on the fine-papers machines were announced in February and April, when two hundred workers were laid off.[17] Wausau thought JR's asking price was excessive and did not make an offer.

To minimize layoffs, James River cut most workers' hours to four days a week. Louise Caouette recalled an unsettling encounter with one employee: "We were trying to balance out the hours so that everybody kept working, even if it might be fewer hours. I actually had a father who came to me and said, 'I don't care if my son doesn't get his forty hours; I'm entitled because that's my machine and my shift, to get forty-four hours.'" Sandy Mason kept getting laid off because she could not count her fifteen years of employment at Campbell's toward her seniority status in Groveton. Her bosses told her they expected the mill to shut down. She took a job at Weeks Memorial Hospital in Lancaster.

By June 1991, James River had found buyers for twenty-two of the thirty mills it was trying to sell, but the three northern New Hampshire mills remained on the market. JR intensified its cost cutting at Groveton by imposing a wage and hiring freeze on both labor and management. "James River had a whole passel of these real small mills that looked like old Number 1 and Number 2 paper machines," Bill Astle, supervisor of shipping, remembered. "Groveton's were state of the art by comparison. There was a guy who was the head of marketing, named Bob Cochrane, who said, 'If I could have this mill, I could make a lot of money by putting all the premium grades on there.' Politically, it didn't happen. And so, Groveton was essentially forced into making this low-end commodity grade of paper."

Late in the summer, James River and leaders of Local 61 began to negotiate a new contract to replace the three-year agreement set to expire on September 1, 1991. JR demanded a wage freeze and that the union accept "flexibility" in the mill's maintenance department. Murray Rogers, later president of Local 61, became involved in union politics at this time because, as a younger worker, he saw benefits in the "flex" proposal. "I could see that we were being held up by having strict trades," he said. "They would contract people in to do the work because they didn't want to fight with us. I was a pipe fitter, and I wanted to be able to weld. Other people in the other trades wanted the flex because of the fact that you would stand there for hours and wait for somebody." Rogers understood that flexibility offered younger maintenance workers a better hope of finding high-paying jobs if the mill failed: "If the mill did go down, I'd be a heck of a lot more marketable if I could pipe fit and weld. You've always

$1.75

Jordan Associates, P.O. Box 283, Colebrook, N.H. 03576

COÖS MAGAZINE

James Wemyss of Groveton Paper Board:
'No Matter What-- We're Here To Stay'

GROVETON PAPER
BOARD INC.

RECEIVING
DOCK

Regardless of what happens to Groveton's James River mill, Groveton Paper Board will continue, says James C. Wemyss.

The cover of *Coös Magazine*'s November 1991 issue that contained
the notorious interview with Jim Wemyss announcing that Groveton
Paper Board "was here to stay." (Courtesy Charlie and Donna Jordan)

got to think about what's going to happen on the next step. There were mills
being shut down all over the country."

In October, James River made its "final offer," a one-year extension that
maintained current wage levels and imposed flexibility. Following its leaders'
recommendations, mill workers voted 274–40 to reject JR's offer. Local 61
president Web Barnett said there were some "glaring issues that we don't agree
on."[18] The union chose not to strike because it realized JR would probably
shut down the mill. "It was a tense time, confrontational," Murray Rogers
recalled. "They weren't negotiating with us, and we ended up working under
an old contract." Eventually, James River forced the union to make concessions — or else. "Nobody wants to give up anything," Rogers said. "That's the
way unions work."

In October 1991, with the local rumor mill working overtime, Wemyss agreed to a rare interview with Donna Jordan, publisher of *Coös Magazine*. He told her the mill faced its greatest crisis and blamed JR for the mill's "deterioration." Jordan asked what was going on with James River. "I don't know," he replied. "They don't talk to me and I don't talk to them about business." Wemyss added that Paper Board had received "little or no management" from JR despite the management agreement. Wearing a cap with a logo reading "Groveton Paper Board" and "Love" on it, Wemyss was emphatic about Groveton Paper Board's future: "No matter what — we're here to stay."[19]

When Jordan's article hit the newsstand, relations between the two mills broke down completely. "James River fired me because they were trying to get at Mr. Wemyss," Shirley MacDow said. "What's it got to do with me? They figured if they fired me, they could make him toe the line. James River wanted him to do things a certain way. And that didn't work, so they went after me. It was not a nice time. I went over to his [Wemyss's] house, and I said, 'I've just been fired.' 'Huh?' He called the board of directors, 'Put Shirley on the payroll.' And so, it was immediate."

Pete Cardin said he and his fellow Paper Board workers "didn't understand the relationship between Groveton Paper Board and JR." As relations between JR and Wemyss worsened, Cardin recalled, Paper Board workers remained confident they would have a job: "It was very nerve-racking in some ways, but we always had this sense that even though we were part of James River, we're somehow protected because Mr. Wemyss would always come along. He's a funny guy; he would always push [James River] a little bit to see if they had any balls, so to speak. Most companies probably would have told him to stay out of the mill, but they didn't seem to. He'd come in the mill, and he'd rabble-rouse and say, 'Don't worry boys, I'm going to take care of you.' By doing that, he would give us a sense of, 'We're OK because Mr. Wemyss is here.' Towards the end, it was obvious that James River was really, really struggling. Mr. Wemyss was in the mill quite often, and I think he was trying to give the whole mill some sense that there was some hope here."

Bill Astle thought Wemyss encouraged Paper Board workers to scoff at JR: "I'm sure Jimmy kind of instilled it in the people — they were James River employees, but they were running Paper Board machines. And they kind of took it upon themselves, 'Hey, we can do whatever we damn well want; James

River can't tell us what to do.' And then there would be the issue of everything done on allocation. Everybody was using the same steam plant; everybody is using the same maintenance group. And how will you allocate the [wastewater] treatment plant? So the Paper Board would always come back, 'You're screwing us; you're screwing us.' So it became certainly a bone of contention."

Jim Wemyss Sr. died on November 24, 1991, at age eighty-eight. He had not been intimately involved in the operation of the mill for decades; however, he deserved credit for reviving and diversifying a rat-infested, moribund operation during the dozen or so years when he dominated every aspect of life at the mill.

On December 15, 1991, James River shut down Number 3 and Number 4 paper machines and laid off one hundred employees. A week later, another 250 employees were out of work, and Number 6 went down as well. Workers could draw on their 1992 vacation time to help them through the gloomy holidays. Others applied for unemployment insurance.[20] Most of the laid-off workers returned to work in early January, but on January 10, Number 6 paper machine shut down for a month, and when it restarted, only 25 of 110 laid-off workers were called back to work.[21]

Unexpectedly, in mid-February, James River announced its corporate restructuring had been completed, and the Groveton, Berlin, and Gorham mills were no longer for sale. But more bad news followed. In May, twenty-six union and twelve nonunion jobs were eliminated.[22]

Many younger mill workers faced the question: "Should I stay or should I go?" Tom Bushey had been working full time for only a couple of years. Even though he decided to stay, he could see that James River was starving the mill: "That was a really tough time. I was making good money, but you always had that dark cloud over your head, and you had to be careful about personal finances because no one really knew where we were headed. James River not giving any money for capital improvements to resolve problems that were causing financial losses month after month after month. They were so crazy about saving money. They would have all these meetings to sit down and talk about ways to improve the plant and whatever. If you couldn't figure out how to go out there and do it without any money, you never did it. After two and a half years of this, it was just screaming that we needed money."

Dave Atkinson had been promoted to superintendent of Number 6 paper machine in 1990. By early 1992, he wondered: "Was it going to survive? That was prevalent throughout the organization. It was an awful way to work. It was not a fun environment." He began receiving calls from executive recruiters. Initially, he wasn't interested in changing jobs and leaving his hometown. Eventually, he "took the bait": "It was for a product development chemist position at Rhinelander Paper Company, which was owned by Wausau Paper Company. I said, 'Sounds interesting, send me some more information.' I ended up going out for an interview and taking the job. That was absolutely gut-wrenching." With two young children, he felt he "had to be ahead of the pack getting out." The move turned out to be "the best thing I ever did."

NORTH COUNTRY ROCKED BY DIAMOND LAND SALE

Sir James Goldsmith held on to the Diamond lands until the stock market crash in late 1987, when his French-based holding company, Générale Occidentale, quietly offered them for sale. The proposed sale of Diamond's one million acres in the northeastern United States shocked the timber and conservation communities of Maine, Vermont, and especially New Hampshire. Ever since the 1890s, Wall Street investors had demanded that large paper companies, such as International Paper and Great Northern, acquire vast timberland holdings to assure an adequate supply of wood fiber for their mills. Throughout the twentieth century, paper companies had viewed their timberlands as "strategic reserves" that played a dual role of ensuring their mills a reliable supply of pulpwood while controlling the price paid to nonindustrial landowners for pulpwood. Before Goldsmith, paper companies did not worry if they managed their timberlands at a net loss, provided there was abundant, affordable pulp for their mills. Papermaking was where the profits lay. After Goldsmith, timberlands had to become "profit centers" or be sold off to avoid a hostile takeover.

Diamond owned sixty-seven thousand acres in northern New Hampshire and another twenty-three thousand in Vermont's Northeast Kingdom. Timber industry leaders, conservationists, and politicians in the two states worried that the selling price, $19 million, or $212 an acre, was nearly double the going rate for large parcels of timberland. They feared only a developer would be willing to pay such a steep price. Henry Swan, president of Wagner

Woodlands in Lyme, New Hampshire, performed due diligence for a possible purchase of the New Hampshire and Vermont lands. To his chagrin, his foresters concluded that the Nash Stream had been so severely overcut that it was worth only $100 an acre as a timber investment.

State political and conservation leaders claimed there was insufficient public funding to acquire the Diamond lands in New Hampshire and Vermont. At the end of May, an obscure Nashua developer, Rancourt Associates, stunned everyone by acquiring these lands. Within two weeks, U.S. senator Warren Rudman of New Hampshire and Paul Bofinger, president-forester of the Society for the Protection of New Hampshire Forests, brokered a deal with Rancourt. The public acquired roughly forty-six thousand acres from Rancourt for $282 an acre — a nifty $70 per acre publicly financed profit for a few weeks' ownership. Nearly $4 million of the $12.75 million purchase price came from the U.S. government. The state established a forty-thousand-acre Nash Stream State Forest; the U.S. Forest Service would own a conservation easement on the state forest.

Bofinger and Rudman, along with U.S. senator Patrick Leahy of Vermont and Carl Reidel, the dean of Vermont conservationists in the 1980s, were terrified that the Diamond land sale was the first of a series of paper company land sales that could transform the character and economy of the region. They secured an additional $250,000 from the U.S. Forest Service budget to fund a four-state study of the so-called "Northern Forest" region. Congress directed the Northern Forest Lands Study (NFLS) to assess the future of the vast undeveloped forests of northern Maine, New Hampshire, Vermont, and New York's Adirondack Park and Tug Hill region. The greater Groveton region was in the heart of the study area.

The commissioner of conservation in the state of Maine, Robert LaBonta, fearing that the NFLS would be a federal stalking horse to wrest control of central and northern Maine's forests from private and corporate owners, threatened to keep Maine out of the NFLS process. To appease LaBonta, Senators Leahy and Rudman wrote a "Letter of Clarification" to the chief of the United States Forest Service on October 4, 1988. The key part of the letter read: "The current land ownership and management patterns have served the people and forests of the region well. We are seeking reinforcement rather than replacement of the patterns of ownership and use that have characterized these lands."[23] Although the intent of the NFLS was to search for a menu of economic, ecological, and political strategies to protect the region's forests and economy, LaBonta's threat effectively gave the Maine delegation to the NFLS, dominated by the chief lobbyist of the Maine Forest Products Council, veto power over the work of the NFLS. He and LaBonta's successor would block any meaningful examination of the condition of the region's forests and the habitat needs of rare, threatened, and endangered species such as wolves, lynx, and cougars. They also kept the Northern Forest Lands Study from conducting an in-depth analysis of the economic weaknesses of a region that relied almost exclusively on the declining paper industry.

The Northern Forest Lands Study, released in the spring of 1990, dealt a blow to those hoping to salvage the status quo. It warned: "The forces and conditions that have given us the Northern Forest of today can no longer insure its perpetuation." "One of the most important challenges will be to convince those within the region that some kind of change is inevitable. Without intervention a series of incremental actions is likely to permanently alter the landscape and lifestyle of this region. Ignoring the problem will not make it go away."[24]

The NFLS recommended that its work continue under the auspices of a Northern Forest Lands Council (NFLC) for another four years. Most council members shared the timber industry's belief that the NFLC's mission was to prop up the status quo. They sought to promote a favorable business climate via lowered property, capital gains, and estate taxes. The council agreed to operate by consensus. Timber industry representatives were not bashful about exercising their "right" to block consensus on any subject they opposed.

The council delegated its work on the timber economy to the "Local Forest Based Economy" (LFBE) subcommittee. The LFBE needed to ask tough questions, such as: Is the region's economy healthy? How competitive are our paper mills with mills in the Southeast and the tropics? How well has the region developed its local value-added manufacturing potential? Are citizens, communities, and schools prospering? How secure are paper mill jobs? Are loggers earning a fair wage? What is the condition of the industrial forest? Will current forest practices promote economic prosperity for timber communities? It asked none of these questions during its three-year existence.

Instead, the LFBE commissioned a study designed to offer strategies for more fully plugging the Northern Forest into the global economy. Mitch Lansky, author of *Beyond the Beauty Strip*, a *tour de farce* critique of the myths of industrial forestry, submitted a series of questions to the committee: Who benefits from globalism? Who pays the costs? What are the impacts of the global economy on local economies, environment, labor force, and land ownership patterns? What opportunities exist for the Northern Forest region to buffer itself from the adverse impacts of the global system? And, if we are assessing globalism, should we not study the likely ecological and economic impacts of global climate change on the region? Those questions were of no interest to the committee.

The council issued its final report in the fall of 1994 and disbanded. Two weeks later, Scott Paper sold its Maine mills and 930,000 acres of timberland to a South African paper company, SAPPI. Throughout the following decade, seven million acres of timberland owned by paper companies in 1988 were sold at least once. Most of these lands changed owners two, three, even four times via hostile takeover, merger, sale of mills, or divestiture of a mill's lands. The new owners were mostly wealthy timber investors, endowments, and hedge funds. Several of these speculators resold the former paper company lands within five or ten years after another round of intensive cutting to defray the purchase price.

Public policy failed the communities of northern New England at a time when it was abundantly clear the dominant industry was in deep trouble. When northern New England paper mills began closing early in the twenty-first century, affected communities and political and economic leaders were unprepared for the magnitude of the collapse of the twentieth-century status quo.

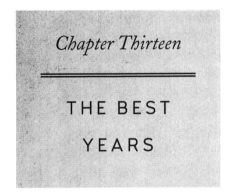

Chapter Thirteen

THE BEST YEARS

WAUSAU WAS A LEAN and hungry company looking to expand. Wausau's executives had very much liked the Groveton mill when they visited in January 1991. With the proper investment, they believed, Numbers 3 and 6 paper machines could produce the colored, premium fine papers Wausau specialized in, and Groveton could give the midwestern firm an entrée into lucrative eastern markets. Wausau's Rhinelander, Wisconsin, mill produced pressure-sensitive labeling, packaging papers, and technical papers. Its mill at Brokaw, Wisconsin, turned out specialty printing and writing papers, 65 percent of which were colored papers. The Brokaw mill was running at full capacity and could not keep up with orders. Early in 1992, Wausau's board of directors had authorized CEO Arnold Nemirow to spend $100 million on a new paper machine and related mill expansions for Brokaw.

Around that time, a senior vice president of James River contacted Nemirow and told him the Groveton mill was on the verge of shutting down. He urged Wausau, Groveton's best customer, to take a second look. Jim Wemyss had also renewed his courtship of Wausau: "I went out and saw [Nemirow] again and said, 'They're getting worse by the hour. It's terrible.' They were going to junk the mill practically. Shut it down. He flew in and met them, and then I took him out to my house for lunch, and I said, 'You've got to move, now.' And I guess he did."

Dave Atkinson had started work at the Rhinelander mill on June 1, 1992. In August of that year, as he recalled, Arnie Nemirow telephoned him: "He said, 'Dave, I'm calling to see if you would be interested in being on the due diligence team. We're looking at the mill in Groveton, New Hampshire. I understand that you used to work there.' Of course I was a nervous wreck; the CEO's calling. I said, 'I only started here two months ago. I'll have to check with my boss.' 'Don't worry, Dave. I've already talked with them; they know I'm talking with you.' I don't think I even knew then what due diligence meant. I said, 'Yes, I would be interested in that.' My contribution was knowing an awful lot about machines, the people, the culture, the capabilities of the operation. I wasn't involved in 'What are they going to pay?' Just 'What is it capable of?' Wausau was pretty much a regional supplier — Chicago, Minneapolis, St. Louis, Denver, and wanted to repeat what was successful for them in the East. That was the reason they bought Groveton."

In October, James River cut the running time for its two fine-papers machines to five days a week, and it laid off one of the four paper machine crews, calling it a "temporary layoff" of twenty employees. The following week, another nineteen workers were laid off for at least a week as Number 6 paper machine shut down.[1]

The due diligence team, led by Wausau vice president Tom Howatt, concluded the Groveton mill was a good buy for Wausau. On October 28, Wausau Paper Mills Company announced it was buying the fine-papers operation at Groveton for $20.2 million, one-fifth the amount authorized for a new paper machine for Brokaw. Wausau would own no timberland and would continue to purchase pulp from Berlin, Old Town, and other mills. Groveton gave Wausau twice the mill capacity of its planned expansion, and the $80 million in savings allowed Wausau to invest heavily in Groveton. The editors of *PaperAge* were so impressed with the transaction that they hailed the deal as the "buy of the decade" and named Arnold Nemirow 1993 paper industry "executive of the year."[2] *PaperAge* was especially awed by the maintenance of the Groveton mill. "Even the windows on the hooded dryers were sparkling clean," editor and publisher Jack O'Brien later marveled. "Have you ever seen that in a mill? Unbelievable maintenance."[3]

According to Cecil Tisdale, Wausau appeared in the nick of time: "My supervisor told me when we were talking about Wausau going to buy the place, 'Now I can tell you. I couldn't before. If Wausau hadn't bought this place, in two weeks the doors would have been shut.' James River was going to shut it down."

The due diligence team morphed into a transition team. During the transition period Wausau executives observed the bad blood between James River and Groveton Paper Board. Pete Cardin recalled: "This one particular manager for Groveton Paper Board — I won't say his name — would walk up to other [JR] managers and tell them flat out, right in front of everybody: 'When we take over, you're gone.' When it didn't turn out that way, those same [JR] people had influence in the Wausau organization. I don't think that was forgotten. Very bad behavior on our part, to have somebody in there like that."

Greg Cloutier believed the transition period allowed some JR managers to avenge past humiliations. "There was one accountant [who] was very bitter about Mr. Wemyss because he got fingered a couple of times, probably unjustly — profit-loss numbers. He was also a guy that Mr. Wemyss had used a little bit to play the cost-allocation game between James River and Groveton Paper Board. I think Mr. Wemyss didn't realize this, but he had kind of baited this guy to go to Wausau and say, 'You are not getting a fair deal.' I think that started the process of being totally separate."

Wausau's transition team had neither the time nor the patience to mediate this family feud. "When James River left," Pete Cardin said, "their advice was, 'Don't get in bed with Groveton Paper Board.' That's what I heard." Wausau insisted on separate corporations with separate offices. Eventually Wausau painted lines of demarcation on the floor of the mill defining where Paper Board employees could and could not venture.

Wausau informed nonunion employees, primarily office personnel and management, they no longer had jobs. Pam Styles recalled: "Everyone was let go, and then they rehired the ones they wanted. They just said, 'The company ended; that's it. You're done working for this company.' We all had to put in résumés. They pretty much hired back most of the same people in their same positions. I think they probably started them at about the same pay that they were making."

Tom Bushey remembered: "You've got the whole drama of whether or not you're actually going to have a job with Wausau because Wausau didn't want anything to do with running Groveton Paper Board, and they also wanted to sift the wheat from the chaff when it came to the managerial team. It didn't take too long for a few people to be showed the door, permanently, right out of the building. Wausau came in and offered jobs to the ones that they wanted to keep."

The due diligence team had devised the mandatory resignation policy. "It was possibly driven," Atkinson speculated, "by the fact that when Wausau came in, they knew they were only going to run one [fine-papers] machine, and you don't need the same staffing level to run one machine as you do two."

Two decades later, Ted Caouette, then superintendent of the paper machines, remembered the period with bitterness: "Wausau, in my opinion, did not do a very good job coming in, particularly to the salaried people. They never told you whether you were going to get hired or not. They said, 'Unless you get a letter in the mail' such and such a date before they took over, 'you're not hired.' This went on for, if I remember right, a few months. That was no fun. Everybody was worried. And then finally get the letter and there it has your salary and it was the very same it was before, and what your title is going to be, and 'Welcome.' That was, for me, too little too late because they'd already done a bad deed by not telling us, and that stuck with me through the time that I worked there, actually. It was hard on those people, and I'm sure, hard on their families. Some of them didn't get hired. [Wausau] came in with a bang, and they went out with a bang."

James River shut down Number 4 paper machine during the transition period, squelching some of the euphoria over the mill's future. Many blamed Wausau for failing to try to buy Number 4. Dave Atkinson demurred: "James River didn't sell it." James River was shedding its fine-papers business so it could concentrate on tissue making. "If they sold it," Atkinson added, "it would have been a machine that would be competing against them. In some of my discussions with Jimmy [Wemyss], even in the good years of Wausau, [*in a funny voice*] 'Why did you guys let that tissue machine go? Arnie Nemirow, if he'd been a better negotiator, he woulda gotten that machine.' But Wausau at the time had no tissue at all. It wasn't something that they knew, understood. So they didn't want it either."

Murray Rogers, the last president of Local 61, had long shared Wemyss's frustration over the demise of Number 4 and the scores of lost jobs. When informed that James River had not initially offered Number 4 to Wausau, he was surprised: "Really? OK, so we thought it was Wausau not wanting anything to do with it."

It had been a traumatic decade for the mill's labor force. In 1984, a year after James River acquired the Groveton mill, there were approximately 800 employees at the Groveton mill and Campbell Stationery's North Stratford converting plant. Nine years later, Wausau acquired a mill with 360 employees. Groveton Paper Board, now an independent corporation, employed about 140. Some 300 out of 800 mill jobs had disappeared. Campbell's, with its roughly 200 jobs, was defunct. Approximately 100 jobs had been eliminated because of the shutdown of Number 4 paper machine and the accompanying reduction in jobs in the tissue finishing room and maintenance.

It was clear that employment levels would never again approach the Wemyss and early James River eras. Bill Astle observed: "[Under Wemyss] it was a case of if you were from Groveton, you always had a job at the mill. By the time James River came it wasn't nearly as much so. And with Wausau Papers, they could care less where you came from, it was what you brought for skills."

Before it would sign the final purchase agreement, Wausau insisted on negotiating a four-year contract with Local 61. The union was forced to bargain from a position of weakness. In addition to heavy job losses, the union's finances were in shambles in the aftermath of an embezzlement scandal. It could no longer pay for arbitration cases or train its officers. It was forced to discontinue a popular tradition of giving each member an Easter ham, and it could no longer contribute to local charities or sponsor scholarships.[4]

Wausau labor negotiators were accustomed to bruising contract talks with their Wisconsin locals. Dave Atkinson recalled they were "pleasantly surprised" by Local 61's "huge, huge sense of cooperation and all-pull-on-the-rope-in-the-same-direction" attitude. Local 61, still operating under the contract that had expired in September 1991, was eager to save the mill, while recovering some of the concessions made in the final James River years. Wausau understood the union's weakness. "I can recollect some conversations, saying: 'Well, they've just been through six or eight really tough years with James River, and we are, maybe, one of their last hopes, so it's no wonder they're being friendly and cooperative,'" Atkinson said. "But [the Groveton union] would have been anyway. I knew that; [Wausau] probably didn't. The union-management relationship that exists in Groveton is much different from what they had seen at Rhinelander and Brokaw."

After an intensive week of negotiations, Tom Howatt and Local 61 hammered out a four-year deal that granted no pay increases for two years, followed by raises of 3 and 2 percent in the final two years. Web Barnett said the negotiations "went very well. It was hard negotiating; there were a lot of issues to cover." In March, the rank and file voted 211–43 to accept the tough deal. Barnett, who would shortly retire, said: "I think there are mixed feelings, but at least we know we have a company that will stay with us."[5]

Groveton Paper Mill Maximum Hourly Wages, 1946–2006, and Purchasing Power in 2006 Dollars

- - - Top union wage ——— 2006 purchasing power

The chart above shows real wages for the mill's highest-paid union job —
paper machine tender (dotted line) and the purchasing power of wages from
1946 to 2006, expressed in 2006 dollars, using the Department of Labor's
Consumer Price Index (solid line). A machine tender received $1.27 an hour
in 1946 and $20.09 in 2006. In 1946, $1.27 had the purchasing power equivalent to $13.13 in 2006.

Gains in purchasing power were modest under Jim Wemyss Sr. They were
steadily higher under Jim Jr. from 1953 to 1968. Under Diamond (1968–1982),
with Jim Jr. at the helm, purchasing power also increased steadily, except
during the two oil crises of the 1970s. Purchasing power continued to rise
under James River from 1983 to 1987 but fell sharply the last five years under
JR, especially after JR forced concessions on the union in 1991. Wausau's first
contract kept purchasing power depressed from 1993 to 1997. Thereafter, purchasing power increased, but never again reached the heights of the Diamond
and early James River years.

Howatt's transition team moved to New Hampshire late that winter to begin the mill's makeover. Wausau assumed formal ownership of the Groveton paper mill on April 1, 1993. "What's amazing," Atkinson later observed, "is that on March 31, 1993, we were owned by James River and unprofitable. One month later, with the same equipment, we turned a profit."[6] The first years under Wausau were "the best years," Atkinson recalled. "The first time in my career it was high energy. The management team that Wausau had was much leaner than the traditional paper mill. Those were long days — fulfilling days." Wausau astutely promoted Atkinson to paper mill manager. The mill community was delighted that a well-regarded hometown boy was slated to play an important role in the new regime.

"I still remember Tom Howatt walking into the conference room for the morning meeting and just strutting in like he was finishing a race," Bill Astle recalled. "He was all business. He was a shrewd negotiator; he allowed Wausau to buy that mill for a song. He got all kinds of concessions, and clearly he was the sharpest guy in the room in the negotiations. I remember what a breath of fresh air it was after the lackadaisical days of James River and kind of floating in and out. Basically in the first ten days, 'You've got to do this, this, this, and this. In the first thirty days, everyone here will do this, this, this, and this.' He even made the observation, 'Change that doesn't come within the first thirty days is very difficult to ever initiate, so make no mistake, things are going to change.'"

"Nobody could outwork Howatt," Astle asserted. "He toured the entire mill every day. He was on a bit of a dead run, but he took it all in. If he'd see something in shipping, he'd take the stairs three at a time, come up to the mezzanine where I was, 'Bill, what's all this over here? How do you deal with that? Do we need that here?' 'I don't know. I don't think so, Tom. It's always been there.' 'If we don't need it, get rid of it.' You knew he was paying attention, because if he came through the next day, and it was still there, he'd be three stairs at a time up, 'What is the reason that's still there?' So what it clearly imparted early on was this guy knows what's going on and makes note of it. By the same token, when everything was as it should be he recognized it, and you were given a leash."

The stresses during the transition from James River to Wausau were bearable because everyone could see that Wausau was pumping money into the long-neglected mill. In the first four years, Wausau spent $25 million fixing mill infrastructure and modernizing mill equipment, while simultaneously reconfiguring the mill's paper production, finishing, and shipping operations to achieve its East Coast marketing strategy.[7]

Tom Bushey, conditioned by James River's parsimony, was flabbergasted by the attitude of the new owner: "That mill goes from what I see as some very dark days of having no money, to you can't spend the money fast enough to get that place to where Tom Howatt wants it to be. I can remember going sheepishly to Tom one day asking him for a small amount of money to fix something that under the James River days would be just so taboo to ask for. He was like, 'Of course. And by the way, I want you to do this, this, and that. And make sure you put enough money in the CFR [capital funds request] to cover these other things.' So I put it all in. 'There you go; hurry up and get it done.' It was unbelievable. You thought $35,000, $40,000 was a lot of money, no — $150,000, $200,000, $300,000, $400,000. It was one project after another under his tenure. You couldn't get it done fast enough. And if the right way to do it is to spend another twenty grand, 'Do it; get it done right because we want this place looking good. We are committed to this place. This is going to be the East Coast producer for us.' Just staggering amounts of money."

Once Howatt chewed out the frugal engineer: "I remember getting hell from him about some work up in the distribution center. He wanted the place painted. We had spent what I thought was an enormous amount of money painting this thing. He got upset because we didn't take the time to go up and cut down a bunch of unused old conduit pipe that was up in the ceiling. We just spray-painted over it. We thought we were doing a good thing by trying to control costs. He looked up there and saw that. That didn't look showcase. That's not like something that you want to see in a magazine with his company name on it. 'Get up there and get that down.' Just mind-boggling. You couldn't write the projects quick enough. Write the justification, and hang on. We were spending [money] so fast, it wasn't funny."

Bill Astle agreed that Wausau spent freely, but he remembered Howatt telling a project engineer, "'Make sure you come in under budget, because if you don't, you have go before the board of directors. And I'll tell you what, it'll be your one and only chance to be in front of the board of directors because that will be the end of your career.'"

Veterans of the transition from James River to Wausau speak of exhilaration and exhaustion in the early Wausau years. Dave Atkinson said: "It was fun for me because all of the problems and opportunities that employees [identified], 'Hey, if we could replace the drive on this machine it would be so much better.' Or, 'If we could do this to that pump over there,' or 'If we could do this to the converting equipment.' All of those things that took money to do that prior owners didn't have and weren't willing to invest. Wausau could see the return."

"At least in the initial years, Arnie Nemirow gave Tom Howatt complete control," Atkinson said. "We were so remote from headquarters that there was not a lot of control. Not a lot of approvals needed. In fact, Tom Howatt was, 'Don't take stupid risks,' but it was an environment where risk taking was not frowned upon. It was rewarded. There's going to be failures, but for every one thing you tried that's a failure, if you had six successes, then keep going. Keep doing it."

Wausau began an $800,000 renovation of the shipping department warehouse before it took ownership of the mill because, as Arnold Nemirow expressed it, this project "put capital where our customer connects with us first."[8] The new owner installed a sophisticated computer program in the shipping department for locating, loading, and tracking each item. Shipping received the night's orders between 3 and 5 p.m., and the loaded trucks would be on the road by 9 or 10 p.m. for next morning delivery. The new shipping facilities were completed in late summer 1993.

Howatt was so impressed by the shipping department makeover that, at the end of the first year, Bill Astle received a large raise: "When Wausau Papers came, jeez, I think my salary doubled within the first year. It was because there were goals that were given to me, and if they were achieved, you were rewarded, and it didn't matter how cheap they could get you, the attitude was, if you're worth the money, we need to pay it."

Although delighted by the raise, Astle thought it represented one of the few times when the normally astute Howatt might have miscalculated: "I think they wrongly assumed that people in Groveton had options, because out in Wisconsin, within a fifty-mile radius there were probably six or seven mills. If you didn't feel you were getting a fair shake at one, you didn't need to sell your house and buy a new one, you just changed jobs. But I found them to be a breath of fresh air. The place seemed to be under control again."

In its first two years, Wausau spent around $2.5 million to computerize Groveton's color paper production system. It installed a large holding tank that mixed pulp and the desired dye mixture, computerization that allowed for more exact color mixing, and scanners at the dry ends of the paper machines that continually checked the color of paper taken up on the reel.

Dave Atkinson said the new color scanners dramatically speeded up production time and reduced waste: "This color scanner is reading: Is the paper blue enough? Is it green enough? Is it too red? Improving the paper mill so you could go from blue to green in fourteen minutes instead of seventy-two minutes that you're making waste. That's very costly. All those raw materials, all those things you're using — energy, steam, fiber, dyes — if you only make fourteen minutes worth rather than an hour and ten minutes worth, you've improved your cost effectiveness greatly. That's what color scanners did."

Lolly LaPointe, superintendent of the stock preparation department, oversaw the process of switching from dry, powdered dyes to all-liquid dyes: "When Wausau came, I think they done some great things with colors. Real deep, deep colors. Very, very top-quality stuff. They had a little niche for that stuff. When Halloween came around, you were doing all kinds of orange, black, and Christmas, your red, your green."

Groveton began producing Astrobrite colored papers on June 30, 1994. Atkinson noted proudly: "Tom Howatt said to me the most efficient, cost-effective, highest-quality producer of Wausau Papers text and cover Astrobrites was the Groveton mill. In fact, we had to mess up the formation, which is one of the measurements you do to make paper, because when we made 'Rocket Red,' it looked so much better than Brokaw's Rocket Red. Because the distribution centers got both, we needed to make ours look more like theirs. So we had to — I call it 'dumb it down' on a few grades."

When Wausau bought Groveton, it ran only the venerable Number 3 paper machine because it was more versatile and reliable than Number 6. Wausau renamed the eighty-five-year-old machine "Number 5" so as to avoid confusion with its Number 3 in Wisconsin. (This caused Groveton Paper Board to change the name of "Love in the Afternoon" from "Number 5" to "Number 1.") Joe Berube, a machine tender on old Number 3, marveled at the variety and quality of the paper he helped produce: "We made over five hundred grades of paper, which is the most grades of any paper mill in the world at that time. We made printing papers, writing papers, computer papers, advertising papers, index cover grade papers. In all different finishes. Over a hundred different colors probably. These real bright neon colors would pull your eyeballs right out of the sockets; they were so bright. They were used in advertising to get people's attention."

In the first eighteen months, Wausau operated Number 6 for only a month and a half. Atkinson said, "The runability of Number 6 paper machine was horrendous. Very challenging machine to keep the sheet threaded, to keep it running all the time. Tears and breaks. Any little upset on the machine's system, and there would be a break. The drive control was 1970s vintage." James River refused to upgrade it. In 1995, Wausau installed a new drive system for the Queen of Diamonds: "I think it was a two and a half million dollar capital expense. That made Number 6 as good a machine from runability and predictability standpoint as what Number 5 was in the last few years."

Ted Caouette appreciated Wausau's investment in production: "They were focused on making paper. 'What do we need to make better paper?' So now, you've got new equipment coming in. Everybody was, I think, tending to their job better because the focus was on production. I think [Dave Atkinson] did a very good job when he was managing the paper machines, but he was doing such a good job, they asked him to do a lot of other jobs, and the focus got lost in the shuffle. Not instantly, but over time. He still did a good job. He did a good job whatever he did."

Atkinson saw things differently. "We certainly grew in the early years — '93 to '95 or '96 — when I was truly paper production superintendent. That is when we developed tons of different grades and became much more efficient at doing it and really honed in on those things; but then we came to a point where the development work, learning to make the Wausau family grades, was done. Now it was a question of maintenance and some of the other things that needed to be worked on. I think that is when my responsibilities were broadened to overall production superintendent, so now all of a sudden I had finishing operations under me. [The production crews] were very good at what they did, and it was very easy to say, 'OK, I'm going to focus now on the finishing operations. That's where the efficiency gains need to be had. You guys are going to handle [production] well.' And they did. There was never a slip-back."

In July 1994, Wausau's president and CEO, Arnold Nemirow, resigned to take over Bowater, a much larger corporation that specialized in newsprint. During his four-year tenure, Wausau's income had increased 42 percent.[9] Late in 1994, Tom Howatt was promoted to vice president and general manager of Wausau's Printing and Papers division, and he returned to Wisconsin after less than two years in Groveton. Tom Craven, head of purchasing, succeeded Howatt.

Wausau was not happy with Groveton's wood chip boiler. In 1994 the company had conducted a three-month study on the feasibility of converting the mill's Number 1 boiler back to oil. At the time, wood chips were eighteen dollars a ton. The mill's appetite for chips pumped $3 or $4 million into the local economy, and according to timber industry estimates, 225 logging jobs depended in part or entirely upon supplying the mill with chips. The mill ceased using wood chips on April 29, 1997. The decision, made in Wisconsin, was based on the relatively low cost of oil at the time and the higher maintenance and capital costs required by a wood-chip-burning boiler.[10]

Portland Natural Gas Transmission announced plans in 1996 to construct a pipeline from western Alberta that would run by the mill on its way to Portland, Maine. Wausau signed a twenty-year agreement to purchase natural gas to power the mill. The conversion to natural gas at the mill was completed by September 1999. Initially, the mill paid $3.50 for a million Btu's (one dekatherm) of natural gas. Tom Craven characterized natural gas as a "cost competitive fuel alternative to oil."[11]

Jim Wemyss, one of the largest private timberland owners in New Hampshire, was infuriated by the switch from chips to oil to gas: "It was a beautiful wood-burning boiler. Then some geniuses got the idea to start burning gas because the gas line went through. I had nothing to do with that. I would never have allowed it. We're in the woods business. Let's stay with it."

Four years into the Wausau era, the mill was profitable and making some of Wausau's highest-quality paper. As the 1997 labor contract negotiations approached, union leaders were determined to reverse concessions they had made to James River and Wausau and share in the mill's profits. Wausau had just enjoyed record second-quarter shipments and earnings, and the union reminded Wausau of its 1993 pledge that if Groveton was profitable, "concessions would not be sought and future contract settlements would be competitive."[12]

Late in January 1997, the rank and file rejected Wausau's first offer by a vote of 263–63, even though union leadership had recommended acceptance. Union president Richard Goulet warned, "The plant is tense." Union members complained that workers at the Otis, Maine, plant, acquired by Wausau in February 1997, earned $16 per hour versus $12.49 in Groveton. The union argued that the disparity in wages paid in other mills would widen under Wausau's proposal, and it demanded an additional thirteen cents an hour increase for each of the five years covered by the contract.

Dave Atkinson explained Wausau's 1997 negotiating stance: "It isn't just wages, it's the overall operation of the mill. I can remember: 'How come they're making $2.50 more an hour than us? We're doing the same thing.' My response was, 'Hey, the cost of living is different. Look at what they're spending here.' I probably said to many employees: 'I hear you, but if you're expecting a $2.50 an hour increase, then you're going to be disappointed. That's why you negotiate.' He added that periodically "out-of-contract adjustments" were granted to some employees.

When I pointed out that Groveton was the lowest-paid paper mill in the country, he responded: "You know why? Each contract that got bought and sold was because of Jimmy [Wemyss]. It stayed that way for whatever reasons. I'm not knocking Jimmy at all, but the wage scale — the base started somewhere." The concessions to James River and Wausau had exacerbated those pay discrepancies. Nevertheless, the average weekly wage of Northumberland residents, $621, was significantly higher than that in any other neighboring town.[13]

In March, by a vote of 211–117, with 34 abstentions, the rank and file rejected a second Wausau offer that raised wages 16 percent over the duration of the five-year contract. The *Berlin Daily Sun* reported "a number of votes against the contract yesterday were voided because comments were written on the ballot."[14] Murray Rogers confirmed my suspicion that the comments had been obscenities.

A day later, the union voted 195–165 to go on strike, but since a strike vote required a two-thirds majority, the vote failed, and, by default, the contract was accepted. Union president Goulet bitterly complained: "The contract in no way was accepted by the workers. They have to accept it because it was shoved down their throats."[15]

In 1997, at the union's request, production workers, but not maintenance, finishing, or shipping employees, went on twelve-hour shifts that began at 7 a.m. and 7 p.m. Each of the four crews would work either three or four days consecutively, then be off for three, seven, one, and three days over the course of four weeks. Each crew would work seven days on the day shift, seven nights on the night shift, and enjoy a total of fourteen days off. Most younger workers liked the change. Joe Berube, a veteran of more than thirty years by then, grumbled, "That was another thing that was wished upon us." Some of the shift supervisors and tour bosses also resented the change because, as management, they had no say in the union vote for the twelve-hour shifts, but they were now required to work those longer shifts.

In February 1997, Wausau bought Otis Specialty Papers in Jay, Maine, for nearly three times what it had paid four years earlier for Groveton. Steve Schmitt, a vice president of Wausau, said, "We intend to grow through acquisition."[16] That December Wausau merged with Mosinee Paper Corporation, a firm that specialized in making tissue paper — an irony not lost on Grovetonians still smarting from the loss of Number 4 paper machine. The new corporation, Wausau-Mosinee, employed thirty-five hundred workers at nine facilities.

The debt incurred by these moves, combined with troubling trends in the paper industry, such as rising pulp and energy prices, low commodity paper prices, and mill closings and downsizings around the country, ended the free-spending days of Wausau's first four years in Groveton. The new mantra became "cut costs."

Early in 1998, Wausau announced one cost-cutting program — a generous early retirement buyout to employees age fifty-five and older. Dave Atkinson explained the corporation's rationale: "There needed to be a downsizing. Groveton was right-sized. Brokaw, Rhinelander, and the other [Wausau] mills were way overstaffed. Groveton was able to produce 330 tons a day on two paper machines with a paper machine crew size of five. Why do [other mills] have sixth hand, seventh hand, beater room helpers? The Wisconsin mills, I think, didn't really like the Groveton mill all that much. [Our workers] really were a high-performing work team."

A consultant proposed the "voluntary early retirement package" (VERP) that included severance pay, retirement and medical benefits, and a financial bridge until the retiree became eligible for Social Security. It would be paid as a lump sum that extinguished the employee's future pension claims against Wausau (but not against James River).[17] Some employees received $150,000–$200,000.

Labor law required that Wausau offer the early retirement package to workers at all its mills, not just its Wisconsin mills. The company expected half of those eligible to accept VERP. When 98 percent opted for retirement, Wausau fired the plan's authors and paid out a great deal more money than anticipated. All but two of the 104 eligible Groveton workers accepted the buyout. One of the men who declined had two or three ex-wives. "Why aren't you taking it?" Atkinson asked. "He said, 'Oh, Dave, I'd end up with none of it, so I'm going to keep working. They're going to have to wait for it.'"

The union reluctantly acquiesced to the buyout. "It was pretty much indicated that if they didn't get 'em from the upper age group, they were going to cut manning, and it would be in the bottom," Murray Rogers said. "Our take was: Let the older people go if they want to go. We're going to need the younger people to run this thing. You get an aging workforce, it's going to catch up to you. That buyout was a blessing for some because they were, I'd say, beyond their peak on ability and things of that nature, especially maintenance guys."

Initially, the buyout hurt Groveton. "It was a major mistake on Wausau's part," Ted Caouette asserted. "It was good for the guys who could retire and get out of the mill. But it was very difficult for years to come to get that experience back. Jobs weren't being automatically filled by experienced workers. After a while, it got better. For us, it was not a disaster, but it made everything very difficult." Customer complaints about poor-quality paper jumped in the fall of 1998 and remained very high for the next six months. February 2000 was the worst safety month in fifteen years.[18]

Atkinson acknowledged the mill suffered from the loss of experienced workers. But, he noted: "It created tremendous opportunities for some of the younger workers. I know that we recovered pretty quickly from it. [Younger workers] were open to trying newer things. You were a much quicker operation. More nimble, which you need to be."

The buyout was a good deal for the people who took it, but many of them invested in the stock market, and the 2007–2008 market crash hit them hard. Fred Shannon was one who lost his buyout money. When I reminded him in 2010 that the market was recovering, he replied: "It's too late for me."

Although Wausau had saved the Groveton mill, there was a dark side to Tom Howatt's dynamic leadership. Dave Atkinson called Howatt a wonderful mentor but conceded, "I never considered him a resident. He built a home in Littleton," a half-hour drive south of Groveton. Bill Astle said, "He was an upwardly mobile guy. He didn't want to end his career at Groveton. He was looking to be CEO."

During the transition period, Louise Caouette sensed the incoming management team — with the exception of Dave Atkinson — did not place a high value on community relations. She was especially troubled by Tom Howatt's attitude toward fraternization between management and labor at the mill: "One of the things that was told to me was, 'There won't be the socialization between the upper ranks and the lower ranks.' It challenged a lot of relationships. Everybody sort of bought on because everybody was glad to still have a job, [but] it was uncomfortable. It hurt relationships. In the mill, social things became strained." She added that after Howatt was promoted and returned to Wisconsin in late 1994, this policy was relaxed, but "by that point, a lot of damage from an emotional standpoint had already happened."

Chapter Fourteen

A BATTLE WE COULDN'T WIN

"IT WAS RATHER TRAUMATIC, to say the least," Shirley Mac-Dow said of the formal split-up of Wausau and Paper Board in 1993. "That mill was like Siamese twins. You had to decide, 'This pipe is yours, and this one is mine, but this one has both so we have to pay you 50 percent.' It was a tough show. There was a lot of antagonism because we were like the enemy, so to speak."

Pete Cardin welcomed the split: "Wausau had a strict focus. Paper Board wasn't part of that focus. When it happened, I said, 'We're going to have to fly on our own, and that's a good thing.' Of course, it's much more complex than that. We discovered that immediately by having to set up our own administration. This is where it started getting a little bitter. The sale had to go through at the same time that they negotiated the contract with the union, and the operating agreement with Groveton Paper Board was dissolved. So all of those things had to happen at exactly the same instant. It was very complex."

A surgical separation, however, was not possible. As long as the two separate companies shared the same mill complex, there would be, Cardin said, "bones of contention." "Wausau realizes that anything that we're involved with that they operate is going to be challenged because we operate on such a slim margin. We look at our budget item by item by item. Every month we'd sit down and go over it and say, 'What's the reason for this few extra thousand dollars?' If that seemed to be coming from something they were doing, we would challenge them. Nobody likes to be challenged in their management, especially in what they would consider petty. But for us, it wasn't petty."

Dave Atkinson thought the operating agreement Wausau inherited from JR "was very good for Groveton Paper Board." The new agreement negotiated with Wausau was not as favorable for Wemyss's outfit. "Wausau took the negotiation much more seriously than great, big, large James River Corporation," Atkinson explained. "I don't think [JR] paid much attention to the operating agreement, and therefore the Groveton Paper Board got a lot of costs not assigned to them that should have been probably. Wausau basically provided steam, electricity, maintenance services. The first operating agreement that Wausau negotiated with Groveton Paper Board made Groveton Paper Board's costs of manufacturing paper go up considerably. A lot of the things that they got for free, or weren't allocated properly, were allocated more properly by Wausau."

"There were times when we had great relations," Cardin remembered, "but when it came down to the operation of the mill, decisions were being made that would affect them and us both. Then the relationship would deteriorate."

The Groveton Paper Board Company operated only one paper machine, Love in the Afternoon, renamed "Number 1" to avoid confusion with old Number 3 that Wausau had renamed Number 5. Paper Board's machine crews, operators of the neutral sulfite semi-chemical mill, and stock prep crews became Paper Board employees. The two companies had always shared maintenance and utility workers. The 1993 separation required that those jobs be assigned to one company or the other.

Paper Board had to negotiate its first union contract before the official separation date of April 1, 1993. "Everything was going fairly well in the negotiations until it came to an issue regarding the folks that worked in the [wood] yard, the folks that were dealing with the chip pile, and the people that maintained the equipment out there," Cardin recalled. "During this negotiation, the union wanted those people as union employees. I could see it from their point of view, because knowing that this was going to be a separate union, they were going to have a very small bargaining unit, and they wanted to make their unit as big as they could. We took a pretty firm stance on that one. These were salaried employees, and we were not going to allow them to become unionized. It just went against the grain. It would be like allowing our office workers to become unionized. We were talking about probably a dozen jobs. These folks felt very strongly that they did not want to be in the union. They felt like they were being used as pawns here."

The union threatened to break off negotiations. Chicago-based lawyers for Jefferson Smurfit, at the time a large shareholder of Paper Board, wanted to call the union's bluff. Cardin remembered Jim Wemyss "was getting pretty emotional about this. He was saying that he has lived through strikes before; he does not want another strike in this town. It's just not worth it. The attorneys are telling him they cannot go on strike. They have no legal course to go on strike because first of all we don't even have to recognize them as a union."

The union negotiators knew that their bargaining leverage was limited because if everything fell apart, the company might shut down. "When we met again, the union said that there was only one person they could trust to negotiate for Groveton Paper Board, and that was Jimmy Wemyss," Cardin noted wryly. "The rest of us were untrustworthy. They didn't put it that kindly. Remember we have a dance going on here. And so, Mr. Wemyss enters the negotiations. The speeches were given and how he loved these folks and we're all family here. In the end, he gave in to the union and allowed those employees in the yard to become part of the collective bargaining unit. They felt like they had been betrayed. There were bitter feelings. But it did resolve the contract issue. After it was all done, we had a big dinner with the union, and I think we invited the yard employees, and everybody was best friends, and we all loved each other. Well, we [supervisors] were [still] despicable guys. But Mr. Wemyss was pretty heroic [laughs]."

As part of the separation agreement, Paper Board had to find office space outside the mill. In May 1993 Shirley MacDow negotiated the purchase of the Weeks Medical Center building in Groveton for Paper Board's new offices. This building, on the corner of Main Street and Mechanic Street leading into the mill, had once been the site of Everett's Diner.[1]

During the transition period, Tom Bushey declined a job offer from Paper Board and remained with Wausau: "The Board Company still retained that culture of almost terrorism of managerial style. The Board Company was very 1950s in their managerial style. Take two good guys and put them in a situation where they're going to become adversarial to one another. Whoever wins was the best guy of the two. If you ask me, that was bred with the Wemyss family, and then continued with different managers."

Jim Wemyss's daily involvement in Paper Board had diminished over the years, except during crises. Every day Wemyss would call Shirley MacDow or Greg Cloutier to learn Paper Board's daily tonnage; "444, and you can see me no more," he would tell them. "If they didn't make 444 tons that day, they had to answer to me if I was in Florida, if I was in Tanganyika. Every day I said, 'What's the number?' And if it was 398, 'What the hell — I'm on my way; I'm coming up.' 'Oh, Jesus, don't do that.'"

Wemyss spent more and more time in Florida. Even during the warmer seasons, when he returned to Groveton, he left the day-in, day-out running of the mill to his small, loyal group of managers. Cloutier believed that Wemyss had set up a management team that only Jim Wemyss could manage: "If you talked to most of these guys, I think you'll find they're all tough, potentially bullies, dynamic, dominant characters. They would cause chaos beyond belief and could never manage a company. Mr. Wemyss was somehow able to control these people who were exceptionally good in their skill set, but their personalities were borderline aggressive. We knew that when he called us all together, we were a team. He had that rare quality to be able to do it. There wasn't a good replacement. Maybe he didn't give it up soon enough. Like family businesses, the father's really got to turn it over early."

Wemyss had installed his son-in-law, Gene Petryk, as superintendent of the mill in the early 1990s. Initially, Petryk, a retired army captain and helicopter pilot, tried to run the mill as if it were a military operation. Greg Cloutier recalled that Petryk's demand "You will show me respect" failed to impress union workers who were governed by seniority, union-management grievance procedures, clearly defined job descriptions, and loyalty to Jim Wemyss.

After a while, Cloutier said, Petryk "realized that the best thing he could do was organize. He started using his helicopter maintenance training to lay out procedures, so when we attacked a problem, there was a little bit more of a structured [approach]. He realized that production increased when Mr. Wemyss wasn't meddling. Towards the end, I found [Petryk] to be pretty good. We must have come up at least a hundred tons [on the machine] before he left."

Cloutier questioned Petryk's savoir faire in dealing with his irrepressible father-in-law: "I remember the day [Gene] came, and it was like the third year, and they were going to build a new house, and we were all interested in how he was going to build it. He said, 'I got a nice piece of land. Beautiful.' 'Where?' 'Right next to my father-in-law's.' 'Are you stupid?' [laughs]. [Petryk] liked to come in around eight o'clock; he'd come in before that if we had trouble. [One morning] he looked all tired. 'Mr. Wemyss was mowing the lawn out in front of my house at six-thirty' [laughs]. Really, what he was trying to do was get Gene to get into work. That's the lawn mower trick."

In 1996 Petryk decided it was time to go to Paper Board's directors and propose it "retire" Jim Wemyss and promote him, Petryk, to president. It was, Cloutier judged, "a suicide mission," especially since Wemyss learned of the plan before the board met. Cloutier described the bloodbath: "Mr. Wemyss was the chair of the board. These were all loyal investors with thirty years. And then [Petryk] got drinking. He never drank at work, but once he got out of work, he'd have some pretty stiff drinks. His judgment was clouded. It was merciless. They just railroaded him out of town, basically. They didn't want you to carry out any trade secrets. A cardboard box. I could not believe that it was done that way. It was bloodshed. The comment I use was, 'Mr. Wemyss, people of that genetic makeup, eat their young if they have to.' And he did. It was terrible."

Shirley MacDow retired shortly thereafter. Pete Cardin recalled her retirement dinner: "That was a nice party they gave for Shirley. It was really first class. Shirley is probably the most loyal employee to that company, I think, that they ever had. Her number-one thing was that company, period. They can't complain about Shirley's performance — ever."

In the summer of 1998, Jim Wemyss finally retired. "I wanted to retire for five or six years," he said. "And Mr. [Ray] Duffy was one of the directors, and he was an officer in Jefferson Smurfit, and very friendly with Michael Smurfit and the whole family. They owned a section of the Board Company, and they had a lot of other paper mills. I said, 'Come on, Ray, you take it over. I don't want to do this any longer.' After that everything went to hell. Ray was a nice person, but he had no paper mill knowledge. I felt he could draw on the resources of Jefferson Smurfit's, and it just didn't work. I don't know what the hell happened. Replacing me with my ideas and way of doing things is — I don't think you can do it [chuckles]. Not that I'm that smart; it's just that I did things so much differently than anybody else."

Greg Cloutier offered a different perspective: "He was forced out. Part of it was me. He was seventy-one or seventy-two. Mr. Wemyss was not there, so we were struggling with day-to-day leadership needs. I'm in charge of operations, and really operations means how well the paper machine was running: the 444 sort of thing. We had come up from like 300 tons to 440 tons on this machine. I did not have the technical science that supported that next level of operations on the paper machine. Mr. Wemyss had that, and he's not around. It really required somebody that understood the science. When the crew made a change, everybody understood why they were making it.

Mr. Wemyss was very dynamic in being able to do that. Had he been there every day, he probably could have taught me how to do that. We got to a point where I said, 'Listen, you've gotta take him off my back. You've gotta let me try to do it my way or find somebody different.' Mr. Wemyss was never going to give it up. What we were basically saying was, 'Let us have our own meetings. Let us do our own problem solving,' and not have a person come in who may not have been involved for two days, and all of a sudden he comes in and says, 'Do all this.' We can't get him to listen to the fact that we've already done that. [Ray Duffy] asked Mr. Wemyss to step aside. That didn't go over well. There was clearly tension, and I felt pretty guilty that we had done that to him, but we probably did it too late.

"We had these ass-chewing, lecture meetings with Mr. Wemyss, and they would go on. The machine was struggling, and the guys were struggling. [Bruce Simonds] was a young guy who had good ideas about what to do, and we were tying his hands. He truly understood the science, and he read about it. He wanted to learn more about it — that rare individual that just loved it. It wasn't fair. You tried to tell [Wemyss], and he just would go off. It was his legacy. I think he was struggling with a lot of personal dynamics, having to turn it over to somebody else. Seeing that he didn't have the energy and the skill to take it to this next level. Part of it was that he just wasn't there every day."

"I just walked away from everything," Jim Wemyss Jr. said. "I didn't say I lost interest in the people of Groveton, but I had no more authority. The worst thing you can do is put somebody in your place and then try to micromanage it from there. Walk away. 'It's yours now.' No excuses. It's yours. You do it. That's the way it should be."

Jim Wemyss III succeeded his father as president of Groveton Paper Board, and Ray Duffy succeeded Wemyss as chairman of the board. Greg Cloutier did not miss Wemyss's meddling, but he did miss Wemyss's vast knowledge of how to produce paper. "Duffy really didn't bring anything to making the company more profitable," Cloutier said. "Monthly meetings he would sweep in for a day and leave. He went and played golf and never spent any more time really thinking about operations other than you're not doing what you're supposed to do. You need to go there and work the problem: 'What do you need? What are you missing? What are we not bringing to the table that I can use my contacts to help you with?' He didn't do any of that."

Pete Cardin offered a very different assessment. Duffy, he thought, was "very professional, super-professional." Cardin explained: "Whereas Mr. Wemyss was a production guy, Mr. Duffy was a financial guy. He really taught me an awful lot about business management. My business management skills were nothing. He really showed me how to read a P&L [profit and loss] statement and make decisions. He had great people skills. He was a top-notch politician. Great negotiator."

"Instead of just having goofball meetings, we'd actually have monthly, professional meetings," Cardin said. "The chairman of the board would come to Groveton and have a meeting with all of his managers, and we'd actually have an agenda that we would have to sit down, and we would have a time limit on our meetings, and each department would have to report, instead of having somebody rant and rave about something. If we didn't meet our production levels, our quality levels, instead of ranting and raving about it, 'Let's talk about why. Give me a reason why.' Very severe if you didn't meet it. He had these cold, blue eyes, 'Give me a rational reason why you didn't meet it, and how are we going to correct this problem?' He wasn't some pushover. He knew. That forced us to become better and better and better. Over the course of his chairmanship, we progressed a lot, and we improved dramatically as a business. We were very, very, very proud of ourselves for all the things that we did."

Greg Cloutier was struggling as head of operations. He had never run a paper machine, but as head engineer, he had supervised the machine's rebuilding: "We had changed so many things in the paper machine. By that time we had done the dryer section over. We'd done the drives over so we could go faster. We'd done the press over. We'd done part of the Fourdrinier over, so I may not have been a papermaker, but I had made the machine. I was kind of the chief mechanic for the operation. You glean a lot in the process, and what it needs to run, but you lose the finesse on how to handle fiber. That was a fairly steep learning curve."

During the summer of 1999, Cloutier remembered, the rewinder could not be made to work reliably: "We'd had a month of poor production. We'd all worked night and day for a month, so tempers were raw. The final blow was Ray Duffy had a friend [who] sold variable speed drives. We put that variable speed drive on the winder, and it just worked terrible."

On August 17, 1999, Greg and Rita Cloutier's wedding anniversary, Greg's frustration boiled over: "I basically told [Jim Wemyss III] to get f-ed, and you can't do that. We had worked every day, eight-, ten-, sixteen-hour days for thirty days, and we were not seeing the solution to this winder problem. Our production numbers were down, and we were shipping paper that was of low quality as well. It was a perfect storm from the point of view of a one-machine operation. We were doing everything wrong, and we really didn't have an answer. We were burned out. 'Shoot me. The disease has overtaken me. Put me out of my misery' [laughs]."

Cloutier, who had survived countless such blow-ups with the thick-skinned father, was fired on the spot by his boyhood chum. Oddly, Cloutier endorsed his own firing: "It wasn't a pleasant thing," he said. "But you can't be in that position and be disrespectful to the president of the company and the things he wants to have done. The interesting thing is my wife congratulated me. Because up to that time, I never had had a vacation. Every vacation I was working on my hydro plants." After his firing, Cloutier built up a successful hydropower company.

Production manager Pete Cardin explained how difficult it is to run a paper mill: "A paper mill is extremely capital intensive. It was heavy industry. You have to reinvest in this thing constantly, otherwise it's not going to make it. So your capital outlay is huge, just your operating capital, not necessarily your projects for nice-to-do process improvement or production increase. Our operating expenses were very high. Mind-boggling. It always blew me away how much money you'd have to spend to run a paper mill because it's such a corrosive environment; it's such a damaging environment that everything has to be replaced almost constantly. As a manager, you really have to be able to predict; predictive failure is where it's at, predictive maintenance. Because you've got to minimize your down time, and at the same time you've got to maximize your life on your equipment and your process. It's a fine line, and it takes a lot of experience to get there, to know how to do it, because you've got to be willing to push it. You'd like to play it safe, but that's not a luxury you have. You're under production pressure. You can't just take the thing down when you feel like it's time."

Entering the twenty-first century, Pete Cardin believed Paper Board's operation had never run better. Management and workers had lowered costs relentlessly: "The irony is we finally got this paper machine humming. We're putting out paper like you wouldn't believe; we're hitting production numbers that are just fantastic. Our up-time is really good; we're putting out a really good product. Lowering our costs. We're operating as efficiently as we possibly can run. Our fiber usage and our energy usage are as low as we can possibly make them."

"We were very proud of what we did to survive," Cardin reflected. "It was a constant battle, and, man, I'm telling you, we fought a lot of good fights, but in the end there was one battle we couldn't win, just couldn't win. In the end, it all came down to the fact that it's a commodity that we were producing, and the demand was disappearing, and so because it is a commodity, we had no control over the price. The price was collapsing because the demand for boxes was going away. There were a lot of people out there that could make it a lot cheaper than we could. The newer, bigger mills down South, overseas. Wider machines, faster machines, just more efficient machines." The decline in United States manufacturing during the 1980s and 1990s reduced demand for boxes. When Wal-Mart required its suppliers use shrink-wrap instead of cardboard boxes, prices for corrugated medium collapsed.

There was one other unwinnable battle: "The price of fuel up here just killed us," Cardin lamented. "Energy killed us." In 1999 Wausau had decided to build a co-generation plant for its Groveton plant, forcing Paper Board to construct its own co-gen plant. "I think they could have put the co-gen in and charged Groveton Paper Board a fair fee," Greg Cloutier said. "And I think the capital costs would have been allocated out."

From 2001 to 2005, the price of natural gas skyrocketed. "The thing with natural gas is just crazy," Cardin said. "When we first went on to natural gas, we could generate all our steam and electricity, and our fuel bill for the month at Groveton Paper Board was about $15,000. When we shut that mill down, that bill was about $100,000 a month. When we first put the turbines on line, we were using 5,000 dekatherms of gas per month. When we shut the thing down, we were using 4,200 dekatherms a month. We were making more paper for less gas."

In 2002, Box USA, headquartered in Northbrook, Illinois, bought Jefferson Smurfit's 28 percent interest in Groveton Paper Board, and Ray Duffy departed. Pete Cardin reflected: "We missed Mr. Duffy because Roger Stone [head of Box USA] was a numbers guy. Cold capitalism. This is very cold capitalism." Two years later, Stone sold Box USA to International Paper, the largest papermaking corporation in the world. Why, I asked Cardin, had Stone sold to IP? "Make a buck," he answered. "This guy knows how to make money. Unbelievable." Did Stone have any connection to the Groveton community? "Nothing," Cardin shot back.

Initially, Cardin was hopeful the new owner would revive the small company: "Their professional papermakers made a tour of the mill, and they said, 'You guys have potential here. We can help you. We can sink some money in this place. We can get more production out of this mill.' We felt pretty good. 'Finally somebody's going to spend money here; we're going to crank up our production; they might even put a new machine in here. Who knows?' I'm the kind of person that loves to hear positive news. I want to be optimistic about the future. I was fifty-six years old. I wanted to know that there was a few more years left in this place, and I really wanted to make it to retirement. Plus I really care about the people in Groveton."

International Paper did not invest in Paper Board. On July 19, 2005, corporate headquarters announced a $10 billion restructuring plan that included selling off or shutting down its higher-cost mills.[2] "We're a New England–based operation," Cardin said, "so if you're going to freight paper out of Groveton, you need to freight it to the New England, New York area, Canada. We were shipping paper to, in some cases, Arizona, the Midwest. There's no money in that. We knew every month as the numbers rolled in, we were losing money; they could not keep us running any longer. That final year the numbers were just getting worse every month."

Lack of orders shut down Paper Board for a week at the end of July 2005. Following Hurricane Katrina in late August, natural gas prices began to soar. On September 11, Paper Board shut down for two weeks. A few days later, International Paper, which by then owned 40 percent of Groveton Paper Board stock, hung a "For Sale" sign on the Paper Board mill.

Cardin's production staff had exhausted itself in cost-cutting and efficiency improvements: "Probably starting in the late summer, early fall of 2005, no matter what we did, it was heartbreaking. I think it was in October 2005, I was talking with Paper Board superintendent Tom Pitts, and he said, 'It's not looking good. Something's going to have to give here before the end of the year, otherwise we'd better be prepared for some kind of long-term outage to get through this energy crisis.' He's looking at the numbers on a daily basis, and he's getting the gas bills, and he's looking at the long-term market costs that are coming in. He keeps asking me, 'What can we do?'

"I'm trying to think of anything, anything. I'm asking my guys, and we're all trying very hard. Everybody knows, 'This is it. We're on the edge.' The guys on the floor are asking me the same thing, 'How are we doing?' I'm answering, 'You guys keep doing the best you can. What you guys are doing right now is keeping us going.' It breaks your heart. These guys at the end of their shift, they see you, and they tell you, 'We did great tonight; we did great today. We never had a skip. We had a real good run. How do the owners think we're doing?' You tell them the best you can, 'They think you guys are doing a great job.' What are you going to do? Are you going to tell them it's hopeless? You can't do that."

In mid-November International Paper announced it must complete the sale of Paper Board before year's end — or else. A month later IP informed Pitts it was shutting down Groveton Paper Board on December 31. "The holiday season is coming on, and Tom has pretty much told me, 'We're shutting down.'" Cardin said. "'On January first, we're down; that's it. We're done.' Merry Christmas." IP spokeswoman Amy Sawyer told a local reporter: "Unfortunately, the smaller mills with older, narrower machines tend to have less capacity and higher costs." In the last half of 2005, United States mills with the capacity to produce a total of eight hundred thousand tons a year of corrugated medium were shuttered.[3]

Cardin orchestrated what he termed a "clean shutdown," as if it were merely another temporary layoff and not the death of a mill: "What we gave for a speech was, 'We're gonna shut this place down. We're going to have a real good shutdown, an orderly shutdown because there's always hope that we're gonna start this place back up again.' We never want to give up hope."

Was there any sabotage during the last days of the mill by embittered workers? "None. None. The morale was good," Cardin replied. "Everybody thanked us for doing everything we could to keep this place running, and we made it absolutely clear that it wasn't anything they did or didn't do that allowed this to fail. Nobody blamed anybody."

Right before Christmas, the local mill managers met with Paper Board workers to inform them of the mill closing and to outline their severance package. Labor laws require that workers receive sixty days' warning of a plant closing — with pay. Accordingly, the official closing date for Groveton Paper Board was March 1, 2006. "We told them what the package was, how they were going to be treated and everything," Cardin said. "[The last day] was melancholy, but it was a time of wishing each other well. It was like life goes on; it was kind of cheerful, in a way."

Murray Rogers, president of Local 61, praised the efforts by Tom Pitts to protect the workers' interests during this nightmare: "Tom Pitts — he did the best he could do. Those guys aren't the guys who are pulling the strings. They do what they can; they take a personal stance for the people." The eighty hourly and twenty-eight salaried workers received the sixty days' pay guaranteed by law, and an additional week of pay for each year's service, up to twenty years. Their medical, life, and dental insurance was guaranteed through March 2006.[4]

The workers in both mills belonged to Local 61, but Paper Board workers did not have seniority or bumping rights in the Wausau mill. Murray Rogers and the union did all they could to help Paper Board workers find jobs with Wausau. A few maintenance workers with specialized skills were able to move over. Dave Atkinson said Wausau would have gladly hired more, but it had been on a cost-cutting, jobs-reducing campaign for years: "Had we been in a market where we were expanding, I guarantee you we would have hired every one we could — the good ones. We wouldn't have scooped up the bad ones. Every operation has its bad ones."

Why didn't Wausau buy Paper Board? "There was never a thought of buying it," Atkinson responded. "If they had said, 'We'll give it to you,' I don't even know that Wausau would have said yes, because it would have been a higher tax burden."

On January 5, 2006, Atkinson wrote a sharp letter to Tom Pitts outlining Wausau's grievances with the Paper Board shutdown process: "The agreements between our companies require us to coordinate our activities and to limit to the greatest extent possible, interference with the other's use of the facilities." Atkinson requested "better communications," pointing out: "Already, your actions in drawing your tanks all at once without coordinating with us has had a negative effect on the wastewater treatment plant." *Wausau Hap-*

penings later reported that the flood of discharged black liquor, chemicals, and ash had "caused a toxic shock to the activated sludge process." Wausau shut down its paper machines for nineteen hours until the wastewater treatment plant's pH was restored to sanctioned levels.

Without Paper Board, Wausau's struggles for survival intensified: "It hurts us from a cost standpoint," Atkinson explained. "We certainly shared and allocated some costs. Mostly on waste treatment at that point. They owned one clarifier; we owned the other, but they operated in concert with each other. There's a lot of things that need to be maintained. There's a big blower for the aeration lagoon that uses a lot of energy. So there was a fairly high cost center associated with waste treatment. I don't think they paid their last couple of bills to us. We said, 'All right, we've got to reconfigure the waste treatment facility, downsize people.' Only one clarifier instead of two. They always paid a little bit more, and it had to do with the fact that they had a pulp mill — their waste had BOD [biological oxygen demand] in it. We didn't have to treat our waste the same as theirs. We reconfigured the waste treatment plant, but we didn't cut the costs in half. They only came down to about 70 percent. That certainly didn't help."

The mill literally became a colder place that January. Atkinson explained: "There were vast sections of the mill that were being heated by their waste heat. Their paper machines were not making paper anymore, so there's not warm air being funneled into [the shipping] warehouse. All of a sudden, our heating costs went up."

Groveton Paper Board ceased making payments to Wausau on December 31, 2005. On September 20, 2006, Wausau filed a $1.1 million lawsuit against Groveton Paper Board charging breach of contract. The suit alleged that Paper Board already owed Wausau $430,000 for overdue payments and other expenses. Wausau sought an additional $29,000 a month until November 1, 2007, when the three-year operating agreement expired. The suit also covered Paper Board's share of costs for sludge disposal, utilities, maintenance, taxes, and insurance, as well as cleanup and repair costs incurred by Wausau when Paper Board's boiler malfunctioned and forced Wausau to shut down some of its work area. IP gave Wausau the runaround.

In 2007 an outside crew of demolition scrappers began to dismantle and remove Paper Board machinery and other assets. Love in the Afternoon ended up being shipped to Vietnam — a bitter irony for many mill workers who had fought in that still-controversial war. The demolition operation caused Atkinson one last Paper Board–related headache: "The people who were in there tearing the metal out, tearing the equipment out, kind of scavenging the place, some of them [were] a little surly, don't follow safety rules. There were a lot of battles that I had with IP at the time because the phone number I had to call was some lawyer in Memphis. It certainly was a lot of time that I, and others on my staff, needed to spend on something that wasn't adding one ounce of value. It wasn't helping our customers; it wasn't helping our efficiency, but it was a necessary evil."

PETE CARDIN: "I HAD EVERY OPPORTUNITY"

Of all the former mill workers I interviewed, Pete Cardin, who had been hired in 1968, was the most devastated by the shutdown of the mill. He had returned to the mill in 1971 following a three-year stint in the army: "I didn't think I was going to go back to the mill. I don't even know why I came back to the area, but I did. Typical lost soul from that whole mess. The [Vietnam] war was highly unpopular, so nobody talked about it. It was like you disappeared for a while into someplace, and you came back, and people just expected you to get on with your life. Uncle Sam had given me a pretty good check when I left the army, and I partied that away pretty quick. Somebody told me, 'They've got to hold on to your job.' I said to myself, 'I'll give it one year, and I'll put some money aside. I'm not going to spend the rest of my life here, no way.' Twenty-one years old. Little did I know. But, like all things, life has a way of going by, and you start tying yourself down, and you get married, and you have obligations. You work because you've got to work; it was a good job, paid well, and people were good to work for. Benefits were great."

Pete thought he had a dream job working on the fine-papers machines from 1971 to 1974. He was progressing steadily toward the highest-paying jobs, back tender and machine tender, when he was ordered off the paper machines by his doctor: "I developed an allergy to the dies and stuff that they used on the machines. When I was told I couldn't work on the paper machines anymore, I swear to God, my heart was broken. I loved it. Oh, I loved the paper machines. It was the camaraderie. It was that esprit de corps. The teams; we're all in it together; it's us against the machine. It was really never that monotonous. You never knew what you were going to get into that night. I really liked the culture of the paper machines. When I was told medically I couldn't work on them anymore, I was devastated."

He transferred from the paper machines to the construction crew: "I went to places in that mill that I had never known existed because we'd wander everywhere, all over the roofs, all throughout the mill. That's when I realized, 'This place is big, all this stuff, holy mackerel.'"

During his stint on the construction crew, Pete was on the lookout for a more permanent job. Eventually, he was hired to unload chemicals for Paper Board's neutral sulfite semi-chemical pulp mill and for the bleach plant that bleached the stock for the tissue and fine-papers machines: "[It was] a very enlightening job. Very dangerous stuff. Extremely dangerous stuff. I learned an awful lot about chemistry on that job. Made a lot of money, worked a lot of hours. Probably the most money I ever made in the mill."

Pete considered his transfer over to Paper Board in 1975 a "life-changing experience." *Why?* "The reason I say it changed my life is that it opened up all the doors for me that I passed through later on," he responded. "If I had stayed where I was, I never would have achieved the level of success that I [enjoyed] in the pulp mill. There were fewer opportunities on the paper machine side than there was in the pulp mill. The pulp mill was in a state of transition. They were building the chemical recovery system at that time. A lot of the older operators didn't want anything to do with the new chemical recovery system because it was horrendously complex, a real beast. I was twenty-four. The next youngest person was probably thirty-eight, thirty-nine years old. And all the other operators were in their late forties, early fifties; some guys were in their sixties. There wasn't that much young blood in the department.

"For a young guy, this was great; I had every opportunity in the world, and I loved the challenge. I found it more interesting than working on the paper machine, much more of a mental challenge. I got a lot of sense of satisfaction of learning the process."

After working for several years in the pulp mill, he was made a fill-in shift supervisor, or tour boss, a part-time salaried job. The rest of the time, Pete continued to work at a union job. He was promoted to full-time shift supervisor of the chemical recovery system and the pulp mill in the mid-1980s. In

1990 he became superintendent of the pulp mill, and in 1996, after a shake-up in management, Pete became production manager for the entire Groveton Paper Board operation, a position he held until Paper Board shut down.

"[After the shake-up] I was faced with a big challenge. People were being demoted or transferred, and I had been promoted. So there was the politics of all of that. Tough times personnel-wise. Tough times for people's feelings. But everybody knew that the more important thing was the survival of the mill, and are we the right people in the right place in the right time? You don't just prove that by saying, 'I'm the boss.' You have to prove that by bringing together a team of people that had trust and respect for what you say. When things happen, and they're not going well, and you're up to your neck in alligators, and everybody is flipping out, somebody has got to make a decision. You've got to take a risk. You have to make the most educated guess you can and go for it. If it didn't turn out right, I would always take the responsibility that it was my decision. 'You guys gave me advice. I didn't have to listen to it. I listened to it; I made that decision; then we get on with it. If it fails, then it's my decision, not yours.'

"So, by behaving that way, plus I had a good rapport with the guys on the floor because I came from there. They respected my ability as an operator. They would always appreciate my help because I had spent a lot of time with them teaching the things that I'd learned. Especially the new guys; I'd work with them and make their job easier because they'd get themselves into problems, and they wouldn't know how to get out of the problem. Instead of screaming at them and give them hell, I'd say, 'Come on, I'll show you what to do. This is what you do. It's real simple' [laughs].

"In the old days, you'd scream your way out of it. Because some of the guys that were in charge didn't necessarily know how to fix the problem, and if they couldn't fix the problem, then 'I'm going to scream at you till you fix the problem' [laughs]. The screaming rolls downhill. I've seen some screaming in that mill."

When the demolition of the mill began late in 2012, Pete often drove over to the old parking area to watch and to grieve. His marriage broke up, and his health deteriorated. In May 2015, at age sixty-five, he died. His death certificate may have said otherwise, but the cause of death was a broken heart.

Chapter Fifteen

CONTROLLABLES

AND

UNCONTROLLABLES

"IT WAS A SURPRISE TO ME," Dave Atkinson recalled of his July 1999 promotion to vice president of operations and plant manager of Groveton. "Probably three or four or five years sooner than I expected. Tom Howatt was on one of his visits to Groveton. He said, 'Dave, I've got an opportunity for you. We're going to be moving Tom Craven back to take over the Brokaw operation,' which needed to improve dramatically. Tom was going to bring a lot of what he learned at Groveton back there. I can remember [Howatt] saying, 'I'd like you to step up.' I said, 'I don't know if I'm ready.' Tom said, 'You're ready.' Wausau was always very good to me, so it's hard to say too much bad, although it didn't end well. 'You're not going to be left alone. You know the operation; you're going to have support.' It was great. That was another good time. All of a sudden, I was in charge, and I was responsible. Before, I always felt a sense of responsibility, but there was always someone else in the front office. That certainly took some getting used to, but I was very supported both locally and at the corporate office, and never did I not like it, except at the end. As the end came, it was no fun."

Atkinson especially treasured a letter from Jim Wemyss: "It was short — one or two sentences. It was on Groveton Paper Board letterhead. 'Congratulations. I'm glad to see that Wausau has promoted a local boy.' Something very nice that I remember today."

Pete Cardin and Groveton Paper Board employees were delighted: "We were so glad when Dave was the guy who came into the mill because he was a local guy; he worked at this mill. I remember working with Dave when Dave was a college guy. Smart guy. Great guy. His father worked at the mill. This was a Groveton guy. When David and that team came into the mill, everybody was very optimistic. There was an awful lot of high morale at the mill at that time. You've got a local guy here, somebody who really knows this mill, knows the people; it's wonderful."

Dealing with energy costs would prove a constant challenge during Atkinson's tenure as mill manager. After converting from wood chips back to oil in the mid-1990s, Wausau again changed its main energy source in 1998, this time to natural gas. In the late summer of 1999 Wausau and Groveton Paper Board began a pre-engineering study for a co-generation plant. Wausau executives in Wisconsin decided in November 1999 to spend $13 million to build a co-gen plant that would only serve Wausau's energy needs.

The co-gen plant burned natural gas in a combustion turbine that powered an electric generator to produce electricity for the mill. The exhaust gases from the turbine, instead of being released into the atmosphere, were sent to a boiler called a heat recovery steam generator. There, mixed with additional gas, they produced enough steam to meet Wausau's needs.[1] Atkinson said, "Wausau wanted to be energy friendly, but ultimately they wanted to spend a lot less to make a pound of paper." The co-gen plant, viewed as a "big cost-reduction project," would be Wausau's last major investment in the mill.

By the time the co-gen plant went online on November 30, 2001, the U.S. paper industry was in deep trouble. Between 1989 and 1999, fifty-two pulp mills in the United States had either shut down or converted to the production of recycled pulp. Between 1999 and 2002, 105 paper machines were shut down in North America.[2] By 2004, nearly all the timberland owned by paper companies in northern New England had been sold off.

Competition with newer, faster mills in the southeastern United States and in China, coupled with rises in pulp prices, fuel costs, and declining demand for paper, caused Wausau's earnings to yo-yo from one quarter to the next. Wausau suffered a $4.7 million loss in the first three months of 2001. The Groveton mill was burdened with high inventories (unsold paper products), and it was forced to make more low-priced commodity runs because it had been unable to expand the market for its higher-priced premium paper.

Atkinson was under relentless pressure from Wisconsin to make the Groveton mill more profitable. Groveton was earning a 7.5 percent return on investment — a respectable profit for a locally owned mill after factoring in all the other benefits it provided the community. This did not satisfy the demands of the directors and shareholders of an absentee-owned corporation who expected a 15 percent return. Atkinson wrote: "We have been in the black, however not 'in the black enough.'" For the first time he addressed the growing concern that the paper mill might not survive. "Does this mean that we are in trouble and close to shutting the doors?" he asked. "ABSOLUTELY NOT! However it does mean that if we don't make a change that longer-term we would be in trouble."[3]

Wausau posted earnings losses in 2005 and 2006. Its Brokaw mill shut down its Number 3 paper machine for six months in September 2005. In March 2006, Berlin's Burgess pulp mill closed; a week later Georgia Pacific shuttered the Old Town mill that Jim Wemyss had transformed in the early 1970s. The demise of the Berlin and Old Town mills forced Groveton to pay even higher shipping costs to purchase pulp from more distant mills.

Desperate to contain costs, Atkinson and his coworkers focused on "controllables," such as reducing energy and water use, generation of broke (low-quality and waste paper), customer complaints, and workplace accidents. "We'd have monthly meetings that I would go to," Atkinson explained. "I would say, 'I understand your concerns [about the mill's survival]. We need to stay focused on what we can control. We can't control the market. All we can control is how efficiently, how cost-effectively we work. Focus on that, and we'll be OK.'"

As the crisis intensified, Atkinson recalled, "There was a conscious effort to say, 'We can't control the price of natural gas. We can't control the price of energy. We can't control the price of diesel fuel. But we can control our usage. How can we use less to do the same thing?'" Engineer Tom Bushey had spent an exciting decade working on Wausau's major capital improvement projects. Bushey's last years at the mill, he said, were "spent exclusively trying to wring operating costs out of that place."

The mill was using twenty thousand gallons of freshwater to make a ton of paper. That water, containing wood fiber and heated to 120° to assure optimal paper formation, was then flushed to the water treatment plant. Because Groveton ran mostly short orders and changed colors frequently, it used much greater amounts of water than if it had done longer runs with fewer color changes. The mill also wasted massive amounts of steam during the paper drying process.

Groveton engineers drew up an $8 million project to address water and steam waste, but Wausau's board rejected it as too costly. "Groveton, in its can-do way, said, 'All right, let's go after it in small, incremental ways," Dave Atkinson said. "'What parts can we do? We can't do the $8 million one, but we can spend $100,000 here.' A lot of those things were done, and they saved our facility money, [and] probably kept us running longer than we would have otherwise."

Bushey and his colleagues hit upon a strategy to reuse the "white water:" "By the simple addition of some three-way valves, we were able to take a lot of the existing tanks and make three major reservoirs for surplus water that was coming off the paper machine. One was dedicated to [Number 5 paper machine], one was for [Number] 6, and one was for non-dyed water that had come off [both] machines. That project was instrumental in us getting from twenty thousand gallons a ton of paper down to five thousand or six thousand gallons a ton, [and] in getting us from fifteen and eighteen mm [million] Btu's per ton down to eight and nine mm Btu's per ton. Huge, huge."

The mill's engineers also took steps to reuse steam. "That really resulted in many, many heat recovery projects," Atkinson said. "We spent a fair amount of money. All that hot air that is used to dry the paper that goes up through the hood, that you see coming out as steam when you drove through town, how can you pump that back in to preheat some water that you're going to heat up with raw steam?"

From January to June 2005 the Groveton mill used 93,000 dekatherms less gas than it had for the first half of 2004, and 176,000 dekatherms less than January to June 2003.[4] Groveton's waste-reduction projects were adopted in other Wausau mills. "Groveton was ahead of the curve on implementing projects like that," Atkinson said with pride. "Many of the things that Groveton implemented became demonstration projects that we brought to the other mills."

Wausau continued to pursue its policy of growth via acquisition despite the intensifying crisis in the United States paper industry. In 2003 it bought Laminated Papers Inc. of Holyoke, Massachusetts. In 2004 Wausau-Mosinee changed its corporate name to Wausau Paper. That autumn, Wausau acquired a shuttered mill in Brainerd, Minnesota, for $9.6 million. Brainerd's two paper machines had been rebuilt in the previous decade. They were capable of producing seventy thousand tons of paper a year, about two-thirds of Groveton's capacity. The mill also had its own small hydro facility.

"The kiss of death for Groveton was when they bought the mill in Brainerd," Bill Astle asserted. "This [Brainerd] mill had some state-of-the art-equipment in it. It had been shuttered because they couldn't sell paper. The idea was, oh, yes, they could fill that with the commodity grades that we were shipping out to the Midwest. When they bought the mill in Groveton, there was already a customer base. With Brainerd, there were no customers."

"Everyone in Groveton was very much up in arms when they bought the Minnesota mill," Tom Bushey remembered. "Time and again it seemed that that mill was going to be the death knell for Groveton." The demoralizing impact on the Groveton community forced Atkinson into damage control. "The biggest question I'm hearing is, 'Does this mean the Groveton mill will be shut down?' ABSOLUTELY NOT!" Atkinson wrote in the Autumn 2004 issue of *Wausau Happenings*.[5] Despite Atkinson's public optimism, Wausau clearly was in trouble. In 2005 it sold off twelve thousand acres of "non-strategic" timberlands, mostly located in northern Wisconsin, to pay down debt.[6]

As superintendent of shipping, Bill Astle was one of the first to sense the growing crisis. Wausau had never garnered as much of the East Coast premium paper market as it had hoped, and after the acquisition of the Brainerd mill, Wausau mills produced much more paper than they could sell. "It just struck me, 'God, inventory level is growing' to where we had every square inch of space filled," Astle recalled. "'Why are we buying another paper mill at a time when we've got such huge inventories?' From my perspective, we can't keep running these paper machines full tilt if we are shipping out ten pounds for every fifteen pounds we produce. We've got a lot of product that's got no place to go. We had the old Campbell envelope building there in Stratford. We finally had to get out because the roof was coming in. Every day it was just this revolving door. I'd have to send somebody up to Colebrook and then make arrangements to send eight or ten truckloads up to dump off, and then go up to try to inventory all of it. It was insane. We had way, way too much inventory."

Astle escaped the excess inventory crisis by taking early retirement in October 2005: "There was almost a sense of dread every time a weekend was coming, because, 'Where are we going to put all this paper?' between Friday afternoon and Monday morning. It had to go someplace, and it was always packed full in Groveton. I'd end up working on weekends just to arrange to shuttle the stuff off-site. I was becoming disillusioned; 'This isn't making sense anymore.' I was in there about quarter of six every morning and left about five every afternoon, Monday through Friday. By the time I came home, I just didn't have anything left to give. I need something better than this. Then it worked out Regina was retiring. I need to look at the numbers. We live modestly, we don't spend a lot of money. We have no kids. I guess that's the real reason I left — a better life. I ended up agreeing to work an extra six months to give them time to replace my position."

In its last years, Groveton enjoyed some success producing premium paper for annual reports for large corporations. Dave Atkinson recalled a large order from United Parcel Service: "Our sales people were out there beating the bushes to get the annual reports for the big corporations. I think [the UPS order] was twelve hundred tons. We're talking eight days, seven days on the paper machine. It was going to be printed in Atlanta. It was done on Graphika Brilliant White, I believe. Lineal, which was an embossed pattern that had value added. It was a super bright paper. It had a good high selling price. Something happened, and [UPS] realized, as they were nearing the end of their run, that they did not have enough paper. They put an emergency order in, and they didn't realize it until way way too late. We ended up saying, 'Yup, we'll go back on and make an additional forty tons.' They didn't need much; they needed two hours' worth, or whatever the heck it was. But we're going to keep that customer happy." There was a problem, however. "It needed to be expedited shipping," Atkinson laughed. "The only way we could get it there was via FedEx freight."

Soaring natural gas prices ate up the savings Wausau's Groveton mill had achieved in its relentless economizing efforts. Energy costs for most light industry are about 1 to 5 percent of operational costs. Energy traditionally had accounted for about 10 to 15 percent of paper mill costs. By 2005, Groveton was spending 15 to 25 percent of its monthly budget on energy. Atkinson termed this huge price jump "a big deal."[7]

Mill engineers contemplated returning the boiler to wood chips. *Could the mill have survived if Wausau had stayed with wood chips?* "It would have certainly extended the potential life of Wausau-Groveton, in my opinion,"

Atkinson responded. "When gas spiked to twelve, thirteen, and fourteen dollars a dekatherm, there were a lot of Monday morning quarterbacks, myself maybe one of them, saying, 'Man, we should have stayed with chips.' It wasn't necessarily a local decision. It could have extended the energy cost viability of Wausau-Groveton. But, honestly, not for much longer."

Wausau's Groveton mill shut down for nine days at the end of 2005 at the time that Paper Board went out of business. "That's a fairly typical time of year to shut down, because printers in the major metro areas shut down, especially if the economy's not all that great," Atkinson remembered. "There's not a lot of people printing; it's not an election year. Inventories were at record high levels."

Early in 2006, Atkinson acknowledged that the preceding year had been "one of the most difficult and challenging years in our mill's history." To the list of "uncontrollables" that were relentlessly driving mill costs up he added "escalating health care costs." "I felt tremendous pressure," Atkinson remembered. "It wasn't fun; but I didn't feel like the end was as close as it was. We were reading about mills all over the country going down. The old mill — the oldest mill. The comeback to that was, 'Yes, we're an old mill, but we've got brand-new equipment. The shell is old, but the guts are efficient.' I think in '05, if you had said to me, 'Will this mill be here ten or fifteen years from now?' I probably would have said yes. But I wouldn't have been as affirmative. If you had said, 'Three years from now?' 'Absolutely.' No question about it."

Throughout the ordeal of 2005, 2006, and into 2007, Dave Atkinson remained publicly optimistic. *Was this a public relations effort to mask a growing crisis, or did he believe the mill would pull through?* "It was one hundred percent sincere," he declared. "I knew that by '05 we made the best-quality [paper], had the best, most modern equipment. We had the best infrastructure of all the mills in the corporation. We had the best paper mill efficiency and finishing efficiency in the corporation. We had a very good operation. In '05 and '06, certainly I was very optimistic, and it was one hundred percent sincere. I think there was no reason not to be."

In the autumn of 2006 there was a flicker of hope. The mill made a profit in the third quarter (July–September) for the first time in nearly two years, owing to a dramatic improvement in the printing and writing business. In the spring of 2007, Atkinson was cautiously optimistic. The paper market had improved, "but not to the degree that supply and demand are balanced," he wrote. He hailed efforts to control safety, efficiency, production, and the quality of Wausau's paper products: "I am pleased with [the] momentum of our mill!" Complaints from customers had declined over the previous four years. Generation of broke had declined each of the past five years. Except for 2006, the mill had boasted excellent safety records every year since 2001. And, for the fifth consecutive year, paper machine crews had reduced the average time required to make grade changes from thirty-three minutes in 2002 to twenty minutes in 2006.

One upbeat story made the local press. The Groveton mill supplied the interleaf paper — the heavy, bright-red paper that was glued to the hardcover book's board — for the seventh and final *Harry Potter* book that was released in August 2007. Two sheets of premium Groveton paper for every book printed. "They made a lot of books," Atkinson said. "My recollection is that was maybe a hundred-ton order. It didn't cost us that much to make, but we got paid probably three times the selling price for a more commodity-oriented grade." It required about ten hours to run off that order, Atkinson estimated: "That was high profile; it got a lot of press. It was the right thing to do, but it literally occupied less than a day's worth of production on the machine."

A four-year union contract was successfully negotiated in the spring of 2007, but by summer, Atkinson gloomily reported that the market for fine papers "is out of balance and shrinking." Manufacturing costs had increased 20 percent in the previous four years, while revenue from sales had risen less than 2 percent.

Chapter Sixteen

F THIS

LATE IN AUGUST 2007, Dave Atkinson received an unexpected phone call from Wisconsin: "At that time I was traveling to Wausau about once a month for a staff meeting. I had a new boss, Dan Trettein, who called me and said, 'Dave, can you come out for a special?' I think I had just been there a week or two before. This was kind of a thorn in my side. You had to drive two hours to Manchester and catch a flight and go through Detroit or Chicago. There were no direct flights to central Wisconsin. So it was an eight-hour trip to travel. Eight hours out and eight hours back, that's if you didn't get weather. It meant I had to travel on a Sunday. I can remember being irritated; I said, 'Dan, I was just there.' 'We really need you to come out.' 'OK, I'll be there.'"

"Dave," Dan Trettein began, "I've got some bad news to tell you." Wausau had decided to close the Groveton mill on December 31. Thunderstruck, Atkinson asked if Tom Howatt knew. Yes. "Something dramatic happened," Atkinson reflected years later. "I believe it was the chairman of the board, San Orr, and the shareholders basically saying to Tom Howatt, the CEO, 'Hey, this business is going in the wrong direction. Printing and writing — sales projections — it's not growing, it's shrinking.' I know a lot of people blame Tom. I don't. I know from conversations with him, Groveton was his baby. On my way back to the airport, I pulled into the corporate office and went in and saw Tom. It was an emotional meeting. I really think he was in a similar position to me. We commiserated about that. He said, 'Dave this is the state of the business, and we need to contract. Groveton is efficient, but it's far away.' One hundred ten thousand tons being made, only sixty-five to seventy thousand tons a year being sold regionally. When diesel was not that expensive, it was less of a big deal. [Wausau] had to shed capacity."

Should Groveton have been the first mill closed by Wausau? "Absolutely not!" Atkinson insisted. "Tom Howatt did say that to me. But given the realities of where the corporate office was and geographically where the sales were, the efficiency of Groveton did not make up for the difference in shipment costs. They were trying to sell into a market that was shrinking."

Howatt, Trettein, and the Wausau board did not consult Dave Atkinson or alert him that they were contemplating shuttering Groveton. I asked Atkinson if it bothered him that such a momentous decision was made without local input. His answer surprised me: "The mere fact that I wasn't consulted maybe even adds something that it was a decision that was made quickly and not the way any decision had ever been made in my years at Wausau. Tom may have wanted to insulate me from ultimately having to be part of the decision. I don't think I would have had any influence. I think I'm glad I was insulated from it because it made me just like every other Groveton employee who I feel strong kinship to. That's what got me through from October to December. 'I heard on the street you're not going to move. You're staying?' I was able to say in good conscience, 'Yes, I am.' I think that helped me live with myself. I never felt like I should have been consulted. I'm glad I wasn't. As odd as that sounds."

Wausau's board would not ratify the decision to close Groveton until mid-October. For the intervening two months Atkinson had to keep the "gut-wrenching" news to himself. "I certainly tell [my wife, Sharon]," Atkinson recalled. "I remember crying. I can feel myself getting emotional now, which is kind of ridiculous, but certainly, not hiding it from her. I couldn't have anyway. In the mill, I never lied, but I was never truly candid for that two months 'cause it wasn't for sure. Tom Howatt didn't give me false hope, but he probably said, 'We can't announce, and you can't talk about it openly.' Because, a publicly traded company, and all those rules that exist, you can't until it's official. Honestly, those two months, as you ask me, they have to be a blur. I got through the day as best I could. I'm sure that employees noticed that I wasn't on the floor as much, that I was in my office more. I know that I withdrew and probably was not myself, which probably indirectly sent a message to the force because, 'Dave's not acting the same; something's up.'"

Comptroller Norm Fortier and human resources director Greg Nolin were the only staff members Atkinson could inform because they needed to begin planning for the shutdown. "I guess we comforted each other as best as that can be," he said ruefully. Pam Styles said, "I remember [Dave's] wife saying he was just sick to death about it."

For Atkinson, September and October were "the *worst* two months of my career." He had to carry on as if the mill had a future. When a big breach in the Brooklyn Dam was discovered that fall, he authorized its repair. Engineers

Tom Bushey and his boss, Steve McMann, thought Atkinson was behaving in an uncharacteristically tightfisted manner. After one tense meeting, Bushey recalled: "My boss [said], 'Get it done. Get it done right. Don't waste money, but don't spare any expense to get it right. We're not going to go back here again.' It's funny, because I've asked Steve if he knew what was about to happen. He claims he didn't. I remember Steve having to go to Dave to get approval for more money because we kept finding more and more hidden damage on that dam. I could tell he was stressed by the whole experience, and he would come back to me and reiterate: 'Get it done, and get it done right. Get this place up and running.' So boom, that's what I did; we charged ahead; we got it done, and spent an enormous amount of money doing it in a short period of time. I don't think that mill pond had been refilled and that mill back on river water for more than a couple of weeks when we finally found out that the place was shutting down."

"We were hearing certain rumors," Sandy Mason, a paper machine crew member said, "but we were always told that they weren't true. Late September, the mill's going to close. Or some jobs are going; some are staying. Different rumors; it wasn't all the same. Then we saw [in] the paper Dave Atkinson said, 'The rumors weren't true,' so we had to go on that."

On Tuesday morning, October 23, 2007, Atkinson informed his management staff: "'Hey guys, the company is coming in; it's not good news.' That was a difficult meeting because I was now Dan Trettein. The reaction from my staff, maybe an hour or two before the company plane came plowing in, was just like me in Wausau two months prior. 'Are you crazy?' 'Does Tom Howatt know?' Same questions." That afternoon, Stu Carlson, senior vice president for administration, and Curt Schmidt, head of human resources, informed the mill's 303 employees that the mill would close forever on December 31.

Everyone knew the mill had been struggling, but no one expected a decision to close the mill had already been made. Pam Styles was expecting another quarterly briefing on the mill's financial status. She recalled that when Carlson said, "I am sorry to report we're closing the mill," there was stunned silence. "I think a pin could have dropped on the floor," she continued. "I remember one person standing up, and it was, 'F this,' and he walked out and slammed the door."

"When I walked into that conference room that day, I had the sense that there was some bad news coming, news about curtailment of the paper mill for a short period of time due to lack of orders," Tom Bushey remembered. "Maybe an announcement that we need to trim a percentage of the workforce to stay in the black. Never dreamed it was going to be a flat-out, utter, shut-it-down. I don't think anybody saw that coming. There was emotion like you wouldn't believe. There was people in the room that stood up and got argumentative. There were a few people that stormed out of the room. A lot of people just cried. So many of us were shell-shocked. We tried to ask a few questions about where everything was headed. And then this Schmidt guy did get it out there that there may be opportunities for some folks at some of the other mills."

Everyone asked, "Why Groveton?" "If they would have been looking out for the stockholders' money, they would have shut the Brokaw mill down because [it] was not economically viable," Bushey said. "It was an energy hog. Groveton had a tremendous amount of automation that Brokaw did not have. I believe there was some smoke and mirrors played as regards to which mill should have been shut down."

Atkinson agreed: "Don Paquette, who was a longtime shift supervisor in Groveton, said to me when he visited Brokaw for the first time, 'Making paper in Groveton is an art and a science combined, especially with the new technology. Making paper in Brokaw, it's an absolute miracle.' Brokaw had good people, but they didn't have modern equipment. If I were going to shut a mill down, it would have been Brokaw."

Many from Groveton thought the troubled Brainerd, Minnesota, mill acquired in 2004 should have been shut down. Atkinson thought Brainerd made "pretty decent paper," certainly better than Brokaw's product: "What did Brainerd have that Groveton didn't? It had geographic proximity to the markets that they had, so it didn't have an exorbitant shipping cost to get the product to the end user that Groveton had. I don't want to sound like I'm a fan of the decision, but that's why."

Murray Rogers and other officers of Local 61 were in Maryville, Indiana, at a Wausau Council meeting on October 23. Stu Carlson called and told him the news of the mill closing and offered to send a private jet for them. Rogers angrily declined: "I found my way over here; I'll find my way back." When he returned to Groveton, he confronted Atkinson: "'You knew when I boarded that plane that this was going down." 'Yes, I did.' I said, 'How dare you do this to the union, knowing that we spent a couple of thousand dollars on airline tickets and hotel rooms to go to a Wausau Council meeting when you knew this mill was going down?' He reimbursed the union for what was spent for that trip. That's the type of guy Dave is."

United States labor law requires companies closing plants to negotiate a severance package with the union, a process called "effects bargaining." Because of Local 61's lack of leverage, Rogers referred to the process as "effects begging." The Wausau severance package stipulated that on December 31 all but thirty-eight of the union jobs would be terminated. A skeletal force of mostly maintenance workers would continue to work at the mill until May 2, 2008. Workers could use seniority to bump for those jobs, although Wausau reserved the right to select the employees it wished to retain after December 31 to maintain waste treatment, utilities, and to perform maintenance.

Wausau would pay severance only if production and safety standards were sustained right to the end, and there was no vandalism. Workers who quit before December 31 (unless given permission by Wausau) and those who were fired ("discharged for cause") lost their severance pay and benefits. Workers would be paid for unused and accrued vacation and would retain health and dental insurance until March 1, 2008, or, if working at the mill after that date, until their jobs ended. Those with less than ten years of service at the mill received four weeks' salary at the employee's normal hourly wage for a forty-hour week. Employees with ten to twenty years of seniority received eight weeks' severance, and those with more than twenty years of service received twelve weeks of severance pay.

The union fought unsuccessfully for the deal IP had given to the Groveton Paper Board employees two years earlier — one week of severance pay for each year of seniority up to twenty years. However, the union could not strike or threaten a work stoppage because Wausau would simply walk away from the mill. The union representatives were so angry over the effects bargaining package that they refused to sign the agreement, leaving only president Murray Rogers and the International representative to sign. Stu Carlson, Curt Schmidt, Dave Atkinson, and Greg Nolin signed for Wausau.

During this painful time, Rogers said, Local 61 did not get much help from the International, its parent union: "That guy was getting ready to retire. He didn't do us any real favors in this whole thing. The International kind of went away. I felt that as soon as they found out that the dues were going away, they kind of stepped out of it." Rogers was grateful for contributions of over $2,000 to the food bank from locals around the country.

Rogers and his fellow negotiators had erroneously assumed "that anybody that was sixty-two after that mill went down would be allowed to collect full pension." "That's a kick," he said. "It was our assumption that got us into trouble. But it was too late." Bruce Blodgett turned sixty-two shortly after the mill shut down, and he took his pension. By claiming it before age sixty-five, he lost one-half of 1 percent per month: "They got me for 18 percent, so they got me for about four hundred bucks. By the time they got done with me, when I cut my wife in for half of my pension, that took me a hundred forty bucks a month to do that. I think I wound up with $1,050, $1,060 for a pension where I should have got $1,473."

Dave Atkinson sympathized with Murray Rogers's unhappiness with the severance package but suggested Local 61 could have done worse. Not long after the mill shut down, the stock market crashed. "Manufacturers across the country were announcing massive layoffs, massive shutdowns everywhere," Atkinson said. "The news picks up on stories about corporate America and Wall Street, and these poor people are left with nothing, and there's no severance. I'm always looking for the silver lining. Had we waited a little longer [to close the mill], and we had been caught up in that whole thing, there would have been less of a perceived obligation from the corporate office to provide the severance that they did for the folks in Groveton. I really believe that. Then the severance package given to the Groveton workforce would have been worse."

Rogers began working with the New Hampshire Employment Services and Southern New Hampshire Services (SNHS) to help everyone, whether union or salaried, write résumés and search for jobs. He credited Ron Giroux of SNHS with keeping him calm: "He's the one who said, 'You're going to go through three stages. You're going to be mad. Then you're going to grieve. But then you've got to get on with life. The longer you stay mad, the less chance you're going to get a job because somebody else that doesn't stay mad is going to move up. You need to get on with life and do what you've got to do.'"

With an eye to future employment, Rogers advised his fellow workers, "The best thing they could do was go out of there with their heads held high running that machine to the fullest capability because they were now trying to be marketable. Show these people that are watching — because everybody's watching this mill — that you can do a good job. They ran it to just about setting records to the last day. They did a good job."

With the regional economy in free-fall, there were few jobs available for anyone, and scarcely any that paid comparable wages. Job specialization in the mill also worked against workers finding a new job. When the mill closed, generalists, such as maintenance workers, enjoyed great advantages finding decent-paying jobs. There were no jobs operating a paper machine or a ream wrapping machine. Some workers went on disability because of age or weight. Rogers thought that fewer than twenty former mill workers moved out of the area to find work. However, they were probably among the younger employees.

Mill workers who were over fifty-five found it especially difficult. "You go out there, and you've got a little of this gray on you, the guys will say 'Beat it,' unless you've got some kind of a trade that they want," Bruce Blodgett explained. "They're not going to hire these guys. A lot of them are trying to get by on unemployment or keeping unemployment until they can get to be sixtyish, at least."

The final two months at the mill were an eerie time. Heartbreak, anger, fear, bewilderment, desperation, and gallows humor settled into a kind of psychological numbness. For ten more weeks Groveton paper workers had to continue to operate machinery safely and make high-quality paper. "I thought I was going to retire from there. Didn't work out that way," Sandy Mason said with a bittersweet laugh. For Tom Bushey, it was a career, not merely a job: "I'm sure I'd still be there tomorrow — today — if the place was running."

"It was sad," Atkinson said. "It was hard, certainly, to get up between August and October. Once the news was shared, it was probably easier because now I wasn't holding this burden, and I could go out on the floor again and be me. From October to December there was a lot of activity related to the shutdown that kept you focused. The hourly workforce were superb. I can't stress enough how orderly and proud and well the workforce in Groveton shut the operation down. Sabotage, sour grapes — no. I was doing a lot of communicating about, 'I'm with you guys. We're all in this together. Let's go down proud.'" He quickly added, "They would have anyway."

"I put in a lot of hours because a lot of the guys were finding other jobs and were taking them," Sandy Mason recalled. "So you got a lot of overtime. By December I was making a pretty good paycheck."

Although Wausau no longer wanted the mill, its midwestern mills coveted some of Groveton's equipment. Tom Bushey remembered: "The announcement was no more than made, and then we had an influx of people from the other [Wausau] mills basically coming to start picking meat off the bones. I spent most of my time sharing drawings and file information, technical information on various pieces of machinery that we had at the mill. The converting equipment, they obviously had intentions of taking that completely out of the mill to some of their other sites. The Brokaw mill was not able to make some of the grades that we were making in Groveton as efficiently as we were making them. We had folks from the Brokaw mill come out and spend time with us trying to understand how we achieved such low energy and water consumption numbers. I had to give them the inside philosophy on that."

Pam Styles and her fellow office workers spent a substantial amount of time disposing of records and supplies: "We had to package up everything that was significant and send it over to Wisconsin. We had to shred everything that might have been confidential or wasn't needed. A lot of stuff was given to the employees. You just had to check with Dave. He told us to take anything that was part of our supplies or office materials. I was the one that stocked the cabinets, so I had quite a bit of stuff to sort through [*chuckles*]. I brought a lot of it here to [Groveton High] school. Labels and paper. I also kept the sample room stocked up, so we had reams and reams of paper. I don't know how many cases of paper I had sent up here."

Tom Bushey and three other managers refused to believe the mill's fate was sealed. They developed a plan to keep part of the mill open to make paper towel grades on a reconfigured Number 6 paper machine. "[We] tried to do some research on what it would take to convert Number 6 paper machine to towel grade," Bushey recollected. "At that time, generally speaking, for a few million dollars, that machine could have been converted. Now, it wouldn't have been the most efficient machine because of line speed and that sort of stuff, but that machine could have been converted to towel grades. We found out Wausau was already buying four hundred and five hundred tons a day of parent roll stock from another tissue manufacturer to satisfy the demand for their Bay West products. This is the sinister part of what they voted to do in

Groveton — you've got four and five hundred tons a day being purchased from China and other mills. The sad part about it is they had a paper mill here in Groveton that had a very good, efficient workforce. They had a modern electrical system, a modern waste treatment plant system, and they just flushed it all down the toilet. Those paper machines — put brand-new tissue machines on those old, existing foundations. Completely doable. Ultimately, they put in two new machines [in Harrodsburg, Kentucky]. Those two machines could have been put here. But for them, it's all about centralization — one great big mother of a mill, I guess."

Dave Auger invited Dave Atkinson to join the effort to buy the mill. He declined: "I probably didn't have the heart to tell Dave [Auger] that it's a lost cause. You don't want to pour water on someone that's just been punched in the face. Out of respect, I let it go. I do remember them wanting to have an audience with Scott Dasher and Tom Howatt, and that's probably where the definiteness of the covenant was communicated more clearly. They knew they can't make fine paper, so I think they nitpicked the covenant. Good for them, from that standpoint. But in the end it didn't matter."

Bushey described their plan to save the mill: "Dave Auger, Steve McMann, and myself, and Norm Fortier put forward a letter to the Wausau corporate office asking them if they would be interested in buying parent roll stock — towel stock — that we would make off the Number 6 paper machine if they would either sell the mill to this group for short money, or lease the facility to this group where an investment could be made. Would they be interested in a contract? If you are, then we would then go and try to secure the money. We had a fellow out of Maine that was helping us with trying to secure financing and that sort of stuff.

"We were at the beginning stages when we found out that not only the place was gonna close, but it was going to be transferred to a new owner, and the new owner was going to have a covenant in the deed that it could never be a paper mill again. The full depth of what they intended to do was not understood by most people. [At the October 23 meeting] they used the words that the mill was being shuttered, and they didn't want that asset to compete against the remaining assets."

They didn't come right out and say: "We're actually putting a covenant on this thing and it's your death sentence"?

Bushey replied: "Right. I personally did not understand that [initially]."

Bushey said that after Eastern Pulp & Papers Corp. had declared bankruptcy, the mill manager and employees of its Lincoln, Maine, mill were able to purchase the mill. "But the difference there," he pointed out, was "they had a bankruptcy court on their side. Whereas Wausau, when they made the decision to shut that place down, they did it from a position of very solid financial footing. They owned it; they didn't have a creditor standing there waiting to be paid, and so they were able to do what they did without any recourse."

Wausau did offer Bushey jobs in Wisconsin and Kentucky. "I refused," he said. "There have been times when I probably kick myself for not doing it. But, on the other hand, once I understood the true realities about what they were doing, and the covenant — I couldn't keep my mouth shut and go to work for somebody that was doing something to my hometown that was completely unnecessary. If this mill was not viable for them to run, then all they had to do was sell the damn thing to somebody else or sell it to the employees and put some restrictions on where the mill can and can't sell paper and be done with it."

Atkinson and his managers developed a schedule for shutting down the mill. The last supplies were delivered by mid-December. To avoid flooding the wastewater treatment plant, they shut down the paper machines on different days. The final run on Number 6 paper machine ended at 9:42 a.m. on December 19.

Old Jim Wemyss had told his son that at all costs Number 3 paper machine must be kept running. When it shut down, he warned, the mill was finished. On December 20, 2007, at 11:44 a.m., the one-hundred-year-old paper machine completed its last five-ton reel. Fred Shannon's niece, Wendy McMann, called him the night before that final run. Fred and his pal John Gonyer went down to the mill: "It was sad. It was sad. When that tail came down over the last time, it kind of choked you. I remember Dave Atkinson come walking by, and we said, 'We're sorry to see it happen.' He said, 'Nobody feels worse than I do.' I looked at him, and I says, 'You wanna bet?' He weren't the only one that felt bad. We all did. A sad day. You figure all those people — just throwed out, done; that's it. They all gotta go find jobs. I feel so damn bad for all those. . . ."

"I had tears in my eyes," John Gonyer confessed. "It was a sad day. Really was. Terrible. All these people standing around with long faces."

Dave Atkinson's memory of the last run was hazy: "I remember standing at the dry end with the whole maintenance force, a lot of the office staff, admin staff. There was probably a hundred people. It was sad; it was surreal. That's probably why I don't remember it all that vividly because it's really not one of those things you like to remember. Jim Wemyss probably called me and said, 'Will you do me a favor and save me a strip off the last reel off both machines?' I personally made sure that that happened. He was in Florida. It was a couple of months later that he finally limped into my office and I said, 'Here you go.' A lot of the guys wanted to sign it. I think we did two. We did one for Jimmy. I think we did one for the Historical Society."

When the last reel had been removed, the washup, cleanup, and boil-out began. Normally, a shutdown requires an additional eight-hour shift. Because this was a permanent shutdown, the maintenance and machine crews spent a week siphoning the dryers and lubricating the massive machine. Perhaps someday the machine might run again. Glimmers of hope remained.

Tom Bushey was impressed by how the workforce shut down operations: "Greg Nolin kept encouraging everybody, 'Let's go out on top.' There was a sense of pride with the entire workforce despite everybody losing their job. So many of the people, that was the end of their working careers. They'll never make that kind of money again, and they'll never have another opportunity like that because of their age and skill set."

Roger Caron recalled the final day: "People were going around, visiting, socializing, and talking to people that they'd spent a good share of their lives with. Kind of gut-wrenching watching people go out the door with their personal belongings and know that they don't have a job to come back to."

"Wausau Papers always felt the Groton operation was hired help," Bill Astle observed. "If you looked at the Brokaw, Wisconsin, area, Wausau Papers was involved in everything — probably every little league team and anything that they could be supportive of, they were sponsors. There was never a sense that Groveton was part of the family. I'm sure when they shuttered Groveton, they thought, 'We'll never be there again.' I'm pretty certain that no one from Wausau Papers in Wisconsin has set foot in Coös County since the mill closed. Nor will they ever have a reason to, because they have no connection." Dave Atkinson subsequently confirmed Astle's assertion.

Epilogue

THEY RUINED
THIS TOWN

DAVE ATKINSON remained at the mill throughout 2008, overseeing the process of shutting down. Tom Howatt urged him to continue working for Wausau as a vice president. "We'd love to have you stay with us," he told Atkinson late in 2008. Atkinson declined: "I got called three times. I'm glad I didn't go." The decision to terminate his career at Wausau and to remain in the Groveton area has endeared Atkinson to the community. Roger Caron spoke for most former mill workers: "No one on the floor blamed Dave Atkinson or the managers for what came down. A good share of us felt this was a Wall Street decision and not a Main Street decision that shut this place down. It wasn't the work ethic by any means that caused this place to go down."

Reflecting on his career at the mill, Atkinson said it was "very satisfying. Too short, for sure. I learned more there about managing people, managing a fairly complex operation that I couldn't have gotten anywhere else. I think because of the remoteness of Groveton, I was probably given opportunities, at a younger age than I might of in a larger corporation somewhere else. I was able to raise my family, make a very good living, stay in the area where my roots were. There's something very satisfying about that; that's why I chose to stay. I was paid well, but it was a fair wage for what I was doing. A great career; twenty years too short. Now that I'm doing something very different, I sleep better at night. I'm sure that not being responsible for the mill has probably added years to my life. Would I like the mill still to be operating? Would I love to be driving there every morning at six a.m.? I would absolutely love to still be doing that, but that's not reality.

"I think one of the things I miss are those friendships that because you don't work together anymore, you don't see them as much. A lot of good friends over the years. There were three hundred people that worked there, and really, I knew all three hundred of them. That was one of the nice things about Groveton is all three hundred certainly knew me, but I knew them, and really tried to know them."

Roger Caron was born into a family of mill workers: "The mill was always a part of my life." At age fourteen or fifteen, Caron got a job servicing the mill's vending machines. He graduated from high school in 1972. "I had full intentions of taking the summer off, but Dean Sanborn stopped my father and said, 'Tell your boy to come down. I want to talk to him.' I got a job immediately after graduation. There were a lot of times I was getting ready to quit and leave. Of course, one thing leads to another, and lo and behold, I've been here forty years." He worked in a variety of maintenance jobs over the years, serving as foreman in the final years of the mill.

After the mill closed, he collected unemployment and made home improvements on his property. In the spring of 2008, he worked for a month on the construction crew of the federal prison in Berlin. "I wasn't real happy with that particular job [as an equipment operator]. It wasn't as structured as mechanical maintenance was in the mill. In the mill we had more planning and more knowing exactly what moves you were going to make and when you were going to make it. I didn't see that there. I said, 'I'm going to try something else.'"

In the fall, Caron was called to help with the auction of machines and equipment because of his knowledge of the mill. He worked there sporadically until March 2009, when he was hired full time — the last employee at the mill: "When I first took over here, I figured it was just for a few months. All in all, it was a real busy job. There's a lot of different hats you have to wear."

He performed basic maintenance on the massive facility — repairing leaks in the roof, pumping out water from the three springs in the mill's basement, and maintaining the mill's water treatment system. He also was in charge of public safety: "The potential for danger is incredible. Out behind the mill, there's still 34,500 volts that comes into the facility at ten feet off the ground. If someone ever touched that in the right way, it would be history. It's extremely powerful." He helped catch thieves who stole thousands of dollars of copper and ruined tens of thousands of dollars worth of equipment in the process.

"I worked for two different companies. One is an auction company, and one's a used-equipment company. The used-equipment company, Perry Videx, would call and ask about equipment, and you'd go out and find the equipment, take pictures of the equipment, dig out any books or files that you could find on that equipment so they could put this stuff in their database and try to sell it to someone. At other times, there would be clients coming in from all over the world, whether it's India or Brazil or what have you to look at this equipment. And you'd give the people tours through this facility."

Sometimes he helped dismantle and remove equipment; other times, he supervised the contractor: "These people would come in here and they'd work for a week or two — long, long hours. Not knowing this facility, a person would have a hard time wrapping their arms around how much equipment is in a place like this. The number of electric motors, the number of pumps, what have you. Quite a place."

What was it like working in an empty mill? "It's been very strange in a lot of ways. The building creeks and groans. There's always noises when you're walking through here. If you had a person that's a little skittish, he wouldn't last very long here. It's extremely dark. I carry a good flashlight with me, and hopefully it doesn't go out. I've had to come back to the front office with a Bic lighter before. That's a hard trip."

How did you feel about being the last employee of a mill that had employed thousands of people over the previous 116 years? "It's not something that I'm extremely proud of. To me, I would like to see this place still hopping and making paper, or something else. What kept me going is that this facility could be repurposed. I jokingly said to CBS News, 'Maybe it could be an electric car manufacturing facility.' The point I was trying to make was that we have an abundance of talented people in this area with a good work ethic. Once the property is cleaned up, another company will come in and see this as a viable site to do something different. This place does hold a lot of memories for a lot of people, and it provided good employment for a lot of people in this area."

The day I interviewed Roger, August 1, 2012, he was optimistic that a new owner would sign the purchase papers later that day. Instead, a few hours after we spoke, he sent an e-mail informing me that the would-be purchaser had failed to secure the funding and had withdrawn the offer. A salvage company purchased the mill a few months later, and that fall the long, depressing yearlong demolition process commenced.

ON THE BEAUTIFUL STRETCH of the Upper Ammonoosuc River that runs through town, there is a vast open space where the mill had been. For generations of Grovetonians, the mill had always been there. Always. And always would be there. . . .

The closing of the mill left the people of Groveton shocked, bewildered, devastated. Despite the mill's struggles in the early 1990s, and despite the closing of the smaller Paper Board operation two years earlier, the Groveton community was utterly unprepared for the October 23, 2007, announcement. "The mill did good for this town, and it's really hurting without it," lamented Hadley Platt, who first worked at the mill in the late 1940s and retired in 1993. "I wouldn't have this home if it hadn't been for that mill. The mill was the life of this town.""It was worth it," said Belvah King. "I wouldn't have what I've got today if I had just been a housewife and depended on Ted's check."

"Nowadays," Shirley MacDow scornfully remarked, "you could walk up the street naked at night and nobody'd notice you. Sad, sad, sad to see what's happened."

"I tell you, they ruined this town," Lawrence Benoit charged. "They bought up all the buildings and tore them down, and what do we got? A parking lot down here. I think they just hated this area or something and wanted to bankrupt this town. That's my feelings anyway." Benoit's sarcasm is not far from the mark. In its heyday, there were more than thirty storefronts on Main Street and State Street. Each boasted a local business. In 2017, a quarter of the storefronts house active businesses; another quarter are gone, replaced by vacant lots; and the remainder are empty.

"I think where everybody missed the boat was how important that place was from not only the roof over your head and the food on your plate, but also it really was a part of you," Louise Caouette observed. "Many of these folks were many generations. Nobody took the time to deal with the mourning of the loss that the people were going to feel. It was literally a mourning period that people went through, and it was sad." Murray Rogers, the last president of Local 61, emphasized: "The big thing I want people to know is that the majority of people that worked there appreciated that they had that job."

Pam Styles was fortunate to find work as the secretary of Groveton High School after thirty-seven years at the mill: "I think it's taken a big effect on the town, especially that tax [not] coming from Wausau that the town was guaranteed every year. Now the slack has got to be picked up by the tax-payers in town. A lot of people not having jobs have moved away. They all have children in the school, so the count for Groveton High School is going down all the time, too." Raymond Tetreault, who retired in 1987, concurred; his property taxes eat up his Social Security and his pension — "takes it all."

Joe Berube was set to retire early in 2008. Although he had his pension, he worried about the community's future: "There's not a lot of opportunities today for any of the younger generation, that's for sure. If they want a job once they graduate [from high school], they're going to have to relocate somewhere."

Something else was lost when the mill died. "[The mill] was like another family," Pam Styles thought. When there was a death in the family, an illness, or a tragedy, the mill community came together. Dave Atkinson concurred: "There was always an envelope [in the lab] — a collection for someone who had a fire, or chemotherapy, or whatever. Significant collections. Each Christmas and/or Thanksgiving, [James River and Wausau] would buy a turkey or a ham for everyone and give it as a thank you. Many of the employees would say, 'I'm here to get my turkey, but I want to give it to the Catholic church [or a local charity].' Typically, we'd order thirty or forty more turkeys, and Wausau would make a donation to Meals on Wheels or whatever. There was a great philanthropic family atmosphere at the mill. It didn't matter — union, salaried, there was an envelope there."

Five years after the mill closed, Tom Bushey worried about the future of the community: "I don't know what it's gonna take to reinvent this area. I'm a Christian guy, and every day since the mill closed, I've prayed to be a part of the redevelopment of this area. I'm forty-four years old, still young. Definitely could move out of this area. I'd like to see my hometown come back to life, to have some semblance of a community. Because that's what it always was. Growing up, you pretty much knew the inside of every home in the town because it was like one great big family. Now, with the closing of the mill, people aren't coming together as much as they used to. I feel like the fabric of the town is unraveling a little bit each day. It's just hard to see it. Three hundred and fifty people coming together every day, and now, boom — everybody's scattered to the four corners of the state and beyond, trying to find employment."

In nearly every interview, former mill workers expressed bitterness toward the last mill owner. Most of them cited the covenant as the cruelest blow. "I feel that Wausau did a gross injustice to this community [saying] that the paper machines couldn't make paper on this facility," Roger Caron said. "I think they were afraid of the competition because of the nature of the people that work here. We had an excellent workforce and a can-do attitude. They probably saw us as a threat, but that should have been illegal. We live in a forest-based part of the country, and it would almost be like 'you can't make flour in Kansas' or something. To me it was wrong."

Pam Styles recalled the grief in the final weeks: "I'm surprised that a lot of people didn't do any damage to the mill because of them closing it that way. I believe there was some stealing of stuff that was supposed to have been left there. I think everyone has a lot of hard feelings about it, the way they did it. What bothered most everyone is the way they did it so that we couldn't survive with another mill there. I think if they had left it so it could be sold to another papermaking company, people wouldn't have felt as bad, at least that they have a chance to survive. I thought it was a raw deal."

"I think that Wausau should have a lot of guilty consciences for what they have done, especially that thing about never making paper in that mill again," Joan Breault said in 2010. "That has to be plain vindictiveness. Just meanness to do that. They had to know what impact that would have on this area. I don't blame all their bosses. I think David Atkinson is one of the top guys I've ever known. He tried his darnedest to help the people of Groveton. He fought to keep that mill open. Nobody could ever blame him for anything wrong like that. He's a good guy. It was the higher-ups in Wisconsin — Tom Howatt and some of them. It certainly has had an impact on this area. Not a good one. I'm glad I was retired. Right now, I've got a son and a grandson out of work. When my son got done as a paper machine tender [after thirty years], he took a college course on welding. He can't get a job around here. I don't know what's going to happen."

Bruce Blodgett grudgingly defended Wausau's right to impose the covenant: "It's a dirty deal, but they owned the mill. What do you want to do? Hey, they own it; so, kind of a lousy hand to get dealt to you, but how are you going to beat it? I think there's crooked deals in it, sure. But when it comes down to it, if you decide you want to sell your house, I can't tell you not to sell it or who to sell to."

"I can't even imagine such a thing [as the covenant]. Can't imagine it," a livid Jim Wemyss said. "I can't even imagine how they thought it up. Somebody must have hated Groveton. I don't know what their thinking behind it was."

A great many people contrasted Jim Wemyss with Wausau. Louise Caouette suggested: "It's real easy to say 'Wausau,' because that's a group; it's a board of directors. I think the difference was, when it was Wemyss, the buck stopped with him. Why preserve the Wisconsin mill and let Groveton go? There is a sense of community in Brokaw with the management because that's where they live, that's where the shots were being called. They could distance themselves from Groveton. They didn't have to face somebody on the street with a decision that was made in Wisconsin. Where if it was locally owned . . ."

Sylvia Stone worked in the accounting department at the mill from 1952 to 1978. "They ruined our town," she said. "I don't understand why they ever did such a thing. Many corporations don't think of the people; you're a number. I feel that I was more than a number working for Groveton Papers."

Wemyss wouldn't have done this, Thurman Blodgett asserted: "I've seen the time when salesmen couldn't even sell paper. It wasn't very long before his plane would take off, and he'd be gone for a little while, and pretty soon he'd come back. The paper machines would start running again, and they was shipping her out as fast as they could. He'd undersell 'em to keep people working."

Several former workers remained convinced that, as Zo Cloutier phrased it, "If [Jimmy Wemyss] was running that place today, it probably would still be running." Joan Breault suggested that Wausau's treatment of the town might cause some people to reevaluate their opinions of Wemyss: "I bet there are people who used to condemn the Wemysses for stuff, but I bet they wish they had the Wemysses here instead of Wausau. The Wemysses never left the people high and dry like Wausau did."

Jim Wemyss agreed: "You think I'd have allowed this company to be shut down if I'd been working? Are you crazy? It never would have happened." He noted that tissue is too expensive to ship more than five hundred miles: "If I'd kept it as a family business, I'd have two big high-speed tissue machines running there right now, on secondary fiber making Vanity Fair products and dominating the goddamn whole East Coast like I did before. No problem in my mind. But you can't do this till you're a hundred years old. You have to turn it over to somebody someday. And I felt at seventy-five it was time for me to get the hell out."

There's the rub: *If I'd kept it as a family business.* The Groveton Papers Company ceased to exist as an independent, family-owned business in June 1968 when Jim Jr. and his father merged with Diamond International. Even though Jim Wemyss ran the mill for Diamond for another fifteen years, Sir

Mill demolition and Cape Horn. (Courtesy Doug White)

James Goldsmith's hostile takeover of Diamond exposed the illusion that the mill remained under local control after 1968.

Jim Wemyss blamed Goldsmith and Wall Street for the death of the Groveton mill. Certainly Goldsmith's rapacious capitalism accelerated the demise of the region's paper industry, but by the 1980s the future of northern New England's paper industry was already bleak. Signs of trouble had become manifest during the 1970s. The shocks of that decade's two oil crises, the costs of cleaning up past pollution and reducing future emissions, combined with growing competition from bigger, faster, newer mills, placed the old paper mills of New England at a competitive disadvantage. As Fortune 500 corporations swallowed up New England mills that formerly had been owned by people with some connection to the region, decisions over the fates of mill-dependent communities were increasingly made from afar.

Between 1988, when Goldsmith sold off Diamond's former timberlands, and 2005, most of the eight million acres formerly owned by paper companies in northern New England had been sold off to hedge funds, real estate investment trusts, and other speculators who typically log intensively before selling off within five to ten years. A small percentage of these lands was acquired by the public or by private, nonprofit conservation groups.

In the past two decades, at least ten paper mills have closed or ceased making paper in northern New England and New York. In Maine alone, there has been a 62 percent decline in paper mill jobs since 1990. Logging jobs declined 24 percent in the same period, and sawmill jobs diminished by 39 percent. Real wages for those lucky to have a job in the depressed region have declined. Many rural townships are barely surviving.[1] These desperate communities are forced to close schools and cut services. They are faced with choices such as accept a prison, a casino, a toxic dump, or go bankrupt.

Late in 2005, Lloyd Irland, a leading forest economist in Maine, wrote: "My own conclusions from scanning the economic landscape is that the U.S. and Canadian wood sectors are in for a prolonged 'Dark Time,' likely to last decades."[2] The spate of paper mill closures in northern New England since then bears out his observation.

Wausau shut down its Brokaw mill in 2012 and Brainerd a year later. It sold its Rhinelander and Mosinee mills in 2013 under pressure from a hedge fund that bought a huge chunk of Wausau stock in 2011. If, in 2007, Wausau had spared Groveton and shuttered Brainerd or one of its Wisconsin mills instead, it is unlikely that Groveton would have escaped its unhappy fate for long. Almost certainly, Groveton would have been shut down by 2013 because of uncontrollable global economic forces. The covenant Wausau placed on the Groveton mill was an ugly reminder of the power of Wall Street–financed corporations' power to destroy rural resource communities. Nevertheless, the covenant probably didn't much matter because, as Louise Caouette observed: "It's inevitable that the [New England] paper industry is going to die anyway. I think that long-term the whole community — Coös County — has got to find a way to diversify itself. At some point, the community was going to have to deal with the death of the industry."

"It's a dying industry," Dave Atkinson said with resignation in 2012. "Even in China, the printing paper market annual tons per year sold is shrinking. The world market is shrinking. It's going to continue because of the e-media."

"It's time for Groveton to move on," Bill Astle asserted two years before the mill was demolished. "Just as there wasn't always a paper mill in Groveton, and there was life in Groveton before the paper mill, there will be life again."

"I feel I was fortunate to have a job," the ever-feisty Pauline Labrecque summed up forty years at the mill. "I wasn't one that because I wanted the night off I would call in sick. I was there. They could depend on me. That makes me feel good. And if they called me today and said, 'Paulie, we're going to bring back some of them napkin machines on Number 4 here; are you willing to come back to work?' *In a heartbeat. . . . . Yup. . . . . In a heartbeat.*"

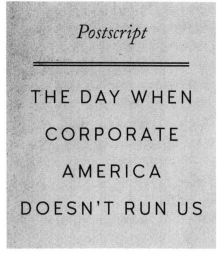

Postscript

THE DAY WHEN CORPORATE AMERICA DOESN'T RUN US

IN ONE of my conversations with Dave Atkinson, I had expressed indignation that Wausau's board never consulted him when it was deciding the mill's fate: *You can see where I'm coming from. A community has been ravaged by decisions from away, and they didn't consult us on those decisions. It's just this absentee — having kind of life-and-death control over our community.* He replied: "Yup. That's what sucks about the corporate world. What's important is quarterly earnings, not long-term. That is Wall Street driven. Do I feel hurt or pissed that I wasn't consulted? Not really. I never felt that way."

I persisted: *As an outsider, I think it's wrong that decisions are made without consulting those who have to bear the brunt of them.* "I agree," he replied. "But that's today's society. That's the Wall Street quarterly earnings society. I look forward to the day when corporate America doesn't run us."

The mill has been demolished. The voices of many who helped me tell its story have been silenced by time. Though the active life of the mill ended a decade ago, the area's economy remains depressed. The story of the Groveton mill community cannot end on such a despairing note. To answer questions posed in the introduction we must examine the economic lessons former mill workers taught me about the successes and failures of the mill.

WHY WAS THE MILL PROSPEROUS FOR SO MANY DECADES? The gorgeous landscape of the Upper Connecticut River Valley provided abundant wood fiber and flowing fresh waters essential for making paper. An unusually loyal, capable, and versatile workforce kept the mill running through wartime, floods, and economic hard times. In its heyday, the mill produced a diverse array of paper products — from fine papers to tissues to paperboard. A strong community, which many likened to a second family, provided support in times of adversity. The mill's postwar prosperity occurred under local ownership that was committed to the community — even when the old-school owners were throwing their coats on the floor and screaming at supervisors.

The American economy enjoyed its greatest period of economic growth and rising standard of living during those postwar decades. Access to cheap energy prior to 1973 kept mill costs down. Government policies such as protections for unions and a steep progressive tax system reduced inequality of wealth in the United States to its lowest point in the last 150 years.

WHAT CAUSED THE MILL'S DEMISE? The decline of the mill after Sir James Goldsmith's takeover of Diamond International coincided with profound changes in national politics and global economic forces. After 1980, the United States government repeatedly reduced the taxes on corporations and the wealthiest Americans. Large corporations, abetted by government policies, successfully weakened labor unions. Global energy prices soared after the oil crises of 1973 and 1979. Free-trade agreements that were ratified in the early 1990s forced mills such as Groveton to compete in commodity markets with newer, more modern, bigger mills located where workers were paid less and environmental protections were lax, or nonexistent. Significantly, the period of decline in important sectors of manufacturing in the United States coincided with a sharp increase in the inequality of wealth in the United States and a weakening of the democratic institutions that nurtured the postwar narrowing of wealth inequality. Today, the gap between the wealthiest and the rest of us is more extreme in the United States than in Europe, and it is worse than it was during the notorious Gilded Age of the late nineteenth century.[1]

Employees of the Groveton mill could not control rising energy prices, falling commodity paper prices, or Wausau's diminished investment in the mill. Dave Atkinson understood this, and throughout those final years, he exhorted the mill workforce to focus on "controllables" such as reducing energy and water use, the generation of broke paper, customer complaints, and workplace accidents: "We need to stay focused on what we can control. We can't control the market. All we can control is how efficiently, how cost-effectively we work. Focus on that, and we'll be OK." Mill workers responded with a variety of ingenious, inexpensive ways to reduce the amount of water and energy needed to make paper. They probably prolonged the life of the mill a bit, but they could not prevent a variety of uncontrollable global economic forces from dooming the mill.

WHAT LESSONS CAN CITIZENS OF THE GROVETON REGION LEARN FROM THE SUCCESSES AND FAILURES OF THE MILL AS THEY STRIVE TO BUILD A VIBRANT LOCAL ECONOMY? The struggle with controllables and uncontrollables suggests an important economic lesson: *To build a strong regional economy that meets local needs, communities such as Groveton need to discover ways to transform uncontrollable threats into controllable assets.* The path to a revived economy begins with an examination of ways to control uncontrollable global forces that pose obstacles to economic recovery.

Energy Prices: Local communities can control their vulnerability to energy price fluctuations by avoiding — or at least minimizing — economic activities that require massive amounts of energy. Conservation, efficiency, and avoidance of wasteful energy uses are key elements in a strategy to diminish greenhouse gas emissions and lower overall energy costs. Local business and industry should, whenever possible, derive energy from decentralized, local, low-carbon sources such as low-impact hydropower and small-scale wood, wind, and solar. The income from locally owned energy production recirculates in the hometown economy instead of disappearing into absentee coffers. "Green energy" projects, however, must truly be "green" and low carbon, and they must be coupled with the decommissioning of fossil fuel capacity. Otherwise, they merely expand energy production without reducing greenhouse gases.

Technological Arms Race: The Groveton mill declined when its absentee owners curtailed investment in state-of-the-art technology. Groveton ought to concentrate on building an economy that relies on smaller-scale, lower-cost technology that requires much less energy to operate. This simple, local business model diminishes dependence on Wall Street investors and global energy markets.

Commodity Production: Paper Board and Wausau could not operate profitably when commodity prices declined and energy and pulp prices rose. A new economy should encourage low-tech manufacturing of niche, value-added products that fetch higher prices and cannot be replicated in other regions.

Economic Diversity: The mill, as Hadley Platt and Sylvia Stone asserted, was the life of the town. Unfortunately, the mill so dominated the area economy that when it closed, that economy went into a tailspin from which it has yet to recover. A healthy, new economy will offer a diverse array of niche products such as maple syrup and maple sugar, local farm produce and goods, high-quality wood products, and low-impact outdoor adventures. Care must be taken to assure that these products and services impose a light carbon footprint and do not degrade ecosystem integrity.

Support Downtowns: Storefronts that are vacant today could sell locally produced goods, *if people shop locally.* Keeping one's friends and neighbors in business is good for everyone. A downtown ghost town discourages tourism and drives talented youth away from their homes and families.

Absentee Ownership: Absentee owners shut down the Groveton paper mill and placed the hated covenant on its deed. Absentee timberland owners have treated forests as a commodity as they overcut and degraded millions of acres of timberlands in northern New Hampshire, Maine, and Vermont in recent decades. Public economic development programs should support locally owned businesses and services rather than continue to offer tax breaks and other subsidies to outside investors with scant commitment to desperate communities.

AT A TIME OF RAPID, HUMAN-CAUSED, CLIMATE CHANGE, HOW CAN WE DESIGN A PROSPEROUS, LOW-CARBON ECONOMY THAT MAKES CREATIVE USE OF OUR NATURAL LANDSCAPE WHILE CONSERVING, PRESERVING, AND RESTORING THE ECOLOGICAL INTEGRITY OF OUR NATIVE ECOSYSTEMS? Perverse as it may seem, Groveton's bleak and protracted economic crisis affords it a rare opportunity to design a new economy that best meets its basic necessities while protecting its greatest asset — its natural landscape. The forested communities of the Upper Connecticut River Valley are wonderful places to live. The mountains of Nash Stream and the lakes of Pittsburg are beautiful, relatively undeveloped, remote, and, by twenty-first-century standards, raw and wild. The Connecticut River divides the valley into New Hampshire and Vermont politically; yet ecologically, culturally, and economically it joins those two states.

Activities that exploit and degrade our forests, soils, farmland, rivers, lakes, and mountains harm our long-term economic health. The great wildlife ecologist Aldo Leopold wrote: "We abuse land because we regard it as a commodity belonging to us. When we see land as a community to which we belong, we may begin to use it with love and respect." When we speak of "community," we are referring equally to both natural and human communities. Our deliberations must include the needs and perspectives of all species native to the region, from humans to loons to lichens.

Half a century ago, anthropologist Marshall Sahlins described Paleolithic hunter-gatherers as "the original affluent society." "There are two possible courses to affluence," Sahlins suggested. "Wants may be 'easily satisfied' either by producing much or desiring little."[2] Desiring little is the surest way to reduce our dependence on the global economy and dramatically shrink our carbon footprint. We are well positioned to follow this path because we are already a frugal, rural culture that engages in considerable barter and often comes together for communal endeavors such as barn raisings and church suppers.

We need to focus on production of necessities such as food, shelter, clothing, fuel, and basic leisure entertainments. Luxuries and superfluities that degrade ecosystems or impose a heavy carbon footprint are not worth the cost. Let us live simply and refuse to be slaves to fashion and frivolities. Freedom, happiness, and fulfillment are discovered in nature, not in material geegaws and the latest technology that Thoreau scornfully described as "an improved means to an unimproved end."

Local business districts will remain ghost towns as long as we patronize box stores and buy commodities produced by cheap labor in factories that degrade the environment. A vibrant downtown is essential to reversing the "brain drain" and luring the region's talented youth back home following college or military service. We can revive our downtowns by offering locally grown foods and niche farm and forest products for sale and services such as Internet cafés, movies, a variety of live music venues, and small museums scattered around the region that celebrate the region's history, culture, and natural beauty.

The mill site in Groveton or the old Campbell's complex in North Stratford would make beautiful locations for a college that offered courses in the ecology, history, culture, and trades that are distinctive to this region. A local college or university would strengthen and diversify the economy, help reverse the

Recreation opportunities abound in the greater Groveton region. In this 2013 photo, kayakers paddle by the Groveton paper mill during the demolition process. (Courtesy Doug White)

brain drain, enrich local cultural resources, and be a boon to local farmers, builders, woodlot owners, merchants, and service providers.

Human-caused climate change threatens the health of forests. In 2007 the Union of Concerned Scientists published a study of the potential ecological impacts of climate change on the forests of New England. The report provided a map showing that New Hampshire's climate a century hence would resemble the current climatic conditions of North Carolina if mankind fails to act aggressively to reduce greenhouse gas emissions. Iconic species of northern New England, such as sugar maples, red spruce, loons, and moose, could lose all or most of their necessary habitat in northern New England. Decline or loss of beloved species will compromise iconic economic sectors such as maple sugar production, leaf-peeper tourism, maple and spruce woods products, and moose viewing and hunting.

Nonnative invasives, pests, and pathogens, such as the hemlock wooly adelgid and the emerald ash borer, have been limited by extreme winter temperatures. As the climate warms in the coming decades, they can expand their range north and wreak havoc on native forest species and the wildlife that depends on them for food, reproduction, or shelter.

Northern New England, one of the most heavily forested regions in the world, can contribute significantly to the mitigation of human-caused climate change in several important ways. Trees and other aboveground biomass sequester and store huge amounts of carbon. Undisturbed soils store even more carbon than aboveground biomass. Species threatened by a changing climate require un-fragmented migration routes to climates better suited to provide for their biological needs. Unsustainable forestry, road building, and development fragment and degrade habitat and pose often-insurmountable obstacles to small, migrating species such as salamanders, worms, lichens, and mosses. Habitat fragmentation isolates populations of stressed species and can cause loss of genetic diversity that is essential for successful adaptation to rapid climate change. Protecting large tracts of undeveloped former paper company forestlands as publicly owned wilderness optimizes long-term forest carbon sequestration potential and improves the chances of survival for climate-stressed species.

It will be centuries before northern New England's forests are again dominated by large, old trees — the ancestral forests that covered the entire region for thousands of years before the Civil War. The degraded condition of so much of today's forests limits, but does not close off, our economic options for niche forest products. Local landowners who placed forest health over a quick buck will enjoy a head start over more shortsighted owners.

Local woodlot owners can earn a respectable return from careful logging if they view forests as communities to which they belong, not commodities to be exploited. Mitch Lansky, author of an important book on low-impact forestry, has written: "For a forest to be 'functional,' it must have all the required parts, and all the required processes." Low-impact forestry (LIF) is, Lansky suggests, "forestry as if the future mattered." It represents a commitment to long-term management and requires the collaboration of landowner, forester, logger, and timber buyers. It utilizes smaller, lighter machines, or, better yet, horses. The cutting standards for LIF are reasonably easy to follow, and they can be profitable, provided that local markets for high-quality wood exist.[3]

To restore healthy forests, public policy must reward responsible forest landowners, managers, and loggers while holding irresponsible actors accountable for their ecologically damaging actions. *Nonregulation of destructive forestry practices constitutes a massive public subsidy to irresponsible landowners and logging contractors and an unjust, counterproductive penalty to caring, responsible woodlot owners and loggers who practice low-impact forestry.* When we internalize the costs of destructive logging by holding landowners, foresters, and logging contractors responsible for the consequences of their logging jobs, profits go to conscientious landowners, and the benefits of maturing, carbon-sequestering, forest habitat accrue to everyone.

TWO APPROACHES TO A FUTURE
FOREST-BASED ECONOMY

The small, water-powered Garland Mill in Lancaster, New Hampshire, and the huge seventy-five-megawatt Burgess biomass plant in Berlin, New Hampshire, offer contrasting visions of a future forest-based economy in northern New England.

The Burgess pulp mill in Berlin was demolished in 2007, but its massive boiler was spared. Six years later, it began to burn wood chips to generate electricity for the New England grid. The output of the biomass plant is marketed as "green energy" that does not release greenhouse gases. These claims are demonstrably false. Each day roughly one hundred truckloads of wood chips are hauled to the plant, a round-trip that *averages* about one hundred miles to and from the plant (assuming a cutting radius of seventy-five miles around Berlin). This amounts to several million miles of diesel-powered trucking annually — an enormous amount of hydrocarbon release for a supposedly clean, green energy source. The fossil fuels burned by chainsaws, skidders, and wood chippers in the woods also release substantial amounts of hydrocarbons during the procurement of the plant's wood chips. And, of course, burning wood chips releases carbon sequestered in trees into the atmosphere.

Burgess is recklessly inefficient, capturing only about a quarter of the potential energy of the wood it burns. A recent report suggests that carbon emission standards for inefficient mega-biomass plants are significantly laxer than regulations for traditional fossil fuel plants. As a consequence, large biomass plants emit more carbon than coal per megawatt-hour generated.[4]

The timber industry and some conservation organizations claim that large biomass plants offer markets for "junk wood" — low economic value, short-lived hardwoods such as poplar, pin cherry, red maple, and paper birch. Supposedly, these markets allow landowners to thin the so-called junk wood while leaving behind vigorous stands of valuable species. Patient, low-impact forestry allows sugar maple, red spruce, and other long-lived tree species to shade out the sun-loving low-value species. However, because of the huge cost of chipping machinery, the relative low price wood chips fetch, the lack of regulations, and the long distances from forest to biomass plant, large contractors invariably practice intensive wood chipping rather than low-impact, timber stand improvement cuts that yield a modest amount of chips but leave behind a healthy forest.

Low-economic-value tree species were relatively rare in the forests that covered northern New England before the nineteenth-century woodsmen arrived. The current abundance of "junk wood" is a legacy of 150 years of overcutting — as if the future did not matter. Another round of clear-cuts or intensive whole-tree harvesting exacerbates and perpetuates the problem that biomass markets were supposed to alleviate.

A 2013 review of research into the impacts of whole-tree harvesting and energy wood harvesting presents compelling evidence that chipping operations cause serious ecological damage. Intensive chipping operations are likely to reduce soil productivity by depleting soil calcium, potassium, and magnesium. Removal of trees, especially whole trees, releases carbon. It takes many decades to sequester the carbon released during conventional clear-cuts. Disturbance of soils during and following intensive logging and wood-chipping operations releases substantially more carbon. Chipping operations conducted at short intervals severely limit the amount of carbon a forest stand can sequester before it is cut again and the sequestered carbon is again released.

The removal of the forest overstory and coarse and fine woody debris on the forest floor can significantly degrade habitat for soil microbes, fungi, and beetles. Small mammals and birds thrive in the forest overstory and in cooler, shaded, moist forest floors characteristic of stands with large trees, snags, or downed wood. Amphibians are more abundant in uncut forest stands than in clear-cuts where sun-parched soils are hotter and drier. Lower-quality habitat reduces reproductive success.

Whole-tree harvesting and energy wood harvesting operations disrupt the interception, retention, and cycling of water, materials, and energy. Less water is stored by trees after aboveground biomass has been removed. Diminished shade increases stream temperatures; this can be lethal to trout and aquatic insects. Removal of most of the living and dead biomass of a stand can increase sediment in lakes and streams and cause long-term reductions in stream productivity and diminished reproductive success of fish and aquatic insects.[5]

In a landscape where intensive whole-tree harvesting is allowed, climate-stressed species will be forced to migrate through a wasteland that is hotter and drier than intact, healing forest ecosystems. The migrators will have to travel through areas with disrupted hydrological cycles and eroding soils. Perhaps a winged creature or a large omnivore such as a black bear can successfully navigate this habitat nightmare. Smaller, less-mobile species — salamanders, soil microbes, mosses, and many native wildflowers — will be unable to traverse a fragmented landscape.

Large biomass plants enjoy tax breaks and incentives, and subsidized rates for the electricity they generate. This misguided public policy underwrites increased carbon emissions and the degradation of our most important terrestrial carbon sequestration system. It undermines the development of a local, low-impact energy policy. Tourists and recreationists don't come to frolic in whole-tree clear-cuts. Public subsidies to mega-biomass plants must be redirected to low-impact forestry practitioners, local value-added manufacturers of niche wood products, forest product marketing co-ops, and public works jobs in ecological restoration, energy audits, and retrofitting buildings.

The Burgess biomass plant, with its huge carbon footprint, rates a zero on the "controlling uncontrollables" scorecard. It is absentee-investor owned. It relies on expensive technology for cutting, transporting, and burning wood chips. Its inefficient use of the potential energy in wood makes it a counterproductive energy policy. Wood chips are commodities that earn the lowest value-added returns for the local forest economy. Burgess's voracious appetite for wood chips drives destructive forestry practices that jeopardize the production of future quality sawlogs that could sustain high value-added woods product manufacturing in the region.[6]

THE GARLAND MILL, founded in 1856, thirty-five years before ground was broken for the Groveton Paper mill, is New Hampshire's last continuously operating, water-powered sawmill. It is owned by a family with a strong commitment to the welfare of the community. It uses nineteenth-century technology to produce a valuable twenty-first-century niche product.

The mill diverts water from Garland Brook to power the sawmill and generate water-powered electricity that it sells back to the grid. After passing through the mill's penstock, the diverted water returns to the brook. The overall ecological impact on the brook and its watershed is slight, and the energy generated helps in a modest way to reduce greenhouse gas emissions. The mill secures its spruce and pine sawlogs from loggers and landowners who cut lightly and protect the ecological integrity of their lands.

The small-scale operation cannot compete in commodity markets with large sawmills that rely on expensive, energy-intensive, high-speed saws to produce huge volumes of lumber. However, the Garland Mill has become a successful niche business by adding great value to its sawed wood. Its skilled and resourceful in-house construction crew creates energy-efficient buildings using the posts and beams sawed by the old water-powered mill. When the mill erects a building, neighbors come to watch the spectacle, and former clients show up to join as unpaid helpers.

The 160-year-old Garland Mill earns high scores on the controlling uncontrollables scorecard.

OVER THE COURSE of seven years, I have received assistance and encouragement from many people. I took a course in ethnography from Millie Rahn at Plymouth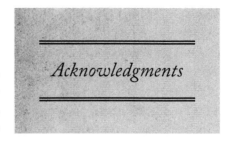

Acknowledgments

State University in the winter of 2009–2010. She required her students to develop oral history projects. Immediately I chose the Groveton paper mill.

Former shipping department employee Bruce Blodgett gave me a tour of the mill and provided me with a list of about a dozen former mill workers to get me started. These early interviews convinced me I had struck gold.

By the end of Millie's course, in late February 2010, I had interviewed eight former mill workers, and by then I realized I was a willing captive of a far greater project. That spring, I continued work on the mill project under the auspices of an independent study with Millie; she challenged me to write a book proposal that spring. I was hooked.

I wish to say a special thanks to my first interviewee, Francis Roby. He couldn't have been more gracious in helping me get started. Thereafter, it was easy to approach potential interviewees. I also wish to thank his wife, Arlene Roby, who shared the 1936 and 1938–1942 diaries of Cy Hessenauer, a logger with a poetic outlook. Selections from his diary were published in "I Have Earned My Place: A Logger's Year, 1936," which appeared in *Northern Woodlands*, Spring 2015.

Early in the project, Joe Berube, paper machine tender, local historian, and author, suggested I contact Gloria White about historic photographs. Gloria, a former mill worker, whose husband, mother, father, and many other relatives also worked at the mill, had been collecting and digitizing photographs of town history. She graciously shared scores of photos she had collected, and she has helped me locate many more. I could not have gathered so many photos of Groveton's paper mill without the assistance of Gloria and her husband, Doug White. Doug also served as a fact checker who answered all manner of questions about the mill and mill photos.

By the summer of 2013 I had accumulated over one hundred hours in seventy-two taped interviews with fifty-six individuals who had worked at the mill or grown up in Groveton. The following people graciously submitted to one or more interviews: Bill Astle, Dave Atkinson, Bill and Iris Baird, Web Barnett, Lawrence Benoit, Joe Berube, Irene Bigelow, Bruce Blodgett, Thurman Blodgett, Joan Breault, Neal Brown, Shirley Brown, Tom Bushey, Louise Caouette, Ted Caouette, Pete Cardin, Roger Caron, Albert and Simone Cloutier, Greg Cloutier, Lorenzo Cloutier, Armand Dube, Leonard Fournier, Kathy Frizzell, Albert "Puss" Gagnon, John Gonyer, Betty Gould, Raymond Jackson, Belvah King, Mickey King, Gerard Labrecque, Pauline Labrecque, Lawrence LaPointe, Elaine LeClere, Shirley MacDow, Wilson "Hoot" McMann, Sandy Mason, Dave Miles, Herb Miles, Gary Paquette, Hadley Platt, John Rich, Rosa and Roland Roberge, Francis and Arlene Roby, Murray Rogers, Fred Shannon, Sylvia Stone, Pamela Styles, Raymond and Lorraine Tetreault, Channie Tilton, Cecil Tisdale, James C. Wemyss Jr., and Sandy White.

I enjoyed each and every one of the interviews I conducted for the mill project. I was always made to feel welcome and was delighted that the former mill workers I interviewed were eager to share their experiences in the mill. Thank you, one and all. You are the chorus for this drama.

Most of the mill photographs are in the possession of the Groveton Region Economic Assistance Team (GREAT). I am deeply grateful to the members of GREAT for allowing me to use some of their photographs for this book and for other mill-related projects. I hope someday there will be a place in Groveton where some of these treasures can be displayed for the public.

I also wish to thank the many people who graciously shared photographs with me: Joe Berube, Roger Caron, Greg Cloutier, Becky Craggy, Becky Crawford (daughter of the late Warren Bartlett), Donna and Charlie Jordan, Dave Miles, Jim Wemyss Jr., and Sandy White.

After I had assembled a good deal of material, I began to offer public presentations in which I showed photographs and played clips from some of the interviews I had conducted. Becky Craggy and Elaine Gray of the Northumberland Town Office were unfailingly helpful arranging these presentations in the town meeting room in the old Moose Lodge. Bill Tobin loaned his sound system for my presentations. On various occasions, Ron Pelchat, Nathan Gair, or Kyle Haley made video recordings of these presentations.

Barbara Robarts invited me to make a presentation at Weeks Library in Lancaster, where she is librarian. Barbara has been a valuable source of information on local and regional history, as well as the extensive historical holdings of Weeks Library. I am truly grateful to Barbara for all the help she has provided me over the years.

Eric Becker guided me through the (for me) tricky task of digitizing the cassette recordings of the mill project interviews. I am technologically challenged, and Eric showed the patience of a saint as I struggled to learn the process.

Jim Wemyss Jr. submitted to ten formal interviews and countless other visits and phone calls. He always grumbled that he was busy, and he always forgot the clock when we began reminiscing about the mill.

Dave Atkinson, the mill superintendent when the mill closed, helped me understand the final years of the mill. He has graciously answered numerous subsequent queries, and he reviewed portions of the manuscript.

Richard Pult, my editor at the University Press of New England, has always believed in the project, and has offered sound, sometimes tough, advice. He has challenged me to improve — and shorten — the original manuscript.

Greg Cloutier, one of the livelier storytellers I interviewed, has been supportive of the project from the moment I requested my first interview with him. Rather than list all the ways he has helped out, I will simply state: *You Had a Job for Life* would not have seen the light of day without Greg's support.

I dedicate *You Had a Job for Life* to my wife, Rachel O'Meara. She has encouraged me, sustained me, endured countless hours of noise while I transcribed the interview tapes, and tolerated never-disappearing piles of papers all over the living room sofa while I organized notes and wrote the book. Thank you, Rachel, my love.

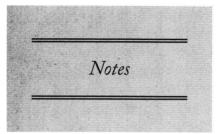

CHAPTER ONE

The Life of the Town

1. *History of Coös County*, facsimile of the 1888 edition (Somersworth: New Hampshire Publishing Co., 1972; originally published by W. A. Fergusson & Co., Boston, 1888), 72. Georgia Drew Merrill is the probable, albeit uncredited, editor.

2. Locals called Rumford, Maine, home of a large paper mill, "Cancer Valley." Maine's Bureau of Health Chronic Disease Surveillance Project found in the period 1984–1988 that the Rumford area had high rates of emphysema, asthma, non-Hodgkin's lymphoma, lung cancer, and aplastic anemia. Mitch Lansky, *Beyond the Beauty Strip: Saving What's Left of Our Forests* (Gardiner, ME: Tilbury House, 1992), 58–59.

3. Undated memo, written probably in August 1954, in possession of the Groveton Mill Oral History Project.

CHAPTER TWO *Feeding the Mill*

1. *Coös County Democrat* (hereafter *Democrat*), August 19, 1891.
2. "The Lumber Business," editorial in *Democrat*, October 3, 1894.
3. *Democrat*, October 12, 1892.
4. *Democrat*, August 2, 1899.
5. *Democrat*, January 20, 1909.
6. *Gropaco News*, Christmas 1920, 6.

CHAPTER THREE *Making Paper*

1. Scientists did not implicate the bleaching process of pulp mills with dioxins until 1983, eleven years after the Groveton pulp mill had been shut down. Peter von Stackelberg, "White Wash: The Dioxin Cover-Up," *Greenpeace* 14, no. 2 (March/April 1989), http://www.planetwaves.net/contents/white_wash_dioxin_cover_up.html.

1. *Democrat,* July 15, 1891. (Note: owing to poor quality of microfilm "283" feet is probably correct. Possibly it could read 233.)

2. *Democrat,* September 23, 1891. It is likely that many accidents and injuries went unreported.

3. *Democrat,* February 10 and 17, 1892.

4. *Democrat,* July 20, 1892.

5. *Democrat,* July 31, 1895.

6. *Democrat,* March 23, 1966.

7. *Democrat,* May 6, 1896.

8. *Democrat,* June 3, 1896; June 10, 1896.

9. *Democrat,* July 22, 1896.

10. *Democrat,* January 30, 1901.

11. *Democrat,* July 17, 1901.

12. *Democrat,* April 10, 1907.

13. *Democrat,* October 9, 1907.

14. *Groveton Advertiser,* March 16, 1910.

15. *Groveton Advertiser,* October 11, 1910.

16. *Democrat,* September 1, 1897; November 8, 1905; February 28, 1906.

17. *Democrat,* May 26, 1897.

18. *Democrat,* May 4, 1898.

19. *Democrat,* April 20, 1898.

20. *Democrat,* October 5, 1898; October 19, 1898.

21. *Democrat,* November 1, 1899.

22. *Democrat,* May 12, 1897.

23. *Democrat,* April 6, 1898.

24. *Democrat,* December 14, 1898.

25. *Democrat,* December 27, 1899.

26. *Democrat,* February 10, 1904.

27. *Democrat,* January 11, 1905.

28. *Democrat,* February 8, 1905.

29. *Democrat,* July 25, 1906.

30. *Democrat,* January 8, 1908.

31. *Democrat,* April 29, 1908.

32. *Groveton Advertiser,* September 3, 1913; October 29, 1913.

CHAPTER FIVE *Ratville, NH*

1. *Democrat*, July 11, 1917.
2. *Groveton Advertiser*, May 11, 18, and 25, 1917.
3. *Paper Makers Journal*, February 1919, 17.
4. *Paper Makers Journal*, August 1917, 8.
5. *Paper Makers Journal*, February 1919, 17.
6. *Groveton Advertiser*, September 7, 1917; *Paper Makers Journal*, October 1917, 24–25.
7. *Paper Makers Journal*, December 1917, 32; January 1918, 8.
8. *Paper Makers Journal*, March 1918, 28.
9. *Paper Makers Journal*, September 1919, 3; "Organizer Parker's Report for June," *Paper Makers Journal*, July 1920, 28.
10. *Paper Makers Journal*, October 1917, 25.
11. *Groveton Advertiser*, May 28, 1920.
12. *Gropaco News*, Christmas edition, December 23, 1920, 1.
13. *Gropaco News*, April 14, 1921, 12.
14. *Democrat*, June 8, 1927.
15. *Democrat*, February 27, 1935.
16. *Democrat*, November 11, 1936, November 25, 1936.
17. *Democrat*, December 9, 1936.
18. *Democrat*, October 6 and 13, 1937; November 18, 1937.
19. *Democrat*, January 12, 1938; February 16, 1938.
20. *Democrat*, April 6, 1938.
21. *Democrat*, September 4, 1935.

CHAPTER SIX *Three Generations of Wemysses*

1. Diary of Cy Hessenauer, 1938–1942, August 13 and 18, 1940. Photocopies in author's possession.
2. "Transfer of Paper Mill Is Probable This Week," *Democrat*, August 14, 1940; *Democrat*, January 8, 1941.
3. "Northumberland a Thriving Village," *Democrat*, March 31, 1937.
4. "Police Guard Paper Mill," *Democrat*, October 18, 1939; November 15 and 22, 1939.
5. "Friendly Relations at Wyoming Mill," *Democrat*, January 8, 1941.

6. "Strike at Paper Mill," *Democrat*, October 1, 1941.

7. Hessenauer diary, 1938–1942, September 23, 1940, and January 15, 1941.

8. "Union and Company Agreement," *Democrat*, July 9, 1941.

9. *Democrat*, October 31, 1945.

10. *Democrat*, July 19 and 26 and August 2, 1944.

CHAPTER SEVEN *Crown Prince*

1. Interview with Irene Bigelow, conducted by her daughter, Gloria White, on October 14, 2010.

2. *Democrat*, September 18, 1946.

3. *Democrat*, October 9, 1946.

4. *Democrat*, September 18, 1946.

5. *Democrat*, September 25, 1946.

6. *Democrat*, November 6, 1946.

CHAPTER EIGHT *The Perfect Balance*

1. *Democrat*, May 14, 1952.

2. *Democrat*, May 21, 1952.

3. *Democrat*, May 28 and June 4, 1952.

4. *Democrat*, June 25, 1952.

5. *Democrat*, April 12, 1950.

6. *Democrat*, September 26, 1962.

7. Anders Knutsson, "Health Disorders of Shift Workers," *Occupational Medicine* 53 (2003): 103–8; Joseph LaDou, "Health Effects of Shift Work," *Western Journal of Medicine* 137 (December 1982): 525–30.

8. The story appeared in Peter Riviere, "'Jimmy, Jr.' Honored at Plant Ceremony," *Caledonian-Record* (St. Johnsbury, VT), July 29, 1998.

CHAPTER TEN *A Fateful Decision*

1. *Wall Street Journal*, June 6, 1968, 34.

2. *Democrat*, September 2, 1970.

3. *Democrat*, September 13, 1973; October 18, 1973; October 25, 1973.

4. *Democrat*, March 22, 1973.

5. *Democrat*, June 14, 1973; July 19, 1973.

6. *Democrat*, July 26, 1973.

7. *Democrat*, August 9, 1973.

8. *Democrat*, October 25, 1973.

9. *Democrat*, March 28, 1974.

CHAPTER ELEVEN *End of an Era*

1. Jack Hiltz, "GM Reviews Events, Progress," *Papermaker*, August 1981, 1.

2. J. Hiltz, "No. 1 Boiler Conversion," *Papermaker*, May 1982, 1–2.

3. Gregory Cloutier, "No. 1 Boiler Conversion Update," *Papermaker*, April 1983, 4.

4. *Democrat*, April 30, 1980.

5. Jack Hiltz, "A Company Newspaper Fulfills a Need," *Papermaker*, December 1980, 1.

6. Susan Breault, "Alkaline Size: Practice Makes Perfect," *Papermaker*, May 1982, 3.

7. *Democrat*, September 16, 1981.

8. *Democrat*, October 7, 1981.

9. *Democrat*, October 14, 1981.

10. *Democrat*, November 11, 1981.

11. Ivan Fallon, *Billionaire: The Life and Times of Sir James Goldsmith* (Boston: Little, Brown, 1992), 359.

12. *Manchester Union Leader*, July 13, 1983; Fallon, *Billionaire*, 375, says JR paid $149 million.

CHAPTER TWELVE *The Worst Years*

1. Jack Hiltz, "New Records Set," *Papermaker*, June 1983, 2.

2. Peter Riviere, "James River: From Wood Chips to Blue Chips," *Democrat*, January 4, 1984.

3. Funding Universe, "Fort James Corporation History," c. 1997, http://www.fundinguniverse.com/company-histories/fort-james-corporation-history/.

4. *Democrat*, August 24, 1983; September 4, 1985.

5. "Campbellettes," *Papermaker*, May 23, 1985, 5.

6. "History is Made in Northern Mountains," *Papermaker*, August 1, 1985, 1.

7. *Democrat*, August 7, 1985.

8. *Democrat*, January 1, 1986; February 19, 1986.

9. *Democrat*, January 15, 1992; March 11, 1992.

10. Bill Sleeper, "Bill's Corner: The Challenge That Lies Ahead," *Papermaker*, April 21, 1988, 2; Greg Cloutier, "What Is Co-Generation and How Does It Affect Us?," *Papermaker*, October 29, 1987, 1; Bill Sleeper, "Bill's Corner: The Beat Goes On," *Papermaker*, August 18, 1988, 2.

11. Harold A. Goldsberry and James E. Maher, "North American Fine Paper Producers Continue Alkaline Paper Conversion," *Pulp & Paper Magazine*, April 1993.

12. Kasy King, "The Alkaline Challenge," *Papermaker*, May 3, 1990, 1, 3.

13. John Kushe, "John's Corner," *Papermaker*, August 31, 1989, 2; John Kushe, "John's Corner," *Papermaker*, November 2, 1989, 2; Jim Bailey, "Manager's Notebook," *Papermaker*, May 3, 1990, 2.

14. James M. Matheson, "James River Restructuring: An Opportunity for Groveton," *Papermaker*, November 8, 1990, 1.

15. *Democrat*, August 22, 1990.

16. *Democrat*, September 12, October 10, November 21, and December 5, 1990. Jim Bailey, "Manager's Notebook," *Papermaker*, December 20, 1990, 2.

17. *Democrat*, January 23, 1991; April 24, 1991.

18. *Democrat*, November 6, 1991.

19. Donna Jordan, "James C. Wemyss and Groveton Paper Board," *Coös Magazine*, November 1991, 4–7.

20. *Democrat*, December 18, 1991.

21. *Democrat*, January 15, 1992; February 5, 1992.

22. *Democrat*, February 19, 1992; April 8, 1992; May 20, 1992.

23. Senator Patrick Leahy and Senator Warren B. Rudman, "Letter of Clarification," in *The Northern Forest Lands Study of New England and New York*, by Stephen C. Harper, Laura L. Falk, and Edward W. Rankin (Rutland, VT: U.S. Department of Agriculture, 1990), 90.

24. Harper, Falk, and Rankin, *Northern Forest Lands Study*, 3, 164.

CHAPTER THIRTEEN *The Best Years*

1. *Democrat*, October 21, October 28, 1992.

2. Jack O'Brien, "Wausau Papers Makes Dream Acquisition — Acquires Groton from James River," *PaperAge*, September 1993, 10; Jack O'Brien, "Wausau Paper Mills' President and CEO Arnold M. Nemirow Named PaperAge Papermaker of the Year," *PaperAge*, December 1993, 8.

3. O'Brien, "Wausau Papers Makes Dream Acquisition," 12.

4. *Democrat*, April 14, 1993.

5. *Democrat*, March 3, 1993; March 10, 1993.

6. Martha V. Creegan, "Colored Paper Still Coming from Mill," *Caledonian-Record*, May 7, 2001.

7. Edith Tucker, "Wausau Union Voting on Labor Contract," *Democrat*, March 26, 1997.

8. Peter Riviere, "Paper Mill Expansion Will Allow Overnight Deliveries," *Caledonian-Record*, August 28, 1993.

9. Journal staff, "Wausau Paper Loses CEO," *Milwaukee Journal*, July 21, 1994.

10. Peter Riviere, "If Paper Mill Changes to Oil Woodsmen's Jobs Could Be Lost," *Caledonian-Record*, April 26, 1994; Peter Riviere, "Workers Are Called Back as Paper Demand Increases," *Caledonian-Record*, September 30, 1994.

11. Pam Bouchard, "Natural Gas Pipeline a Step Closer to Reality," *Berlin Daily Sun*, January 30, 1996; Edith Tucker, "Wausau Will Invest $8 Million at Mill," *Democrat*, July 23, 1997; Tom Craven, "No Correlation?," *Wausau Happenings*, April 1999, 1.

12. Edith Tucker, "Wausau Union Voting on Labor Contract," *Democrat*, March 26, 1997.

13. "Go to Groton for County's Best Pay," *Berlin Reporter*, April 4, 2000. Berlin, another paper mill town, averaged $600, Lancaster averaged $440, and Colebrook $368.

14. Barbara Tetreault, "Wausau Contract Rejected," *Berlin Daily Sun*, March 27, 1997.

15. Edith Tucker, "Wausau Union Voting on Contract," *Democrat*, March 26, 1997; Peter Riviere, "Union Vote Today on Five-Year Wausau Paper Mills Contract," *Caledonian-Record*, March 26, 1997; Barbara Tetreault, "No Strike

at Wausau," *Berlin Daily Sun*, March 27, 1997; Peter Riviere, "Strike Vote Fails," *Caledonian-Record*, March 28, 1997.

16. Eoin Cannon, "Wausau Papers to Buy Mill in Maine," *Berlin Reporter*, February 13, 1997.

17. Editorial, "Painful Decision Will Pay Off for Paper Company," *Wausau Daily Herald*, March 25, 1998.

18. Tom Craven, "Pretty Scary Stuff . . ." *Wausau Happenings*, October 1998, 1; Tom Craven, "Our Customers Are Talking . . ." *Wausau Happenings*, November 1998, 1; Tom Craven, "No Correlation," *Wausau Happenings*, April 1999, 1; Dave Atkinson, "S.O.S.," *Wausau Happenings*, March 2000, 1.

CHAPTER FOURTEEN *A Battle We Couldn't Win*

1. *Democrat*, May 19, 1993.

2. "International Paper Announces Plan to Transform Its Business Portfolio and Performance," International Paper news release, July 19, 2005.

3. Edith Tucker, "IP Owns Controlling Share of GPB," *Democrat*, January 11, 2006; Donna Jordan, "Paper Mill Closing Comes at 'Ironic Time,'" *Lancaster Herald*, January 6, 2006.

4. Edith Tucker, "Local 61 and GPB Ink Closure Contract," *Democrat*, January 11, 2006.

CHAPTER FIFTEEN *Controllables and Uncontrollables*

1. Dan Chancey, "What Is Co-generation?" *Wausau Happenings*, April–May 2001, 3.

2. Lloyd Irland, "Paper Making in Maine: Economic Trends, 1894–2000," Irland Group Forestry Consultants, working draft, April 5, 2003, 12.

3. Dave Atkinson, "Ready, Set, Go!!!," *Wausau Happenings*, September–October 2002, 2.

4. Dave Atkinson, "2005 — a Roller Coaster Ride for Sure!!!!??," *Wausau Happenings*, Summer 2005, 2.

5. Dave Atkinson, "Times Are Changing — for the Good!!!," *Wausau Happenings*, Autumn 2004, 2.

6. "Wausau Paper Launches Strategic Timberland Sales," *Wausau Happenings*, Summer 2005, 11.

7. Dave Atkinson, "Unprecedented Energy Prices Cause Dramatic Shift in Groteon Operations!," *Wausau Happenings*, Fall 2005, 2.

EPILOGUE *They Ruined This Town*

1. Mitch Lansky, "*Beyond the Beauty Strip*: A 20th Year Retrospective," 30–31. PDF, written in 2012, can be downloaded at http://planetmaine.net/meepi/lif/.

2. Lloyd Irland, "Maine's Forest Products Sector and Regional Disparities," in *Spreading Prosperity to the "Other Maines": Reflections on Regional Disparities*, ed. Lisa Pohlmann and David Vail (Maine Center for Economic Policy, November 2005), iii.

POSTSCRIPT *The Day When Corporate America Doesn't Run Us*

1. See Thomas Piketty, *Capital in the Twenty-First Century* (Cambridge, MA: Belknap Press of Harvard University Press, 2014).

2. Marshall Sahlins, "The First Affluent Society," in *Stone Age Economics* (New York: Aldine de Gruyter, 1972), 1–2.

3. Mitch Lansky, "Principles, Goals, Guidelines and Standards for Low-Impact Forestry," in *Low-Impact Forestry: Forestry as If the Future Mattered*, ed. Mitch Lansky (Hallowell: Maine Environmental Policy Institute, 2002), 22.

4. Mary S. Booth, "Trees, Trash, and Toxics: How Biomass Energy Has Become the New Coal," Partnership for Policy Integrity, April 2014, http://www.pfpi.net/wp-content/uploads/2014/04/PFPI-Biomass-is-the-New-Coal-April-2-2014.pdf.

5. Alaina L. Berger, Brian Palik, Anthony W. D'Amato, Shawn Fraver, John B. Bradford, Keith Nislow, David King, and Robert T. Brooks, "Ecological Impacts of Energy-Wood Harvests: Lessons from Whole-Tree Harvesting and Natural Disturbance," *Journal of Forestry* 11, no. 2 (March 2013): 139–53.

6. For a comprehensive examination of problems associated with large biomass plants, whole-tree harvesting, and the carbon sequestration potential

for older forest stands see Mitch Lansky, "The Double Bottom Line: Managing Maine's Forests to Increase Carbon Sequestration and Decrease Carbon Emissions," April 2016, http://planetmaine.net/meepi/lif/.

NOTE: Page numbers in *italics* indicate images; page numbers with "n" indicate endnotes.

Index

and Greg Cloutier, 3–5, 161–62; and Groveton Paper Board, 100–1, 115–16, 180, 202–7; and James River Corp., 157–58, 168, 174–75, 180–81, 187–88; management style of, 1–3, 157–63, 190, 204–7; on mill closing, 242–43; mill owner, 1–3, 108, 110–11, 118, 126; Number 4 paper machine, 94, 189; on pollution, 20, 37, 144; Shirley MacDow and, 164–66, 180; on strikes, 67, 89–90, 113, 137–39, 153–54; unions and, 24, 108–9, 113–14, 137–39, 160–63, 191, 198; Wausau mill acquisition, 177, 186; World War II, 84, 87, 109; Wyoming Valley mill, 101–3

Wemyss, James C., Sr. (Old Jim): 104; death of, 180; Diamond International, 1, 130–33, 155–56; diversification of mill, 87, 92–93, 100–1; employees, relations with, 83, 97–98, 106–8, 134; illness, 98–99; involved owner, 97–98, 159; and Jim Wemyss Jr., 97–98, 108; revival of mill, 1, 75, 79–81, 83; unions, 81–84, 88–91, 191; Wyoming Valley paper mill, 76, 102–3

Wemyss, James C., III (son of Young Jim), 109, 207–9

Wemyss, James S. (father of Old Jim), 76–79, *80*, 88, 99, 137

Wemyss, Margaret Campbell, *80*

Wemyss, Walter, 79

Westab, 145

Weston Dam, 64, 100–1

Weston Sawmill, 12–13, 27, 51, 60, 67

Whitcomb, Lee, 64

White, Cassandra (Sandy), 8–10, 114, 168–72

Williams, Robert, 173–74

Wilson, Charles, 52–53, 69–70

women in mill: in finishing rooms, 103–6; James River and, 170; labor unions, 58–59, 70–72; lower pay rates for, 105, 164–65; and men's jobs, 141–42, 170–73; and World War II work force, 82, 87–88

wood chipping, 29–30, 149, 197

wood piles, 13, 22, 25, 26, 33–35, 67, 135, 150

wood room, 2, 26, 30, 33, 37, 53–54, 68–69, 82, 135

Woodward, Patricia, 72

wood yard, 24, 33–34, 57, 102, 150, 203

World War I, 63, 66, 85

World War II, 1, 82–85, 88, 109–10, 125

Wyoming Valley paper mill, 75–79, 101–3, 137, 145